Women March for Peace

A Volume in the Series
AFRICAN AMERICAN INTELLECTUAL HISTORY
Edited by
Christopher Cameron

Women March for Peace

BLACK RADICAL WOMEN'S
ANTI-KOREAN WAR ACTIVISM

Denise M. Lynn

University of Massachusetts Press
AMHERST AND BOSTON

Copyright © 2025 by University of Massachusetts Press
All rights reserved

ISBN 978-1-62534-903-3 (paper); 904-0 (hardcover)

Designed by Jen Jackowitz
Set in Minion Pro
Printed and bound by Books International, Inc.

Cover design by adam b. bohannon
Cover photo by unknown, *Claudia Jones Delivering a Speech While on Japan Trip*, circa 1955–1964. Courtsey Schomburg Center, New York Public Library.

Library of Congress Cataloging-in-Publication Data
A catalog record for this book is available from the Library of Congress.

British Library Cataloguing-in-Publication Data
A catalog record for this book is available from the British Library.

To Andrew, Christy, and Tammy

Contents

List of Illustrations   ix

Acknowledgments   xi

Introduction   1

CHAPTER ONE
Opposing Hot and Cold War   29

CHAPTER TWO
Sojourning for Peace   59

CHAPTER THREE
No Freedom Here   95

CHAPTER FOUR
Charlotta Bass for Vice President   134

CHAPTER FIVE
The High Price of Peace   162

Conclusion   190

Notes   201

Index   237

Photo gallery follows page 121

List of Illustrations

Figure 1. W. E. B. Du Bois and Shirley Graham Du Bois on his 87th birthday, February 23, 1955. W. E. B. Du Bois Papers, Robert S. Cox Special Collections and University Archives Research Center, University of Massachusetts Amherst Libraries.   122

Figure 2. Claudia Jones, Alamy Stock Photo.   123

Figure 3. Charlotta Bass with Paul Robeson, Alamy Stock Photo.   124

Figure 4. Beulah Richardson, known as the actress Beah Richards. Bill Cosby Show, 1970. UtCon Collection.   125

Figure 5. Lorraine Hansberry, ca. 1960. Courtesy: CSU Archives / Everett Collection.   126

Figure 6. Paul Robeson, his wife Eslanda Goode Robeson, and their son Paul Robeson Jr., at their house in Enfield, Connecticut, ca. 1940s. Everett Collection Inc.   127

Figure 7. Louise Thompson Patterson, ca. 1930s, Louise Thompson Patterson Papers, Stuart A. Rose Manuscript, Archives, and Rare Book Library, Emory University, with permission of family.   128

Figure 8. W. E. B. Du Bois with fellow defendants during trial in Washington, DC, November 1951. W. E. B. Du Bois Papers, Robert S. Cox Special Collections and University Archives Research Center, University of Massachusetts Amherst Libraries.   129

Figure 9. W. E. B. Du Bois and Shirley Graham Du Bois with Mao Zedong, 1959. W. E. B. Du Bois Papers, Robert S. Cox Special Collections and University Archives Research Center, University of Massachusetts Amherst Libraries.   130

Figure 10. Louise Thompson Patterson, ca. 1930s. Image provided by Daily Worker Photo Collection; PHOTOS223; Box 236; Folder 13505; Tamiment Library & Robert F. Wagner Labor Archives, NYU Special Collections, New York University—Courtesy of Longview Publishing / *People's World*.   131

Figure 11. Henry Wallace (far left) with Eslanda Robeson, Image provided by Daily Worker Photo Collection; PHOTOS223; Box 258; Folder 14706; Tamiment Library & Robert F. Wagner Labor Archives, NYU Special Collections, New York University—Courtesy of Longview Publishing / *People's World*.   132

Figure 12. Eslanda Robeson with a delegation of women to speak to a UN representative to urge a ceasefire in Korea, Image provided by Daily Worker Photo Collection; PHOTOS223; Box 258; Folder 14706; Tamiment Library & Robert F. Wagner Labor Archives, NYU Special Collections, New York University—Courtesy of Longview Publishing / *People's World*.   133

Acknowledgments

This project came out of some of the adjacent research that influenced blogs I wrote for the African American Intellectual History Society's *Black Perspective's* website. A colleague and frequent collaborator, Phillip Luke Sinitiere asked me in passing once if I was going to write a book from the research and before he asked, the thought had never occurred to me. I must thank Phil for planting the seeds for this project and for engaging me in several projects that helped to form my thinking. There are also several scholars whose writing on this and adjacent topics have influenced me including the late Marilyn Young, Mary Dudziak, David Vine, Ruth Wilson Gilmore, Barbara Ransby, Vincent Intondi, Leilah Danielson, Erik McDuffie, Dayo Gore, Keith Gilyard, Suhi Choi, Robin Kelley, Keisha Blaine, Gerald Horne, Christine Hong, and many others. I am also thankful for other collaborators like Charisse Burden-Stelly, Tony Pecinovsky, Zifeng Liu, and more whose ideas have informed my own.

I want to extend thanks to my students who are very patient with my ramblings on the Korean War, the Cold War, and the women that I write about and research. They have often humored my incoherent thoughts, but just as often asked difficult questions that forced me to engage more deeply with what I research and teach. This research influenced three classes—one on women and the civil rights movement, another on the Cold War, and one on the Korean War—these allowed me to continually engage students in thinking about the histories that we often forget. I want to also thank my friends and colleagues at the University of Southern Indiana: Cacee Mabis, Stella Ress, Anya King, Jason Hardgrave, Kelly Kaelin, Kristalyn Shefveland, Steve Casement, Sukanya Gupta, Veronica Huggins, Sandy Davis, Brittney Westbrook, Mary Lyn Stoll, and all the people on the Gender and Sexuality Studies and Africana Studies committees. I would also like to extend my gratitude to Shannon O'Neill at the Tamiment Library who helped secure images for this book from an as yet unprocessed collection.

I am lucky to be in regular conversation and contact with so many of my friends from graduate school especially Greg Geddes, Gaylynn Welch, Dee Gillespie, Mellissa Wrisley, and Mary Weikum and the others who remain in touch via the often-troublesome medium of social media—Shannon King, Jennifer Cubic, Marian Horan, Melissa Madera, Gulhan Erkaya Balsoy, Meg Engle and others. I want to also thank my colleagues at the Historians of American Communism and some of the other historians that work on Communist Party (CPUSA) histories that have been friends, colleagues, and collaborators: Vernon Pederson, Katie Sibley, Melissa Ford, Tionne Parris, Elizabeth Armstrong, and Derefe Chavannes. I recently had the amazing opportunity to talk to Louise Thompson and William Patterson's daughter Mary Louise about her mother; I look forward to continuing that conversation.

In March 2020, just as the world was shutting down for the COVID-19 pandemic, I was furiously looking through the Louise Thompson Patterson Papers at Emory University. Little did I (and the world know) what would follow. Through the global crisis and my own health crisis that followed, I was lucky enough to have the support of my friends and family. I want to thank my siblings Dan Lynn and Corinne Lynn as well as their families—Ang, Megan, Ryan Lynn, and Erin Dupree. I have been lucky to have a chosen family—my closest friends Danielle Copeland, Ang Bacon-Reap, Nicole Russell, and Sue Wee-Hickman and their families. Many thanks to my partner Adrian Gentle and my daughter Cybele Lynn-Colon for their patience and support. I want to dedicate this work to Andrew McVicker—forever in my heart and thoughts, who has been gone for nearly ten years, but who I still think about every day. I would like to also dedicate this to my cousins Christy Lynn and Tammy Terns Toups who also left us too soon. Most importantly, I want to thank the women in this book. I am still astonished at their endless optimism in the face of harassment and ongoing war and conflict that the world could be a better place and that inspires me every day.

Women
March for Peace

Introduction

In a September 1951 column in the Communist Party's *Daily Worker*, Claudia Jones reported on a Joint Congressional Committee Report on US incomes. What the study found was that one-third of Americans in 1948 were living on less than $2,000 per year. A simultaneous Commerce Department report found that a single mother with one child was living on significantly less: $1,436 per year. The congressional report described how some of these same families had prospered during World War II because of wartime jobs and higher wages and it asked, "Have peacetimes no counterpart to offer?"[1]

Black, Mexican, and Puerto Rican families were overrepresented among low-income families and Jones described how they were forced to survive on meager rations in overcrowded housing. Social workers had compiled data for Congress on the family's survival strategies and these included limiting meat to Sundays, milk rationed except for infants, and families surviving primarily on starches like potatoes and macaroni. In the first year of the Korean War, inflation rose 8 percent; meanwhile, Jones noted that President Harry Truman had imposed wage freezes that harmed these same working families already rationing. He eventually, and according to Jones, reluctantly, advocated price controls. Jones argued that these struggles revealed the shortcomings of the free enterprise system, which could "only prosper and avoid economic crises in war." The fact that so many families were struggling at a time when the United States had entered another war meant for Jones that "you can't have guns and butter too."[2]

Her opposition to the Korean War and Cold War anti-communism centered on her criticism that capitalism and freedom were not synonymous and that a nation that had never truly exercised democracy could not export it elsewhere. Opposition to the Korean War is part of the historical elision surrounding that war for Americans. Those who spoke out against the US-led intervention in Korea, like Jones, opposed it for many reasons. Some feared war in the nuclear age, others were committed to pacifism. The Black radical women in this book opposed the US anti-communist policy that defined its relationship with its wartime ally the USSR and its role in geopolitics. In other words, they opposed the US Cold War policy in its entirety. Their opposition was characterized by several factors. First, their belief that the USSR was a friend to people of color in the US and in the colonized nations that were seeking independence after the war. Anti-communism transmuted empires, like the US, into defenders of freedom and nationalist movements in postcolonial states into Communist conspiracies. Operationally, the US embraced its role as the primary global military force preventing the spread of that conspiracy. This fed radicals second opposition to the war; the growth of US militarism in service to monopoly capitalism, a term used by radicals to describe the power capitalist interests had over government decision-making. They feared that should the US embrace policing liberation movements abroad, it would abandon democracy at home. They predicted that this abandonment would commit US taxpayers to endless war, the destruction of liberation movements, and the evisceration of the New Deal state, limited as it was.

Black radical women feared the growth of US militarism, the empowerment of monopoly capital, the spread of US neo-colonialism, and primarily what this meant for social justice. The activists in this book argued that a segregated military deployed by a segregated country could not bring democracy to others. A nation at war with itself over the rights of its citizens did not know peace or democracy and could bring neither to other countries. The women in this book are only some of the voices opposed to the Korean War, but their significance resides in how they defined peace. Peace was not simply the absence of war, peace required social justice, which they argued could only be found in a socialist state where systemic barriers to equity and justice would be eradicated.

This book centers on the anti-Korean War activism of Louise Thompson Patterson, Claudia Jones, Charlotta Bass, Shirley Graham Du Bois, Eslanda Robeson, Lorraine Hansberry, and Beulah Richardson, all Black women who were radicalized by their experiences with racism and misogyny. These experiences informed their anti-war position. These women believed that the absence of military conflict was not enough to secure peace. Peace required the liberation of the most oppressed, thus, it meant Black liberation, women's liberation, and self-determination for the colonized. I argue that anti-Korean War activists protested US intervention because it disrupted a liberation movement in a nation of color, a liberation movement that had resisted one colonial power (Japan), only to face another (US). Korean independence, they argued, was intertwined with their independence, as capitalist imperialist powers in the US sought to secure power by subjugating nations of color and people of color. Their vision of peace mirrored the concept of positive peace, a concept articulated in academic literature by Johan Galtung which defined peace as both the "absence of war" and the "presence of justice."[3] However, the women in this book believed that positive peace could not exist under capitalism. Peace meant securing justice and justice could only be secured under socialism; for these women, peace required capitalism's destruction.

This project contributes to the broader scholarship on Black radicalism by demonstrating that Black radical women were influential in organizing and theorizing a conception of peace that was anti-racist, anti-sexist, and necessarily anti-capitalist. They adopted a vision of the future that embraced socialism as key to securing peace and a prerequisite for liberation. They were viewed as a threat because they challenged US claims to democratic leadership and revealed that the US democratizing mission was a colonizing project founded on war and terror and used to enforce capitalisms power. The US sought to hide its anti-democratic practices behind the veneer of righteousness while those that challenged it were violently silenced. This book excavates the forgotten activism against the Korean War and its links to the long durée of Black radical resistance to racist oppression.

BECOMING RADICALS

The women in this book argued that the US Cold War policy was fascist in intent and practice and that it perpetuated the oppression of people of color globally. This book describes them as radicals in contrast to liberals because liberals sought to reform the existing economic and government structures. Instead, radicals recognized that oppression was systemic in existing institutions and that reforming such a system would require constant struggle. Though only two of them were CPUSA members (Louise Thompson Patterson and Claudia Jones) each of them was drawn to party campaigns and practices which influenced their anti-Korean War activism. Louise Thompson Patterson and Claudia Jones were drawn to the CPUSA in the Depression decade because of its vocal and devoted anti-fascism and anti-racism, which they believed were synonymous. Racism was akin to fascism and the persistence of US racism was not anomalous but embedded in its institutions and traditions. Erik McDuffie argues that it was the Scottsboro case that ushered in a new generation of Black women activists into the Communist Party. This new generation was more self-assured, rejected respectability politics, and felt less invested in traditional femininity, and instead showed "intellectual sophistication, political independence," and scandalously, "sexual modernism." The Scottsboro case proved to party members that the US was not free from fascism.[4]

On March 25, 1931, nine youths, Roy and Andy Wright, Eugene Williams, Heywood Patterson, all from Chattanooga, Tennessee, and the only ones of the group that knew each other; Ozie Powell, Clarence Norris, Olen Montgomery, Charlie Weems, and Willie Roberson, all from Georgia, were traveling through Alabama on the same train. The police met the train in Paint Rock, Alabama, after a fight was reported. They discovered two young white women, Ruby Bates, and Victoria Price, among the youth on the train. Bates said later that she and Price claimed they were raped to avoid charges of vagrancy and prostitution. The police arrested the nine boys, ranging in age from thirteen to nineteen. Within a matter of weeks, all but Roy Wright, who was only thirteen years old, were tried, convicted, and sentenced to death by all-white juries in Scottsboro, Alabama.[5]

The International Labor Defense (ILD) with support from the CPUSA rallied around the Scottsboro Boys using a mass action tactic that involved legal assistance, fundraisers, marches, rallies, and publicity. This tactic would eventually save the men from execution, but the case would be long and drawn out with the last defendant released from prison in the 1950s. The Scottsboro Boys exemplified "lynch law," a phrase the party used to describe the use of the legal system to unfairly imprison and kill Black Americans. The phrase described how police, courts, and juries became the new lynchers, and this unfair system was used to placate those who once engaged in vigilante violence. White supremacists were secure in knowing that no Black American could find justice within the courts and prison, the system and those working in it were the new vigilantes.[6]

Louise Thompson Patterson was a leader in the ILD's national movement for the Scottsboro Boys. Thompson Patterson was a fellow traveler of the party when they were arrested; the case inspired her to increase her involvement. A westerner by birth, Thompson Patterson moved frequently as a youth until settling in California during her college years. In 1928, she moved to New York into the heart of radical activism and the cultural ferment of the Harlem Renaissance. During the Scottsboro trials, she took a job with the ILD, an organization devoted to defending the oppressed, including the Scottsboro Boys. Eventually, she joined the party and worked with various adjacent organizations including the International Workers Order (IWO), the Civil Rights Congress (CRC), and the Council on African Affairs (CAA). In 1940 she married attorney and head of the ILD William Patterson.[7]

As an ILD organizer, Thompson Patterson organized the march on Washington on May 8, 1932 to encourage the federal government to enforce the constitution in Scottsboro. She was critical of mainstream civil rights organizations like the NAACP and the ACLU who she argued never organized people in the streets. The NAACP did assist in the Scottsboro Boys' defense, but the ILD and the NAACP never quite agreed on how to conduct the campaigns and even competed to convince the defendants' mothers to side with one or the other organization. This competition never dissuaded the ILD, and it and Thompson Patterson continued mass action campaigns, something the NAACP feared alienated and inflamed white people in the localities of some of these cases. Thompson Patterson gained important organizing experience in the ILD, an experience she would bring to her anti-Korean War activism.[8]

Thompson Patterson organized a march on Washington on May 8, 1932, to pressure the federal government to intervene in the Scottsboro case. She was critical of mainstream civil rights organizations like the NAACP who she described as "mis-leaders" because they never organized people in the streets and placated government officials. The organization of the march took months and Thompson Patterson was left with many of the logistical issues like organizing charter buses, hosting organizational meetings, fundraisers, and rallies to raise awareness and funds. William Patterson, in a pre-march rally gave a speech linking the Scottsboro boys to the larger class struggle. This was part of the imperative for Black Communists like the Patterson's, to demonstrate to the white working class that racism was a tool used to divide and keep conquered the working masses, that it was the greatest enemy of working people and the greatest asset to capitalists. The best indicator of this was the defection of Ruby Bates, one of the alleged rape victims of the Scottsboro boys to the ILD's cause. Bates would travel to marches and rallies giving speeches about how she was compelled to lie on the stand at the trials.[9] Thompson Patterson declared the march a success. The marchers were joined by others from Philadelphia and DC, they had the mass meeting and made their presence known, and all were returned safely to New York. Days later the marchers held another meeting to share their stories of the trek. At it, Thompson Patterson told the audience "You are the United Front" and "not the misleaders."[10]

Across the country in California, Charlotta Bass raised awareness of the Scottsboro case in her newspaper *The California Eagle*. Born Charlotta Spear on February 14, 1890, in Little Compton, Rhode Island, in 1910, Bass traveled to Los Angeles under a doctor's orders for her health. After convalescing, she began working at *The Eagle* under the leadership of Joseph Neimore. Bass was initially hired to sell subscriptions, but Neimore's trust in Bass grew and, on his deathbed, he asked her to take over the newspaper.[11] Bass renamed it *The California Eagle* and transformed it into one of the most important Black newspapers of the twentieth century. For the next forty years, under her leadership and the efforts of her husband Joseph Bass, whom she married in 1915, the newspaper would balance political advocacy and action on behalf of the disenfranchised, with the social news that was so important to community papers. Bass faced off with the Ku Klux Klan which threatened her on numerous occasions, and she worked on desegregation and voting rights campaigns in her community.[12]

During the major organizing around the Scottsboro case, Claudia Jones was not yet the central CPUSA figure she would become in the postwar years, but the party's work on the case was one inspiration that drove her into its ranks. Jones was living in Harlem where street speakers informed the public about the Alabama frame-up and the Communist efforts to free the Scottsboro Boys. Jones was born in Trinidad and immigrated to the United States in 1924 as a child. Her family battled poverty and racism in their new homes in New York City, and Jones would later cite this as the birth of her radicalism. As an immigrant and child of working parents, she knew well that racism and sexism had costs besides limited economic opportunities. She cited her mother's death at her place of work as an example of the near-total exhaustion forced on Black workers for wages that could hardly provide for a family. The Scottsboro Boys, "stirred [her] up," and she joined the party in 1936. From there she rose in the ranks eventually becoming a noted theoretician and head of the party's Women's bureau.[13]

Jones became a leader in the Young Communist League and was a speaker and organizer for Scottsboro rallies. In 1939, she was a headline speaker at an eighth anniversary rally commemorating the Scottsboro boy's "frame-up" trials. The rally attendees and speakers planned to advocate for an anti-lynching bill and for the release of the remaining imprisoned Scottsboro boys, Andy Wright, Heywood Patterson, Charlie Weems, Clive Powell and Clarence Norris. In 1937, the other four were cleared of all charges, and the others were serving lengthy prison sentences, from seventy-five years to life sentences. The remaining defendants would eventually be pardoned between 1943 and 1950, except Heywood Patterson who escaped from prison in 1947 to Detroit. Michigan refused to extradite him, but Patterson eventually returned to prison after a bar fight ended in murder. He would die of cancer in 1952 at thirty-nine.[14]

Reflecting on her work in the Scottsboro campaign, Thompson Patterson believed that the case helped to break down some barriers that so often divided working people. She believed that Ruby Bates's reversal on the rape charges helped undermine some of the mythology around poor whites being the enemies of Black people. She argued that poor whites were used as "agent[s] to do the lynching" but that behind them were the state, the courts, the police, and the federal government who were instrumental in Black oppression. The party sought to organize the working classes and recognized that it was the state and its agents that exploited white working people and perpetuated the oppression of Black Americans. The goal was therefore to undermine the state's hold on working people by exposing it as an agent of capitalist interests invested in exploiting the labor of all poor Americans. The most efficient means of ensuring this was to ensure the working class would not unite, and racial division served that purpose. This would be a theme that emerged in the anti-fascist sentiments of party members and their fears that the US was only ever a hair's breadth away from fascism.[15]

The Scottsboro cases were foundational in the articulation of an anti-imperialist, anti-fascist, and anti-war thinking that would predominate in the party at the advent of World War II. Communists did not see domestic fascism as divorced from American terror abroad, in fact they were in direct relation to one another. Scottsboro specifically was important in drawing Black members into the party or into its inner circles. It was this case that drew the attention of Claudia Jones and the active participation of Louise Thompson Patterson. But the Popular Front policy begun in 1935 would lay out an anti-fascist program that linked police violence at home to fascist dictatorship abroad and draw in an even larger Black membership for the party.

As Alberto Toscano has argued, Black Americans have experienced racial fascism in the United States in the form of discriminatory laws, and in legal and extralegal violence. In other words, the Black American experience of fascism in the United States is "beyond analogy." Black Americans, long the targets of over policing, economic disenfranchisement, and punishment systems, have lived under racial fascism.[16] Fascist governments are built on foundations of racialized and gendered exclusions and Communists recognized that US policy was not so different. Pro-natalist policies in Germany that valued women's maternity were likened to American restrictions on birth control and abortion access. Germany's Nuremberg laws were compared to US Jim Crow laws, and later during the Spanish Civil War, Spanish women's political gains were quickly eliminated under the new fascist regime demonstrating that political reforms were tenuous at best. Among Black women Communists, the triple oppression paradigm highlighted Black women's particular struggles against racist, sexist, and class oppression, and emphasized their vulnerability within a fascist state. This furthered their commitment to socialist change since liberal reforms were fleeting under fascist regimes.

The Communist Party took a stand against the rise of the fascist states and simultaneously recognized fascist elements in the US. When Italy invaded Ethiopia in 1935, the party organized aid for Ethiopians and condemned Italy's colonial ambitions. That same year the Communist International (COMINTERN) in Moscow announced its People's Front of Struggle Against War and Fascism, also called the Popular Front. It encouraged Communists to engage in anti-fascist alliances with other liberals and leftists. In 1936, when fascists in Spain attacked the democratically elected government there, the CPUSA again mobilized in defense of the antifascists. Some radicals traveled to Spain to fight in brigades and Louise Thompson Patterson traveled there as part of a relief committee. Jones was drawn to the party's defense of Ethiopia and Spain, and she later cited the party's anti-fascism and support of the Scottsboro Boys as the reasons she joined.[17]

Traditionally the Popular Front refers to the period 1935–1939 when anti-fascism defined party policy. Mary Helen Washington argues that for Black radicals, the Popular Front continued until 1959. WWII encouraged "Black militancy" which fed postwar struggles and encouraged left-progressive cooperation. This Black Popular Front included "internationalizing" the Black struggle by petitioning the United Nations for redress against US racist policy. Black radicals also worked to "cast racial justice" in the interest of the country and all its people. In formulating their anti-Cold War and anti-Korean War objections, the individuals drawn to the party and its campaigns during the Popular Front, like Thompson Patterson, Jones, and Bass, integrated anti-fascism into the Black freedom struggle and articulated emancipatory claims in cooperation with their progressive comrades around the world.[18]

For Shirley Graham (later Du Bois), it was the treatment of Black soldiers during World War II that radicalized her. Racist abuses in the criminal legal system, the rise of fascism, and a segregated US military led to the realization that US policy resembled fascism and that capitalism perpetuated it. Graham Du Bois was born in Indianapolis, IN, in 1896. Her biographer Gerald Horne argues that Graham Du Bois was a "race woman," whose parents instilled in her a pride in her heritage. She was a playwright, writer, and politically committed activist who would become more radical by the end of World War II.[19]

She worked as the "director of negro work" with the YWCA-USO stationed at Fort Huachuca in Arizona where the soldiers and Women's Auxiliary Corp were segregated. The fort was isolated, and nearby communities were hostile to the Black soldiers making it a difficult place to be assigned. Horne argues that this work had a "catalytic impact" on Graham Du Bois's political identification. She lost her job after some of her writings about the racist treatment of Black military personnel caught officials' attention. This would be Graham Du Bois's first experience with censorship, but she would not be dissuaded, and she would become more committed to the radical liberation of Black America.[20]

After World War II, Jones, Thompson Patterson, Graham Du Bois, and Bass would be joined by other radical Black women like Eslanda Robeson, Lorraine Hansberry, and Beulah Richardson in their concern that the US was committing itself to constant war against "the darker side of the color line." Barbara Ransby, Eslanda Robeson's biographer, notes that Robeson participated in Franklin Roosevelt's 1944 presidential campaign; but, it was in 1948 that Robeson began to recognize the political ramifications of foreign and domestic policy, particularly Cold War anti-communism, and she became more active in the political left.[21]

Robeson was born to a middle-class family in Washington, DC, in 1895. After her father's death, her mother brought her and her two brothers to New York City and then eventually to Chicago where she finished high school. She met Paul Robeson in 1919 and the two were married in 1921. Ransby has argued that three events influenced Robeson's political commitments. In 1934 she traveled to the Soviet Union where she encountered anti-racism as state policy. Two years later she traveled to Africa where she confronted the "ugly realities of racism and colonialism." The third experience occurred during her travels as she met leaders in the diasporic freedom struggles across the world. Imaobong Umoren sees even more significance in Robeson's world travels, something unique among Black women in the early twentieth century. She argues that it cultivated an internationalism in Robeson that expanded her understanding of herself, and Black Americans, as "belonging to a larger world" along with other people of color. This went beyond the African diaspora as Robeson recognized that Black America shared its liberatory aspirations with people in Africa, Asia, and Latin America. This shaped her opposition to the Cold War and her support for Korean self-determination. Robeson would go on to author several books and befriend and work with other radical women like Jones and Graham Du Bois.[22]

Lorraine Hansberry was what Soyica Diggs Colbert describes as a "movement baby." Both of her parents were interested in racial uplift ideology, a respectability politics that Hansberry herself would later reject. Her father, who died when Hansberry was still a teenager, had been a Federal Marshall and an important member of Chicago's NAACP and Urban League, he was also central to the movement against restrictive covenants. Her father bought the family home in a white Chicago neighborhood where they faced racist hostility. Eventually, a court case with the Hansberry name on it made its way to the Supreme Court challenging the restrictive covenants that were used to keep Black families out of white neighborhoods. In the 1940 *Hansberry v. Lee* decision, the court agreed that Hansberry could contest a covenant that had been upheld in court previously. It did not strike covenants down but helped lay a foundation for later decisions undermining the power of restrictive covenants and was an inspiration for Hansberry's play *A Raisin in the Sun*. Both her parents were active in the local Republican party and she and her siblings were taught to be devoted to the "family and the race," so much so that her brother refused induction into the segregated military during WWII.[23]

Hansberry's success as a playwright and her association with figures in the civil rights movement has often obscured her earlier radical commitments, and the concomitant legal harassment she faced by the FBI. She early on criticized Cold War policy and as Fanon Che Wilkins argues, "reached her political maturity in the mid-1950s." This activism, he notes, challenges the widely held belief that opposition to the Cold War represents a "sharp break in the international thrust of postwar" Black radicalism that continued to rebuke American empire. Wilkins focuses on Hansberry's commitment to African liberation and its persistence despite legalized harassment. I argue that even before the mid-1950s, Black radicals, including Hansberry, forged their internationalism and opposition to US empire during the Korean War.[24]

Beulah Richardson was born in Vicksburg, Mississippi in 1925. She graduated from Dillard University in New Orleans in 1948 and traveled to Los Angeles to launch her acting career. She met Louis Thompson Patterson and her husband William Patterson in California. She lived in both San Diego and Los Angeles and as Dayo Gore has argued, she met radicals associated with the Communist party in both cities, but the Patterson's and Paul Robeson were important in introducing her to radicalism. Richardson would eventually go on to become the well-known actress Beah Richards but in these years she found her way to New York where she began to work more closely with other radicals becoming one of Louise Thompson Patterson's closest collaborators and allies.[25]

The Scottsboro Boys case and the party's anti-fascism drew Black radicals into and around the party. It was in this period that they expanded on the existing analysis of US racial fascism and argued that the US had never practiced democracy; lynch law cases like the Scottsboro Boys proved that. Though they hoped that World War II and the US alliance against fascism would usher in a multiracial democracy, Cold War anti-communism dashed their dreams. They came to see the Korean War as the advent of a dangerous national security state committed to white supremacy, bolstered by capitalist imperialism, and committed to constant war. This convinced these radicals that peace required justice, and justice could only be secured under socialism.

KOREAN WAR IN HISTORIOGRAPHY

This project has benefited from a renewed interest among scholars in understanding the Korean War; this scholarship suggests that the Korean War is a far more consequential war than generally recognized. In the United States, its history and ferocity are wrapped up in a lingering anti-communism in which the US is constructed as a heroic savior to the (South) Korean people. The war justified the permanent national security state, surveillance of citizen activists, and a large military budget. Timed as it was at the cusp of the Cold War and following what State Department officials considered the loss of China to communism, the war served as a justification for the United States' bloated military budget. This military investment would allow the US to stay armed and keep and expand its base infrastructure while demanding the largest military spending in world history. The war taught US policymakers how to fight a conflict without the permission of constituents or Congress, and it justified the ongoing anti-communist repression of the civil rights and labor movements, permanently damaging both and limiting their efficacy. As Christine Hong argues, the war justified the US's "formidable infrastructure of violence" which became essential for its position as a global superpower. The Korean War helped to create many of the problems the US continues to face—it is a country that spends more than its allies and enemies on its military, it is a self-perpetuating war machine constructing enemies to justify overseas incursions at constant war even when war has not been declared, and a country whose people do not question its foreign entanglements while paying for war costs ostensibly in the interests of democracy. The Black radical women in this book warned that the Korean War was setting the US on this path, and according to historians, many of their fears came to pass.[26]

Significantly, the Korean War and the people who opposed it are an enigma for the US public. Suhi Choi has studied the Korean War and its memory in documentary films and public memorials; she argues that the US involvement in Korea does not reside in US "collective memory" like other wars have, instead, there is a "collective amnesia" about its history, and the US role in it. It has been seen as a mission to save the Korean people from the ravages of communism. That narrative, she argues, has "safely been maintained because there is little chance that the account would be contested." Part of the reason for that is there are so few "cultural products, the paucity of academic discourse as well as the absence of iconic images of this period in history." The reasons for this include that it was situated between World War II and the Vietnam War, both of which have taken pride of place in US memory. Choi argues that it could also be because it was "hidden behind the aura of the Cold War," sometimes literally as photographs and other evidence were largely in Communist countries. Another reason is "lingering McCarthyism" and the "unconnected information channels" between North and South Korea.[27]

Scholars have begun to reject the foundational narratives that the US has leaned on to justify its role in the war. Challenging the narrative of the US as anti-communist saviors and North Korea as unprovoked aggressors, historian Marilyn Young insists that the US helped to precipitate the war. That included ignoring its history as a colonized nation. After the Japanese victory in the Russo-Japanese War in 1902, Japan began to exert its power in the region. In a series of treaties between 1905 and 1910, that were "forced upon the Korean emperor and ministers through threats," the Japanese Empire took control of the country, imposed colonial administrators, and suppressed Korean culture and nationalist movements. After Japan's defeat in World War II, Koreans hoped that the US would support the nation's independence. Instead, US officials actively worked against Korean independence. During its postwar occupation, the US reimposed Japanese colonial authority and suppressed efforts toward independence; in contrast, the US and other Western allies were moving to end their occupation of Germany and actively worked with and protected Nazis. US policymakers made these decisions based on racist understandings of the Korean people. As Charles Kraus argues, the US occupation government created an "inverse image of themselves" in depictions of South Korean allies as "politically immature, culturally backward, and prone to dictatorship." These "discursive representations" both created a distance between Americans and Koreans and "justified-even necessitated" the US's occupation and continued influence there.[28]

In November 1945, the US occupation government issued ordinance number 21 which reaffirmed Japanese colonial laws. In December, the US "outlawed the People's Republic of Korea," which was a government created by Koreans who hoped the US would support self-determination. Instead the US positioned itself as a "benevolent sovereign," denounced Korean attempts at self-government, and passed ordinances that mirrored antiradical laws in the United States restricting freedom of speech.[29] For the next five years, the US backed the controversial and unpopular right-wing leadership of Rhee Syngman (known also as Syngman Rhee) and helped him to conduct suppression campaigns against leftist critics and the nationalist movement which had popular support. It also armed and trained the South Korean military, pushed for UN monitoring of elections in the South operating as if it was and would remain a separate government, and ignored the South's hostilities against the North at the 38th parallel. For Mary Dudziak, this means that the US justified intervention as the protection of democracy, but the reality was that it aided a government that "massacred its political opposition."[30]

As Monica Kim has argued, while the US claimed it was not a colonial power, it had to simultaneously exert its power while proclaiming to be liberators. This led to "two kinds of military action." The first was "liberation through military occupation," this was framed as "decolonization" from the defeated Japanese. Meaning the US could claim it was helping to liberate Korea while actively suppressing liberation. The second military action was a "war of intervention," in US parlance a police action. Naming it a police action was part of the larger obfuscation of the war. As Kim argues, the US was moving away from the civilizing rhetoric traditionally used to justify imperialism and instead was constructing an image of itself as respecting gradual Korean liberation. Motivated by the racist beliefs that Koreans were incapable of self-government, liberation would be gifted through US benevolence.[31]

Young argues that an important lesson the Korean War taught political administrations was that wars could be prosecuted without "public enthusiasm or understanding." Dudziak has described how Truman's decision to go to war in June 1950, was a "deeply flawed [and] anti-democratic decision-making process" during which he not only did not seek congressional approval but saw Congress as a barrier. Truman acted unilaterally, did not call it a war and instead described it as a police action, and acted even before the United Nations agreed to enter, setting a precedent for presidents to commit the country to conflict with neither domestic nor international approval or support. For Young, it was during the war that American "public acquiescence" to the death toll and suffering "represented an achievement . . . that would serve future administrations." The federal government was able to "wage an immensely bloody war" and behave as if it was not happening. The war effort and the Cold War depended on preventing Americans from knowing what US forces were doing in Korea.[32]

Then as in now, few Americans understood the conflict, and in 1950, many saw it as the first confrontation with the Soviet Union and the federal government encouraged that assumption. Masuda Hajimu argues that those who were paying attention feared that US intervention in Korea was the start of World War III, and few if any discussed Korea. He reasons that there was no Cold War until the Korean War as local politics across the world created the "reality of the conflict." While traditionally, scholars have looked to politicians to place the blame for the Cold War, Masuda instead argues that "local contexts" helped to transform a "cold war" that had not escalated beyond rhetoric into a "Cold War," as conservatives in some places used it to justify suppression, and elsewhere it was used to violently root out undesirable elements. Dudziak notes that in the end Truman's reasons for committing the US to war, that it was part of a "Soviet plan to extend its power," were proven incorrect. The Korean War became the first of many twentieth-century wars the US entered on pretenses, and it created a precedent for unlimited presidential power which Dudziak calls the "legal order of the contemporary forever war." This book highlights the activism of Black radical women that predicted and warned against this path, but they faced violent suppression at the hands of the US government; therefore, their opposition, like the war, has little hold in US consciousness.[33]

ANTI-KOREAN WAR

The cultural elision about the war, I argue, influences the lack of historical memory about those who opposed it. This, however, is not the only reason Cold War peace activists have been marginalized in historical memory. There are several reasons for this amnesia. First, opponents were fractured across political lines, many were pacifists that embraced anti-communism and rejected alliances with the women in this book. There were socialists opposed to the war, but who kept their distance from radicals in the Communist Party orbit. Some liberals were opposed and feared war in the nuclear age but kept quiet to avoid being linked to communism. These political fractures are why it is difficult to describe it as an anti-Korean War "movement." Second, radical opposition to the Korean War was part of a larger opposition to Cold War policy; these activists rejected the propaganda that positioned the US as a democratic savior and the Soviet Union as a menace to freedom.

Perhaps more significantly, opposition to the war and anti-communist policy became increasingly dangerous as a variety of institutions deployed punitive measures against radicals. The foundation for antiradicalism was already in place by 1950, and politicians and law enforcement used old laws and enacted new strategies to silence dissent.

Finally, those who opposed the Korean War did not engage in some of the dramatic and overt displays that would come to characterize the anti-Vietnam War movement. There were no large-scale marches on Washington nor were there public draft card burnings or occupations of university buildings. Instead, their opposition could be seen in electoral challenges, petitions, conferences, speeches, publications, and alliances with radicals abroad. Most important, these activists integrated their resistance to the Cold War state in the movement against racist violence highlighting the lack of democratic protections for some Americans. This too was dangerous for people already being targeted by law enforcement officials, but radicals challenged the US image of itself as a country that valued freedom; a mythology that resonated with large parts of the American public. Radical challenges to it further marginalized them.

Black peace activism pre-dates the Korean War and demonstrates a tenuous relationship between white activists in organizations like the Women's International League for Peace and Freedom (WILPF) and its few Black members, or allies. As Melinda Plastas has shown, Black peace activists envisioned their peace commitments as part of "race-conscious" work for equality. Plastas explores WILPF's close working relationship with some Black club women and the few women that were members of the organization, most famously Mary Church Terrell who was the first Black woman to join. The work these women engaged in fostered an internationalist perspective that influenced how they would confront Jim Crow inequities at home. They, like the women in this book, understood peace as part of their larger efforts to securing democracy in the US. Though their work with white activists was often fraught with conflict, Plastas argues that these women contributed to an expansive liberatory politics that was not confined to US borders. Thus the radical women in this book are part of a larger genealogy of Black peace activists; however, theirs was deeply anti-capitalist and grounded in the belief that war and capitalism were twin evils.[34]

Joyce Blackwell demonstrates that Black peace activists were not pacifists but instead felt that "peace and freedom were inseparable." This means that war and violence could sometimes be justified to achieve peace and freedom. For Black Americans, after the US began seizing its own colonial possessions, their peace activities were integrated into "nonpeace organizations" that resisted US colonial power as white supremacy masked as democracy. Blackwell notes that the Women's Peace Party (WPP), the US branch of WILPF, adopted "non violent resistance or nonviolence" which meant that the group both rejected violent solutions, but committed to ending the "causes of violence- political, economic, and social inequalities." This stand did appeal to Black women, but the organization struggled to recruit Black women into the group, until later in the century when the anti-Vietnam War movement drew in members, especially those already organizing in civil rights and other social justice groups. Blackwell's analysis does not include the Korean War arguing that while some activists continued their peace work, anti-communist harassment made it difficult, if not impossible to continue.[35]

Black wartime participation was often framed as a means to secure a place in the larger body politic, but Black soldiers most often faced segregation, hostility, and violence from their fellow countrymen. This did not stop attempts by Black leaders to seek expanded rights during wartime; continued failure, however, most often pushed leading activists into the peace movement. Those that pushed for expanded rights during war, and protested the poor treatment of Black troops were also considered "disloyal and unpatriotic, bordering on subversive." This did not quell wartime activism.[36]

In a now notorious historic moment, W. E. B. Du Bois, who believed that World War I originated with the European contest over African territory; nevertheless, advocated for Black participation. Shane Smith has argued that Du Bois's stand on the war was often paradoxical, and far more complex than historians have described it. In July 1918, Du Bois published an article in the NAACP's *The Crisis* magazine titled "Close Ranks" which counseled Black Americans to work toward the war effort as part of the commitment to expand American democracy. This article has been cited as a departure from Du Bois's anti-imperialism; Smith argues that in fact, it is one of many editorials in which Du Bois supported Black military service.[37]

Du Bois's advocacy is infamous because of his later anti-war stance, the assumption he did it to secure an officer's commission, vehement opposition from his peers, and his later peace activism, particularly during the Korean War. Chad Williams has chronicled Du Bois's complex emotions on the first world war and shows that this incident would eventually lead to his radicalization and later rejection of war and wartime service. This moment also reveals the complexity of war and Black wartime service. Du Bois's article and commission led to fierce denunciations and conflict within the NAACP, with some leaders like Joel Springarn defending Du Bois, while some of the membership accused him of "abandoning the race." William Monroe Trotter of the National Equal Rights League, denounced Du Bois, accusing him of being "not only no longer a radical, he is a compromiser, he is a deserter, he is a rank quitter of the fight for rights." Williams argues that Black radicals "went in for the kill." Journalist and radical Hubert Harrison published an article in his newspaper *The Voice* titled "The Descent of Dr. Du Bois." In it, he described Du Bois's actions as "cowardice" and accused him of surrendering "life, liberty, and manhood."[38]

This controversy notwithstanding, there were others in the Black press that counseled cooperation during World War I. But after the war, Black Americans, including veterans, continued to face violence and segregation. Wartime participation had not expanded equality. Mitchell Lerner argues that Korea represents an often-overlooked shift in how Black Americans viewed both military participation and equal rights struggles. Disillusioned by the World War I experience, there was a shift during WWII toward "cooperation alongside struggle." The "Double V" campaign, which advocated victory at home and abroad, launched by the *Pittsburgh Courier*, took a middle-of-the-road approach, which advocated for pushing for Black equality at home and engaging in patriotic work for the war. As Lerner shows, scholars have shown that renewed disappointment after the war became "struggle over cooperation" during the Vietnam War. He argues that Korea needs to be part of this trajectory as the movement and many of its leaders continued "cooperation alongside struggle," and thus it was a continuation of WWII efforts.[39]

The Korean War was supposed to be different since President Truman had ostensibly integrated the military with an executive order in 1948. However, "cooperation alongside struggle" presented new challenges as many Black soldiers continued to report poor treatment and continued segregation on US bases and in Korea. Some soldiers questioned why they should be committed to a war and a country that failed to secure democracy for them. Among some activists, early war support dissolved in the face of military racism and continued racist violence at home.[40]

Lerner argues that the war was important in motivating the Black freedom struggle to take on a more "confrontational position." Because of military integration, civil rights leaders often argued for cooperation with officials and embraced a "pro-American, integrationist" position. That would not last as racist incidents in the military and at home led to increased opposition. For Hong, US leaders billed its integrated military as a paragon of its democracy, but the reality was that this "militarized multiculturalism" only served to obscure the "structural linkages and entanglements between differently subjugated populations." The ostensibly democratic military participation of Black soldiers served the US's geostrategic goals and allowed it to launch its "experiments in neo-colonial control" in Asia first.[41]

Increasing discontent, attacks on civil rights, and racist violence continued, and US policymakers ignored calls to enforce integration. The wartime Fair Employment Practices Committee (FEPC), created in 1941 to prevent discrimination in war industries, disappeared amid calls for a permanent committee. This increased frustration as cases of discrimination against soldiers came to light. Bases in southern states continued to practice segregation, and the federal government failed to enforce the desegregation order claiming that it was forced to honor local segregation laws. Even in Korea, after capture, Black Prisoners of War (POW) faced hostility from their fellow white POWs. Some white prisoners created Ku Klux Klan units in the camps and policed their fellow prisoners. These Klan members were seen as more loyal and anti-communist by US intelligence after the war and were "praised for their discipline," while Black soldiers remained under suspicion despite their political affiliations.[42]

Lerner notes that gradually "the sense of patriotic support for the war . . . dissipated" as did any hope that Black soldier's service would lead to an extension of civil rights, as cases of racism against Black soldiers and government failures to take them seriously made the national press. Black soldiers continued to fight but "with a bitterness and resentment" that was stronger than during the world wars; this would pave "the way for the more militant response to Vietnam." For Lerner, the conflicts over the Korean War are important context to understand Black resistance to military service during the Vietnam War.[43]

However, calls for peace and Black equality during the Korean War were complicated by US Cold War policy. Women peace activists found that anti-communism hindered their operations. This was as true for peace liberals in WPP and WILPF as it was for radicals and Communists. Marilyn Young has shown that there was general confusion about why the US was committing to the Korean War so soon after the world war and this fueled anti-war sentiment. This opposition was more widespread than generally acknowledged. As Young shows, Americans feared another world war, and desired peace, but believed that if the country was going to war it had to be a total victory. As Young argues, US troops were equally confused, it was not clear why they were in Korea, and many were not sure why China, a recent ally, was now the enemy. Many of the soldiers, veterans of WWII, were still "mad at the Japanese." The existence of nuclear weapons also made war more frightening.[44]

Some of the most vocal anti-war activists were pacifists who feared the nuclear age. A. J. Muste is one of the most well-known; he was associated with several pacifist groups including the Fellowship of Reconciliation (FOR), the Peacemakers, and the Committee for Non-Violent Action.

Muste, a former Marxist-Leninist, was a critic of US Cold War policy and as Leilah Danielson argues, he was as "prescient" as other critics who feared the policy would set the US on a permanent warpath. Muste felt that the US containment policy which committed the US to contain the spread of communism, made the world "profoundly insecure" as it fed the military machinery of several nations, which only made war and conflict more likely.[45]

Muste was critical of liberal support for peace through defense spending arguing that it was the very thing that compromised peace. The investment in military materiél that countries used to guarantee their defense was the "greatest obstacle[s] to the attainment of genuine or permanent collective security." He found that this was a sentiment that was especially prominent among liberal Protestants who displayed a "moral complacency and self-satisfaction" that excused the US from any responsibility in the Cold War. Muste was an anti-Stalinist and was suspicious of the Soviet Union, but he also believed that US depictions of it "naturalized and de-historicized the Soviet Union" and became a justification for oppressing the civil liberties of Americans. He rejected claims that containment would stop the spread of communism and argued that it would instead foul the US's already precarious reputation with the emerging liberation movements. He feared containment would put the US on the side of "reactionary elites" and in the US's attempts to stop indigenous movements for independence, it would instead push these nations into the Soviet camp.[46]

This book shows that Black radical women were committed to anti-Korean War activism even as they faced punitive measures and accusations of treason. The women in this book believed the war was a new phase in US capitalism that would permanently wed the military and civilian economies to the detriment of global emancipation. Thus war and capitalism were intimate compatriots, and to secure peace and democracy, monopoly capital had to be defeated. This stand directly contradicted US claims to democratic and capitalist superiority and elicited an aggressive response from US law enforcement, civilian patriotic organizations, and intelligence agencies. Using and expanding upon the existing anti-radical legal foundation, US law enforcement deployed punitive measures to silence Black radical women and their anti-war criticisms.

CRIMINALIZING PEACE

The most important reason why little is known about Korean War opposition is that many of those most vocal against it were radicals and some were

Communists. This radical opposition to the war was international, linked to the Soviet Union, and emerged from the anxieties produced by the bilateral contest between the US and USSR that predated the war. They believed that liberation could only be secured with the destruction of the capitalist war state and the creation of a socialist United States. This put them at odds with their government, conservatives, and liberals.

After WWII, while several nations were in the process of reconstruction, including the Soviet Union, the relatively unscathed United States appeared to be intent on and eager for war. The CPUSA's leaders and members attacked the US's growing military behemoth, defense spending, and the escalation of conflict with the Soviet Union. In the first year of the Korean War, as Mark Clapson argues, a large number of civilian deaths, especially from US bombings, led to "parallel propaganda" between Communist nations and Western nations. Communists in the CPUSA and the Communist Party of Great Britain (CPGB) published exposés on the violence. This explains why the US was so vehement in silencing the anti-war movement.[47]

These anti-communist purges marginalized the war's most radical critics and therefore, disciplined other liberals and progressives who distanced themselves from them. Young has shown that there was widespread opposition, and many referred to it as "Mr. Truman's war," but this opposition was targeted by intelligence agencies as part of the growing anti-communist campaigns in the US and it was denied legal recognition, as its leaders were monitored, arrested, harassed, imprisoned, and deported. As Young argues, any opposition to the Korean War was "tainted with association to communism." This has contributed to the amnesia about war opposition.[48]

While anti-communist hearings and legal harassment of radicals were not new in 1950, the war precipitated a more virulent and widespread campaign targeting radicals. Being a radical in the US carried great risk, and opposition to US militarism was particularly risky. Charisse Burden-Stelly has shown that far from being anomalous, anti-communism is a "durable mode of governance" that all levels of government employ. Anti-communism "served to manage and criminalize racial and political "others" whose ideas and beliefs, as much as actions, threatened to transform the racialized class order." Targeting Black radicals and their white allies essentially served to uphold capitalist power, maintain racial hierarchies, and justify political repression. It is an ever-present tool that "worked through and with white supremacy to encourage cross-class collaboration that obfuscated economic exploitation and discouraged interracial class solidarity." Anti-communism has become a means by which US politicians and capitalist leaders effectively stigmatize all challenges to power, but specifically Black radicalism, in order to perpetuate inequality. Liberals have often sided with anti-communists to their own detriment. They have participated in undermining even their own modest goals and prevented unity against divisive power structures, which undercuts all liberatory goals.[49]

The modern passage of federal anti-subversive laws was rooted in US colonial wars in the Philippines. Starting with a 1901 Sedition Law, colonial administrators pushed through legislation to "crush native resistance." In 1903 the Reconcentration Act "authorized mass incarceration" in concentration camps; this was followed by the Philippine Libel Law in 1904 which made "public hatred, contempt or ridicule" of the colonial regime illegal. Nick Fischer argues that authorities in the US went further even than the Philippine colonial administrators to silence dissent during its war in the Philippines, and they used similar language in domestic laws. This legislation expanded limitations on freedom of speech with the nations and its empire's growth and was used to suppress criticism of the US, especially during wartime.[50]

One of the more significant repressive laws was passed in the wake of William McKinley's assassination. In 1903, the Immigration or Anarchist Exclusion Act was passed which barred anyone who "advocated or associated with organizations" that sought the "forcible overthrow" of the US government. Anyone living in the US for less than three years alleged to advocate overthrow of the government could be deported.[51] The outbreak of war in Europe in 1915 and the US entrance in 1917 were used to justify further suppression. The declaration of war granted April 6, 1917, included "authority to censor and monitor telegraphic and telephonic communication." This was followed in June with the Espionage Act which gave the federal government "almost total authority [to] define and proscribe" acts or deeds that would turn people against the war. In October of that year, the Trading and Enemy Act allowed the president to censor and monitor any mail suspected to be subversive. In the spring of 1918, the Sedition Act made it illegal to denounce the war effort and attack the US's form of government. The 1798 Alien Enemies Act was "revived" and empowered the office of the president to deport "unnaturalized subjects of an enemy power."[52]

Deportation was one of the most powerful anti-communist tools in the federal government's arsenal. It was used after the 1903 law, but few radicals were expelled until the post–WWI purge. In fall 1918 the Dillingham-Hardwick Act was passed, also known as the Alien Anarchist Exclusion Act. It expanded on the 1903 law and allowed for the deportation of radicals. The law was used to deport 250 people in 1919 alone, including anarchists Emma Goldman and Alexander Berkman.[53]

The federal government did not operate alone and some of the most vicious and virulent anti-communist laws and committees were found at the state level. One of the most significant was New York State's Lusk Committee, created in 1917, it produced a gargantuan document titled *Revolutionary Radicalism*. Burden-Stelly shows that the Lusk Committee and its report created the foundation for radical repression. It pioneered tools that would be used throughout the twentieth century against radicals. These tools included "conflation of ideas with actions . . . the establishment of guilt by association," using surveillance material in later conspiracy cases, using punitive measures against members of radical organizations, "imprisonment and deportation for possessing radical literature," and using contempt charges to try and coerce testimony. All these tools would be used against anti-Korean War activists.[54]

Even in the Great Depression crisis years the surveillance state found the time and resources to harass radicals and used war in Europe as justification. The Dies Committee, the precursor to the House Un-American Activities Committee (HUAC), was created primarily to monitor fascists in the US; but its chairman Martin Dies, continued to focus on radicals, particularly labor activists. In 1935 the Bureau of Investigation (BI) became the Federal Bureau of Investigation (FBI) and without legal permission, the agency under J. Edgar Hoover expanded its surveillance powers and began to operate with local law enforcement. In 1938, the Foreign Agents Registration Act was passed which required disclosure from those acting in the interests of a foreign government. War abroad and the possibility of US entrance into the war excused the government's increased focus on targeting radicals. Donna Haverty-Stacke argues that it was war preparation that fueled fears of labor insurgency. With the potential for US involvement in the war, officials feared that radicals could disrupt industrial production. Labor resistance suddenly appeared treasonous and labor unions and radicals were targeted. The passage of the 1940 Smith Act (Alien Registration Act) further empowered the state. The act repeated some of the language of the 1903 law that criminalized the overthrow of the US government and included a "compulsory alien registration." It also set penalties for those that did not comply, including deportation. Initially it was used against the Trotskyist Socialist Workers Party (CPUSA rivals), and the Party "cheered the prosecution." But after World War II the government continued to liberally interpret intent to overthrow the government, and the Smith Act would be widely applied against CPUSA leaders. Haverty-Stacke argues that the targeting of labor activists during the war was a preview of the anti-communist trials to come.[55]

The Office of Naval Intelligence, the FBI, the US Army Counterintelligence Corps, the Secret Service, and after its creation in 1947, the Central Intelligence Agency (CIA) were all engaged in surveillance and intelligence gathering of US citizens—precisely what anti-communists accused Soviets of doing. But the federal agencies did not act alone and civilian organizations embracing racially specific patriotism actively promoted antiradicalism. The American Legion is one example. Tens of thousands of its members volunteered to act as confidential informants against radical organizations across the country and it cataloged people it suspected of communism. The FBI also communicated with these organizations encouraging protests against radical artists like Paul Robeson and the 1948 Henry Wallace campaign (see chapter 1). Anti-communist and anti-radical propaganda were used to construct a false sense of unity and arouse anger against dissenters.[56]

Young has argued that anti-Korean War activism was "as great as" and as mobilized as anti-Vietnam War protests, but it faced severe legal harassment and association with communism that de-legitimized it in the eyes of the US public. This means that the similarities between these activists have been obscured. The tactics they shared included "personnel, practices, anti-capitalist yearning, and occasionally tactics." She concludes that the anti-Vietnam War movement was the "culmination of the powerful protests" during the Korean War.[57] The radicals in this book centered their opposition to the war on their belief that despite the image it was trying to construct of itself, the US lacked basic democracy. It was evidenced in the persistence of segregation, racist violence, undemocratic elections, discrimination in education and employment, and the federal government's refusal to defend the constitutional rights of its citizens.

Further evidence included the suppression of peace activists and the punitive measures used to silence criticism of the US war state. This suppression was not something abstract to these radicals as they each cited their own experiences with racism and sexism as part of their radicalization. As Burden-Stelly demonstrates, a Black Scare and Red Scare have operated together to criminalize Blackness and Redness. She defines the Black Scare as the "debasement, distortion, criminalization, and subjection of Blackness," which targeted movements and individuals advocating equality. The Red Scare is the "criminalization and condemnation of anti-capitalist ideas, politics, and practices," and like the Black Scare, depended on discourses of "radical takeover" or the "displacement" of white authority. This ensured state suppression and popular support. Using this paradigm, Burden-Stelly demonstrates that "Blackness and radicalism [are] treated as vectors of subversion." Therefore, the anti-democratic measures taken by the Cold

War state to simultaneously crush liberation movements abroad and in the United States proved that the US could not commit to spreading democracy when it actively undermined it. This fueled anti-war activism.[58]

BLACK RADICAL WOMEN AGAINST THE KOREAN WAR

Even in the face of anti-communist campaigns, the CPUSA, its membership, and fellow travelers organized against the war, party members believed that a contest with the Soviet Union would commit the country to perpetual war; this opposition to anti-Communist policy influenced their understanding of the Korean War. If the US decided that it had to be the world's police force to preserve democracy, its policies would lead to tyranny, war profiteering, and an erosion of social conditions in the United States. The subjugation of the African, Asian, Latin American, and Middle Eastern countries in the name of anti-communism would come at the price of people of color everywhere and the living standard of Americans.

Together Thompson Patterson, Jones, Bass, Graham Du Bois, Robeson, Hansberry, and Richardson imagined a peace that not only rejected war as a tool of capitalist control and wealth accumulation, but also sought a peace based on social justice. Peace could not be achieved without first guaranteeing the right to an equitable and humane existence for all people. The first campaign to encapsulate this goal was the Progressive Party coalition behind Henry Wallace's bid for president in 1948. While the campaign failed, those involved were inspired to continue their work for peace. Wallace chose to run for president out of concern that President Truman was escalating tensions with the Soviet Union and that it would lead to another war. His campaign for president not only worked to try and prevent war, but it also sought to confront the injustices in the United States, end nuclear proliferation, and promote progressive policies. The campaign envisioned the kind of peace radicals sought, one that was grounded in the rights of citizens in the US and abroad. Though it did not go so far as to promote socialism, the Wallace campaign tolerated Communist participation at a time when association with radicals was increasingly precarious. This coalition of radicals, progressives, and liberals was a preview of the mass struggle needed to make substantive systemic change; because of this, it was targeted by federal officials and red-baited into oblivion.[59]

Journalism was essential to anti-war activism. While some of the women were central figures in campaigns, like the Progressive Party, they each produced written work that expressed their commitment to peace, socialism, and racial justice. They were also connected to international networks of radicals that organized peace conferences. These peace conferences became a central organizing engine for the global peace movement, which meant that the US government regularly monitored them and worked with friendly governments to limit travel to them. These legal restrictions meant that not all the women were able to attend the conferences, but they used their journalistic skills to report on their significance and promote a commitment to an international effort to counter US hegemony.

Fear of the nuclear age also drove anti-Cold War activism. Those involved in the postwar peace movement expressed discomfort and fear when the US dropped two bombs on Japan in August 1945. Five years later, in the months before the US intervention in Korea, Truman announced the US would work to create an even more powerful and deadly hydrogen bomb. Activists already on high alert scrambled to oppose this move, and when war broke out in Korea, centered opposition to nuclear weapons in their peace campaigns. One campaign in the anti-nuclear movement was the Stockholm peace petition, known as the Ban the Bomb signature campaign. Radicals worked to secure US signatures on the petition; meanwhile, the federal government labeled it Communist propaganda and targeted those who promoted it. The petition galvanized peace activists globally against Cold War tensions they feared would lead to a nuclear war. These radicals also emphasized that nuclear weapons had only ever been used against a nation of color and were wielded against liberation movements to secure independence on the US's terms and not their own. Nuclear power, they argued, prevented social justice and liberation, and allowed the US to hold the world hostage.

The Sojourners for Truth and Justice (STJ) was founded out of Black radical fears that racist violence and war were kin and used against Black America and the colonized to prevent liberation and maintain white supremacy. The Sojourners, founded by Louise Thompson Patterson and Beulah Richardson, was a pioneering organization of Black women most well-known for its activism against racist violence and legal lynching. But it was also critical of US containment policy and its alleged mission to secure democracy abroad. The STJ called for an immediate end to the Korean War and pointed to the paradox of Black Americans serving in a neocolonial war while they could not enjoy democracy at home. The organization was short-lived but highlighted the women's investment in a social justice-based peace.

Central to their anti-war activity was opposition to lynch law. While the Scottsboro Boys case radicalized a generation of Black radical women, the death penalty case against Willie McGee who allegedly raped a white woman came to define legal lynching during the Cold War. The US predicated its anti-communism on the notion that it was a bulwark against anti-democratic forces, but McGee's conviction and execution based only on the questionable accusations of a white woman proved US democracy was illusory. McGee's case, coupled with racism against Black soldiers in Korea, specifically the case against Leon Gilbert who fled battle, the firebombing of activists Harry and Harriette Moore's home, and the case against Rosa Lee Ingram who defended herself against the sexual advances of a white man, fueled anti-war activism. These activists argued that democracy could not be spread by a racist state and the failure of the US government to ensure the democratic rights of Black America proved it could not spread democracy abroad.

The Progressive Party made another go at the Presidency in 1952 and put Charlotta Bass on the ticket for vice president. This was a historic moment as a Black woman had never been included on a major party ticket before. Bass campaigned with presidential candidate Vincent Hallinan on much the same platform as the 1948 campaign. But in 1952, the stakes were different, the nation was at war, and Bass and the campaign faced right-wing and liberal critics; even Henry Wallace had abandoned the Progressive Party. For Bass, the campaign was not about victory, it was about protest. She told audiences that a vote for the Progressive Party was a vote against the Cold War, against anti-communism, against racism, sexism, and fascism. Most importantly, a vote for the Progressive Party was a vote for peace.

After years of activism and devotion to social justice, what these women faced in return was law enforcement harassment, arrest, prison time, loss of jobs, separation from family, deportation, seizure of travel papers, and the list goes on. What the nation faced was a legacy of hostility toward social programs and a knee-jerk reaction to scream "communism" or "socialism" at anything resembling social legislation; weakened freedom struggles that were dismissed as Communist agitation when they called for the most basic recognition of rights; the use of taxpayer funds for endless war and the enrichment of capitalists; and a deep-seated ideology that chose to ignore systematic abuses and blame the disenfranchised for their oppression. These activists warned that any hope for democracy had always been aspirational in the United States and that fascism was ingrained in US racist policy. Even in the face of anti-communist harassment and punishment, they believed in the US and hoped to see a more democratic future.

The women featured in this book argued that peace was not just a commitment to end war, peace was a commitment to justice and equality. They argued that while anti-communism claimed to promise a democratic future, the reality was that it led the United States into endless conflict, and while policymakers claimed this conflict was to secure democracy in other nations, Black Americans had yet to enjoy the fruits of democracy. This book explores anti-Korean War activism as a moment when radicals, under attack by repressive Cold War legislation, articulated a position that held that ending the war was a precursor to women's and Black emancipation. War, they argued, secured the power of the state, required the suppression of dissenting voices, and made the US a neocolonial power. Additionally, war was a capitalist tool to perpetuate racial and gender inequality, create divisions in the workforce, and prevent labor organizing all to ensure profits. Radical Black women activists argued that war had to be eradicated to achieve liberation. While anti-communism was ostensibly about spreading democracy, it prevented liberation, stymied independence movements, and prevented the spread of democracy. Most importantly, capitalism ensured that war would continue; therefore, ending war required ushering in socialism. Without radical change, these activists predicted a future of near-constant warfare within and outside the US borders, a country with virtually no social programs, and endless poverty; many of their fears came to pass.

CHAPTER ONE

Opposing Hot and Cold War

On March 5, 1946, former British Prime Minister Winston Churchill delivered a speech at Westminster College in Fulton, Missouri, that has become widely known as the "Iron Curtain" speech. In it, he began to imagine how the postwar world should look, and he hoped that the newly created United Nations Organization with US membership would be a tool to prevent war. But he was also very clear that worldwide cooperation did not mean worldwide trust, friendship, or camaraderie. He did not believe that nuclear knowledge should be shared, particularly not with Communists, and he insisted, without irony, on free elections; something Black America did not enjoy. Churchill spoke at length about fraternal compacts between the US and UK in the event of war, later formalized in the North Atlantic Treaty Organization in 1949. Then he moved to the most unforgettable part of the speech in which he noted his affection for Russia but also his growing concerns. In the most famous line, he said "From Stettin in the Baltic to Trieste in the Adriatic, an Iron Curtain has descended across the continent." Behind this curtain were nations that were now under what he described as "control from Moscow." He claimed Communist fifth columns were operating in other countries and taking orders from Moscow; however, he did not believe there were any in the United States because the number of Communists was so small. This did not influence US anti-communists who imagined a revolutionary force trying to undermine and overthrow the government.[1]

Claudia Jones took issue with several parts of Churchill's speech. First, it was given at an institution that practiced segregation. Second, it was clear to her that Churchill's Anglo alliance between the US and UK, which he phrased as "English-speaking peoples," was not dissimilar from Hitler's goal of Aryan supremacy. Moreover, she saw Churchill's peace overtures, which encouraged US military strength, as "sabre-rattling" and setting the stage for a future of war. Finally, Jones argued that this alliance would once again exclude Black people and others in the diaspora as the old empires combined with the US empire to solidify control through militarization. In 1946,

Jones was becoming increasingly concerned that the wartime alliance was dissolving in favor of anti-communist military posturing.[2]

Charlotta Bass shared Jones's concerns. Only days after Churchill's speech she wrote in her weekly column titled "On the Sidewalk" in her newspaper *The California Eagle* that "fifteen million dark Americans . . . listened to Winston Churchill's **words of wisdom** with a degree of apprehension and foreboding." She expressed her doubts about Churchill's awareness of the concerns of Black Americans and people in the decolonizing nations across the world. Churchill claimed that democracy lay with the capitalist democratic nations, Bass argued that those nations did not have a history of democracy when it came to their colonies nor the people living in the metropole. Like Jones, Bass noted that the college was segregated, she wrote: "I wonder if friend Churchill knew that Black American soldiers returning from overseas where they went to fight Hitler are not allowed to matriculate at Westminster College." She emphasized the hypocrisy of the US and UK demanding democracy at a segregated institution.[3]

Both women believed that the Soviet Union, which Churchill accused of aggression, was, as Jones wrote, a "proven friend [to] millions of Black and Brown colonial people." They both insisted that accusing the USSR of aggression ignored the US's aggressive stance and they were concerned about the abandonment of the wartime alliance with the Soviets. Bass wrote of a lynching that was averted in Tennessee the same day Churchill gave his speech, and that it was only the Soviets that were standing up against this "undemocratic democracy" while the US government failed to pass anti-lynching legislation. Jones wrote that it was Black people who would have to stand up as leaders in the struggle against another war, a war that Churchill and Harry Truman seemed to be inviting.[4] Years later Shirley Graham Du Bois used Churchill's metaphor to warn of an "Atlantic Curtain," a curtain that blinded the American people to the reality behind the Cold War. This reality was that the United States manufactured a crisis with the Soviet Union to justify overseas intervention in nations of color, an increased military budget, resistance to disarmament, and the suppression of the US Black freedom struggle. It was all in service to a growing military-industrial complex that fed American fears and encouraged the alliance of the civilian and military economies.[5]

On the precipice of the Cold War, Bass, Jones, Graham Du Bois, and other radical activists feared that the sacrifices in the recent war against fascism were wasted and that the US anti-communist policy was itself fascist. It was in these years that activists reimagined a peace that was at odds with the US government policies which committed the country to a campaign against an alleged Communist menace. The government along with corporate interests pushed to create an anti-communist consensus that justified overseas intervention, military spending, and the internal purges of radicals all ostensibly to prevent Communist totalitarianism and preserve democracy. Jones, Bass, Graham Du Bois, and others attacked these policies as authoritarian, and justifications for military proliferation and wartime profiteering. They argued that peace required equity, humanity, and an ethos of care and cooperation. The peace movement predated the Korean War, and in the years between 1946 and 1950, radical activists watched as the US used anti-communism as justification for overseas intervention, alliances with undemocratic regimes, and justification to suppress internal dissent.

Claudia Jones most effectively theorized a social justice-centered vision of peace, which, she argued could not happen under capitalism as capitalist interests, driven by profit, pursued war, and conflict abroad to secure resources and labor. Jones was one of the party's most prolific writers and theorists, and she defined peace in opposition to US anti-communist policy. She instead reasoned that anti-communism was fascist because it centered on war and conquest to secure the US government and capitalist interests. To do so, it suppressed criticism, violated the constitutional rights of citizens, and deployed violence against liberation movements. US policy, she argued, was predicated on war.[6]

The 1948 Henry Wallace presidential campaign was the first organized effort to challenge anti-communist policy. The Black women involved found that their voices were important in imagining and theorizing what peace should look like. The campaign created a progressive coalition that helped the women to visualize a just world. Influenced by thinkers like Jones, peace was imagined as the absence of war and the hope for an equitable future. A democratic nation, they argued, could not wage war abroad and against its own people.

The Cold War peace movement was internationalist as it drew these activists into the global peace movement, a movement spearheaded by radicals that the US intelligence apparatus identified as subversive. This did not dissuade them. Shirley Graham Du Bois was especially active in the global peace movement as she traveled to peace conferences abroad to connect with other women who were concerned about the US military's aggression. This early opposition to anti-communist foreign policy informed women's opposition to the Korean War. US intervention in Korea would not have been possible had the US not pursued what became known as containment and radical activists knew that the Korean War was not a proxy war with Soviet communism; rather, it was a war against the independence of people on the "darker side of the color line."[7] It was in the years before 1950 that Claudia Jones, Charlotta Bass, Shirley Graham Du Bois, Lorraine Hansberry, and Eslanda Robeson would all help to envisage a peaceful future as one that achieved racial, economic, and gender equity and rejected capitalist control.

SOVIETS AND PEACE

What drove US policymakers was the belief that the Soviet Union engineered a global peace movement as a cover to spread communism; therefore, Americans who supported the Soviets and peace were believed to be treasonous Communist agents. The peace movement coalesced against US policies like the 1947 Truman Doctrine. The Truman Doctrine came out of a speech President Harry Truman gave before a joint session of Congress on March 12, 1947. In the speech he requested funds to the tune of hundreds of millions of dollars to be given to Turkey and Greece to "withstand Soviet pressure." Before the speech, this funding request was "put into the framework for a new global foreign policy," in the State Department. The doctrine was a key moment in US Cold War policy as it committed the US to insulate other countries from Soviet influence.[8]

In response, in 1948, the Soviet Union announced the "Struggle for Peace in All the World" campaign, which informed its foreign policy until 1954. Timothy Johnston argues that the Soviet's Struggle for Peace campaign was a "vital platform" to communicate an "early Cold War vision of the world" to the Russian people. This focus on peace provided the Russian people with a way to define peace and was not, as some scholars suggest, a way to trick Russians. In other words, recovering from the world war led many to imagine different ways to achieve peace. This was something the Russian people who had experienced war, desperately needed. In contrast, the American people, most of whom did not witness battle, appeared to be posturing for another conflict. The Soviet peace movement was also an attempt to cover for the country's military deficiencies.[9]

US intelligence agencies viewed the Soviet peace platform with suspicion. A 1949 State Department report claimed that the Soviet peace program was a propaganda campaign to rally "non-Communist foreign support" and to influence labor organizations. The Soviet's program, the report claimed, misunderstood US intentions. By 1949, the Soviets had successfully tested its atomic bomb and had advanced the message that its nuclear program was committed to ensuring peace and preventing the US from holding the world hostage as the only atomic power. The Soviets hosted peace congresses across the world and the State Department attacked them as a front exploiting intellectuals' desire for peace. It made recommendations for a reverse propaganda campaign to emphasize US efforts at peace. The document was also remarkably self-aware about the danger of US racism in the Cold War contest and urged that the State Department emphasize "the advance made by the American Negro" when in African nations and India and focus on the "violent nature of communism" and the role of the UN in securing peace.[10]

Its recommendations for dealing with domestic issues regarding the Soviet Peace initiative included an internal propaganda campaign highlighting US progress in the labor movement and recommending a focus on the "vertical mobility of social structure" in the US, the right to "juridical defense," and the right to protest. These were remarkable claims given the persistence of legal segregation and the harassment and arrests of Communists and fellow travelers, especially those in labor unions. Additionally, the State Department recommended downplaying differences among Americans and "exploitation of the emotional loyalties of man to country, religion, family and local traditions." The report recommended a focus on propagating the idea that Soviet culture was failing, that communism meant abandoning individuality, and that there was "dwindling membership in Communist parties" around the world. This latter claim was paradoxical given that US containment policy pivoted on the assumption that the Soviets were successfully spreading the Communist conspiracy and that Communists were proliferating. The State Department's goal was to convince Americans that communism and the Soviet Union were a detriment to democracy and free expression.[11] Radicals were not dissuaded from criticizing the new containment policy and actively participated in the global peace movement, despite its links to the Soviet Union.

THEORIZING PEACE

Claudia Jones led "theoretical innovation on the left" on peace, gender, and race. She theorized a notion of peace that envisioned an equitable socialist future and argued that peace was a prerequisite to global emancipation and that war and militarism affected the most vulnerable and the most oppressed. For Jones, war was endemic in capitalism and the machinery of war required the subordination of nations of color and the global working class. This appeared especially true with the increasing tensions between the US and the USSR. She viewed the struggle for peace as a gendered and racial struggle, and she believed it was women who had to lead the movement arguing that war affected women and people of color disproportionately because it was their children's and husbands' bodies that were sacrificed for capitalist gain and their labor that was used to produce war materiél.[12]

Jones's peace theory was influenced by her experience in anti-fascism in the 1930s and how the CPUSA viewed peace during the war. Communists have been accused of having a confused policy on World War II that alienated many people in its orbit and those in the party itself. When the Soviets and Nazis signed the non-aggression pact in 1939, the CPUSA took up an anti-war position. With the Nazi invasion of the USSR in August 1941, the party became aggressive supporters of the war and urged US involvement. This moment has been used to prove the party's obeisance to Soviet policy and it was correctly criticized for abandoning some of its anti-Nazi campaigns. But scholars have recently seen it as an indication of the members' different views on war and aggression. This elision also reflects the failure of some historiography to recognize Claudia Jones as a party leader.[13]

Christina Mislán has argued that Jones used a "DuBoisian" framework modeled after W. E. B. Du Bois's 1935 book *Black Reconstruction* in her WWII journalism. What this means is that Jones's support for the anti-fascist alliance during the war and her opposition to anti-communist policy afterward were a resistance to a new slave system. During the war, the US fought against fascism, and after the war the US engaged in fascism shutting down liberation and democratic movements abroad and at home. This was a sentiment that predominated in the Communist Party. Erik McDuffie argues that during the Cold War, the CPUSA believed that the US was "on the precipice of fascism." As a result, it abandoned its Popular Front policy of cooperation with liberals and once again advocated for "socialism and world revolution."[14]

Sarah Dunstan and Patricia Owens have explored Jones's stand in the war years through an international relations lens. At the time, a trend in "geopolitical discourse" against white supremacy was to center the colonial experience and imagine the US as part of a global resistance to fascism, rather than in an alliance with imperial powers. Jones was engaging with a liberatory ethos that centered on the colonized, both abroad and especially within the United States. What Dunstan and Owens argue is that Jones was not part of empire-making, but instead, she engaged in an anti-colonial discourse that centered on anti-fascist resistance. Additionally, Jones and other Communists saw the fascist states as a threat to socialism, particularly in the Soviet Union. Her wartime anti-fascism was embedded in her socialist and anti-colonial commitments.[15]

Jones's support for the war after the CPUSA's policy shift was predicated on the fear that Nazi fascism endangered Soviet communism and could reverberate to the US which had a tenuous grasp on democracy. Fascists were committed anti-communists and targeted radicals in their own countries, and this influenced her criticism of US Cold War policy. In 1947 she wrote an article criticizing the Truman Doctrine. That same year, she signed a statement along with other Black party leaders protesting it. The protest statement argued that US support in Turkey and Greece, outlined in the doctrine, amounted to imperialism, and it was part of an "Anglo-American drive . . . toward atomic war." This had been presaged in the Churchill Iron Curtain speech, and the doctrine formalized it as US policy. The other signers included Black radical comrades Ben Davis and Audley Moore, and it claimed that the US's "imperialist ambitions abroad" were reflected in its indifference and inaction against racist violence at home. The statement noted that there was a rise of fascism within the US evidenced in the loyalty oaths created by Truman in an executive order signed days after the doctrine that required all government employees to affirm their loyalty to the US against communism. In Executive Order 9835, government employees had to pledge loyalty to the US and denounce communism. Jones reasoned that anti-communism coupled with the US commitment to militarism and capitalism was fascist, and forcing consensus behind this policy proved that. Cold War policy allowed the US to use its military to intervene across the globe under the pretense of securing democracy, and that pretense was used to convince Americans that wars conducted by the US were righteous. Meanwhile, Black Americans continued to face racist violence at home, and attacks on labor organizing increased.[16]

Charisse Burden-Stelly argues that Jones recognized this as the manifestation of US fascism, which is consistent since it was the party's anti-fascism that drew Jones to it. She theorized that US fascism was expressed as "white supremacist terrorism," which could be seen in the criminal punishment system that targeted Black Americans as well as in racist violence by fellow Americans that went unchecked and unpunished. Wall Street imperialism was another of Jones's targets, and it was global since it exploited labor within the US and abroad, and this was supported by US military action and occupation. This "warmongering and militarism" was one aspect of US fascism and it encouraged the suppression of "all progressive thought and activism."[17]

Jones also recognized the anti-Blackness of anti-communism. Burden-Stelly argues that Blackness equals "value minus worth" in US racial capitalism; this describes the regular degradation of Blackness in political economy and that leads to it being a "constant source of profit and extraction." Radical challenges to the social order threaten the white supremacism in domestic and foreign policy because radicals reveal that oppressive institutions deploy and normalize stereotypes about Black inferiority. Cold War anti-communism is no different and is a progenitor of racial capitalism. It deployed both a "Black Scare" and a "Red Scare" to suggest that challenges to the racial and military status quo were un-American and suggested that the goal was to undo US culture and usher in a new racial and economic system. Therefore, government agencies believed that Jones and her fellow Communists and radicals sought to "topple exploitative racial and economic relations" thus the anti-communist purges wedded anti-Blackness with anti-communism and "radical Black peace activists" embodied the threat to the US white supremacist world vision.[18]

Julie Powell has described this as the racialization of communism. In the anti-Communist imagination, radical ideology was imported by unwanted outsiders, particularly immigrants who disrupted otherwise peaceable people. Discontent with the US system was unheard of for anti-communists who used "racial overtones" to describe radicals. These descriptions made their way into popular culture where the white working class engaged with anti-communism to "secure their own purchase on whiteness." Believing that outsiders were riling up contented and passive Black Americans justified the oppressive measures that the state deployed, and it also constructed claims to rights as radical (foreign) agitation. Jones knew this, and she importantly knew that this racial divisiveness penetrated the left too. Jones criticized her comrades as being in league with capitalists when they ignored Black oppression. She was also aware that racism hurt the US overseas. For McDuffie, this was the foundation of Jones's writing on peace.[19]

Central to Jones's analysis was that women were the most vulnerable under a war economy and that it was women who had to take the lead in the peace movement. But McDuffie argues that Jones "essentialized women as naturally inclined to peace." Other historians like Jacqueline Castledine concur and argue that Cold War peace activism reflected a maternalism that positioned women as more committed to peace. However, Castledine does note that women deployed maternalism as a tool to strategically place violence against the vulnerable as central in anti-war debates. This was meant to undermine war as a diplomatic solution.[20]

Suzy Kim argues that Cold War women's rights advocates deployed a maternal feminism that centered on the experience of women and children, but she argues that they did not universalize women's experiences. The women she studied in the Women's International Democratic Federation (WIDF) an organization that was linked to the anti-Cold War movement in the US, articulated a socialist feminism that included an "explicit acknowledgment of difference based on material conditions." For Kim, these women "spearheaded the structural critique" that laid the foundation for an intersectionalism that included class, race, gender, nationality, and coloniality. Maternalism helped some women who advocated war against imperial powers, and those who sought peaceful coexistence to appeal to and cooperate with liberals.[21]

There were, however, women like Jones and the others in this text who invoked the threat war and militarism posed to children and the home to recruit women into the peace movement. Jones rejected essentialism and any naturalized category of woman. She placed women at the center of political resistance and did not subscribe to gendered universalism. Maternalism is ultimately a reductive understanding of the complexity of Jones's and others' thinking. In addition, maternalist politics is about the disciplining of women of color and the belief that progressive women should be empowered to intervene in others' lives and neglects the ways gender and race politicize and circumscribe women's existence. More importantly, radical women believed the home could be the site for revolutionary change, and reducing their politics as maternalist universalized their commitment to women's rights when they rejected this reduction. Jones did not argue that women were naturally inclined toward nurturing or were biologically similar, nor did she believe women were more peaceful. Indeed, Jones and other radical women believed that bourgeois women were integral to the functioning of the violent militarized state and were part of the oppressive capitalist class. What Jones did argue was that it was women's responsibility to push for peace because only peace could lead to liberation and that the CPUSA had a responsibility to organize and empower women to lead.

She articulated this in a June 1949 article titled "Peace Is a Woman's Business." In it, she reasoned that investment in peace meant the realization of some of the most important goals in advancing the rights of women and all the oppressed. The article described a Congress of American Women (CAW) meeting in New York City. The CAW was the US branch of the WIDF. The meeting was attended by 300 women who demanded price controls, childcare subsidies, equal funding for education and housing, and equal rights as part of their peace commitments. All of these were compromised by US foreign policy, Jones specifically blamed the North Atlantic Treaty Organization (NATO). In April of that year, the collective security system in the treaty organization committed the founding nations, including the United States, to each other's defense. It was intentionally created to counter Soviet power. The CAW had issued a protest stating that if the US Senate ratified US membership, it "would be a step toward war rather than peace."[22]

Jones and the party denounced the military alliances embedded in NATO as an escalation of conflict with the Soviets. The meeting attendees spoke about the need to focus on domestic issues including integration, housing, education, and primarily peace. Instead, US policymakers were posturing for war. The meeting concluded by passing a resolution that stated: "Peace was a Woman's Business" and used the language of women's maternity to support it. However, it did not assume that women's maternity made women more peaceful, that maternity was women's sole role in life, nor did it conclude that domestic issues were only women's concerns. Jones also emphasized recognizing the specific and different needs of Black women as they were the most compromised in a war state. Jones's language targeted progressive women as the vanguard of a peace movement recognizing that nonprogressive women operated as agents of oppression; gender identity was not itself a guarantee that social justice would be prioritized.[23]

Eslanda Robeson echoed this in a 1949 book she and writer and activist Pearl Buck coauthored titled *American Argument*. The book was a debate about "race, patriotism, capitalism, world affairs, gender, and sex." As Barbara Ransby argues, in the book Robeson took "populist views" on intellectual issues and argued that the Soviet Union was more effective at addressing racism than the United States. She was also forward thinking about sex and gender arguing that sex need not be confined to marriage.[24] Her views on gender were in line with Jones's arguments that women could not be considered indistinguishable and that they too were agents of oppression as much as tools of liberation. Robeson wrote in *American Argument* that when women's only companions are "a boiling pot and a crying child and when four walls make her world" she becomes mindless, unstimulated, uninformed, and apolitical. She once believed that "women wanted a different world," but many are "docile although often irritable and petty." Robeson was not engaging in stereotypes, instead she believed that women needed relief from domestic requirements and the expectation that they would share political views with their husbands. Essentially, she wanted women to be liberated from maternal expectations. But even then, they also just as often voted with the "conservatives and militarists." She described a time when she went to Washington to testify before a Senate committee against universal military training along with two other women. She assumed that the women were compatriots and would take her side, but the other women argued that military training would provide young men with needed discipline. Robeson described how there were military figures there watching the testimony; she chose to be a "reckless woman" and vehemently stated her objections to universal military training. But at that moment, she had become afraid of other women: "women, who worship uniforms; women who put Hitler into power in Germany; women who blindly believe what they are told; women, millions strong, who never think and never know; women who breed sons and send them into the Army without protest." The experience disabused Robeson of the idea that women were devoted to peace.[25]

As Robeson noted in the book and Jones would emphasize elsewhere, all women, whether aware of their oppression or not, were vulnerable to the violence of the war state but Black women were superexploited. Additionally, white women just as often subscribed to and promoted white supremacy. McDuffie argues that Jones's most famous work, her 1949 "An End to the Neglect of the Problems of the Negro Woman!" article, articulated "key arguments she proffered a few years later in her articles on the Korean War." In it, Jones argued that Black women's super-exploitation was the "highest manifestation of capitalist exploitation." And she linked Black women's oppression to their "second class citizenship [and] to the genocidal conditions in which African American communities lived." McDuffie writes that according to Jones, US anti-communism "further immiserated black women, revealing the fallacy of American democracy." Jones had been writing about peace and women's oppression for years, and in her neglect article she would articulate her most important thoughts on women, racism, and peace, and how she saw the way forward against US fascism.[26]

She wrote that Black women were super-exploited and that progressive leftists (she called them left-progressives) had to yield to their leadership in the working-class movement as well as recognize their participation in racist and sexist institutions. Super-exploitation described Black women's position as the most exploited because she was triply oppressed because of race, gender, and class. But Jones argued that by emancipating the most oppressed Black woman, then emancipation could be achieved for all. This was the larger point of the article and what it is most remembered for. She wrote that recruiting Black women "for the struggle for peace is decisive for all other struggles." She worried that the "bipartisan warmakers" in both the political parties were winning women to their side, including Black women, by appealing to women's organizations. Women could be part of the military establishment, and women could be appealed to by warmakers, thus women could be and were part of the institutions to agitate against. She noted that they were not more peaceful and some women's organizations that had claimed to take an anti-imperialist stand had endorsed Cold War policy. Jones was not essentializing peace as women's work, she was arguing that women had to confront the war apparatus because only with peace could they be free.[27]

She insisted that the party's Marxist-Leninist principles made it a leader in peace, and it was only under socialism that peace could be achieved, peace based on the principles of "full economic, social, and political equality." She urged the party to not just recognize Black women's leadership but to end the patronizing practices of wanting to instruct them on how to be political. She argued that historically Black women had always engaged in politics and taken leadership. It was imperative now for American women to take leadership in the anti-imperialist peace movement because their government was largely to blame for the devastation facing women abroad, and it was important for the party to foster that leadership. Peace was a prerequisite for all struggles for emancipation, but first, the peace movement had to overcome its oppressive practices.[28]

Despite her anti-war position, Jones did not embrace pacifism, she recognized that violence was necessary to resist oppression. In the summer of 1947, she participated with fellow Communist and veteran Nathan Albert in a radio debate on universal military conscription; while her opponents tried to discredit her because of her CPUSA membership, she asked why the US needed military conscription during peacetime. She told the radio audience that: "Our position holds that military might alone cannot contribute to the peace or our own national security without being combined with a democratic foreign policy." The others in the debate asked if she supported the mandatory conscription in the Soviet Union and she countered that the Russians had recently been invaded and had been invaded in the past, it was within that nation's right to prepare for an invasion, especially while the US was posturing for unprovoked war. The US had never been invaded, had seen virtually no action in its territory during WWII, and was not threatened by an outside force; thus, the US's impulse for mandatory conscription was offensive, not defensive. She and Albert insisted that "such a preparedness program in which millions are spent for war preparation . . . can hardly be said to be contributing to peace." Jones would later support the Soviet atomic bomb as a necessary balance to US military power.[29]

Months before the official start of the Korean War, on International Women's Day in March 1950, Jones gave a speech that further articulated her understanding of peace. The celebration that year was even more important, she told her audience, because of President Truman's "cold-blooded order to produce the hydrogen bomb and to inaugurate a suicidal atomic and hydrogen weapon race." That January, Truman announced that the United States would pursue the research and development of a hydrogen bomb, more powerful than the bombs dropped on Japan. Women's groups, she claimed, condemned the order and tensions with the Soviet Union as a whole; this posture kept the US on the precipice of war. She quoted a statement released by the liberal Women's International League for Peace and Freedom which condemned the call for a hydrogen bomb. Jones called these protests an "index of the readiness of American women" to protest the policies of Truman and his Secretary of State Dean Acheson. These women objected to what she called the "Truman-Acheson doctrine" of the inevitability of war.[30]

The speech and the article were another effort to rally the party behind the organization of women and to understand the need for their leadership. She counseled the party to "inspire the growing struggles of American women and heighten their consciousness of the need for militant united-front campaigns around the burning demands of the day, against monopoly oppression, against war and fascism." Here again, Jones noted that women were just as susceptible to the influence of capitalist and imperialist propaganda, and nowhere did she naturalize a sense of women's peace sentiments. She argued that women were "offered the fascist triple K (*Kinde-Küche-Kirche*) pattern of war and 'war psychology.'" The fascist triple K referred to an old German slogan that celebrated women's natural role as caregivers. She believed that the celebrations of women as wives and mothers were a cover for preventing their activism in progressive movements and a tool to lure women away from peace. Jones was clear that women had to be organized because they were being exploited by the military state, and it was the state that deployed essentialist arguments.[31]

During WWII, some federal dollars were made available for childcare so that women could do war work, this was a recognition of the social worth of their reproduction and their labor. But these subsidies were gone at the end of the war as they were expected to vacate jobs and stay home. For Jones, this verified that reproduction was in service to the war state, and rewarded during wartime, women were meant to stay home during the peace and resume their reproductive labor in anticipation of the next conflict. Jones saw these assumptions about women's domesticity to be akin to Hitler's glorification of women's natural role; she counseled activists to revolt against this capitalist propaganda.[32]

She included in her analysis opposition to the Equal Rights Amendment (ERA). The party had opposed the amendment from the beginning because of its vagaries and the problems of reform in a capitalist system. The party argued that a blanket amendment could not correct the abuses within the system and, as other amendments had proven, constant legislation was required to enforce constitutional mandates. Reform necessitated regular correction, and Jones believed that socialism was the only way to end all systemic abuses. Jones also opposed the amendment because its "equalitarian concept of women's legal status . . . in the atmosphere of the cold war, [carries] with it a mandate for drafting of women into the armed forces for the war economy." An undifferentiated equality would further integrate women's labor in service to the capitalist war state.[33]

Jones's peace was grounded in Marxism, which she believed was needed to secure women's rights and dignity; therefore, she concluded that "Complete emancipation of women is possible under socialism." Capitalist exploitation made women's emancipation impossible because their labor, which included their reproductive labor, was needed to secure monopoly capitalism. Jones believed that a socialist state did not turn to aggression and warfare for its maintenance because it was not required for the capitalist class to secure its profits. Rights in a capitalist system required "constant struggle" as capitalists, in league with the government, undermined rights in favor of profit and that profit meant the exploitation of workers globally. In a socialist state, and Jones pointed to the Soviet Union as an example, rights were guaranteed and she reasoned that women's rights required different treatment from men. Treating people equally did not address the unique needs of individuals, in a socialist system, she argued, dignity would be in the design. Jones wanted to organize women into the peace movement to "help raise consciousness to the understanding of the bipartisan demagogy." Raising their consciousness would help convince women that "the final guarantee of peace, bread, and freedom, and the full emancipation of subjected womankind, will be achieved only in a Socialist America."[34]

Jones's vision for peace reflected the positive peace that the Progressive Party advocated in its electoral attempt in 1948. Peace was meant to usher in a world without war, but also a world where gender and race justice existed. Jones reasoned that capitalism guaranteed war. Labor exploitation and imperialism were a fixture in capitalism; therefore, for radical women, a peaceful future required a socialist future.

HENRY WALLACE FOR PRESIDENT

Black radical women not only campaigned for Wallace they took up leadership roles in organizing the Progressive Party, articulating its platform, and even convincing Henry Wallace to be its candidate. Eslanda Robeson and her husband Paul were central to Wallace's campaign, even traveling with him on the campaign trail. Shirley Graham Du Bois, helped organize the party, formulate its anti-racist platform, and convinced Wallace to run. Charlotta Bass was a delegate to the party convention and helped put

Wallace on the ballot in California; and Lorraine Hansberry led a campus Wallace group. The 1948 Progressive Party campaign was a demonstration of interracial organization and unity that those involved hoped to replicate throughout the country.

The Progressive Citizens of America (PCA), an organization formed in 1946, asked Wallace to be the keynote speaker at its founding meeting. The PCA sought a "progressive victory" in 1948 and denounced the Truman Doctrine. It wanted a third-party alternative to the Democratic and Republican Parties because, despite their differences, the two parties were committed anti-communists and prioritized conflict with the Soviets rather than domestic issues. Henry Wallace recently had a falling out with Truman over escalating tensions and as a seasoned politician he had a record that appealed to several progressives. Wallace had been Secretary of Agriculture in Franklin Roosevelt's cabinet and in 1940, became Roosevelt's vice president. Wallace was outspoken against colonialism and imperialism, and he was an anti-racist, which some Democratic party leaders did not like, so he was replaced in the 1944 election with Harry Truman. Wallace was appointed Secretary of Commerce, a role he would continue into Truman's first term after Roosevelt's sudden death. As early as 1946, Wallace began warning the American people that the US should not alienate its wartime ally the Soviet Union. But as tensions soured, and Truman's anti-communist rhetoric increased, Wallace became more outspoken.[35]

In July 1946, Wallace wrote Truman a letter expressing his concerns about his harsh rhetoric against the Soviet Union. He wrote about his worries that a new war was on the horizon and that peace could not be secured if the US committed itself to military proliferation. Truman did not respond. In September 1946, Wallace delivered a speech at Madison Square Garden titled "The Way to Peace." Even though he included criticism of the Soviet Union, critics accused him of being pro-Soviet. The speech became an opportunity to oust Wallace from the cabinet; Truman asked for his resignation, and Wallace complied.[36] In 1947 when Truman gave his speech that became the Truman Doctrine, Wallace criticized it as a "turning point" when the United States would back a "reactionary" government in Greece, by-pass the newly created United Nations whose job it was to maintain world peace, and expand US military aid to other governments. The doctrine has been seen as a blueprint for later US interventions and appeared to be a moment when the US began its commitment to act as a global police force committed to interfering in the political and military conflicts in sovereign nations. Wallace knew what generations of Americans would later realize; this commitment put the US on a path to perpetual war.[37]

The PCA spent the remainder of 1947 building its third party and seeking its candidate. In December 1947, Ada Belle Jackson from the PCA wrote to Graham Du Bois asking her to sign on to a Christmas letter to Wallace urging him to run for President. The letter from over 100 "Negro leaders," noted that Black Americans needed his leadership, and arguably, his name recognition. Graham Du Bois agreed and signed on as did W. E. B. Du Bois, who was a member of the PCA National Board. On December 29, 1947, Wallace announced his candidacy for President on the Progressive Party (PP) ticket, Glen Taylor of Idaho joined Wallace as his running mate for vice president.[38]

Wallace embraced "progressive capitalism," which accepted basic capitalist tenets but sought a just system that shared wealth more equitably. The PCA, while not a Communist organization, did not discourage Communist involvement both because of Communists' organizational skills and because it rejected the growing anti-communism of the two political parties as an assault on freedom of speech. This stance, and the Progressive Party's anti-Cold War rhetoric, along with its support for women's and civil rights, drew in radical supporters. According to Mary Hamilton, many Black leftists poured time and energy into the Wallace campaign leading to a gender and race-integrated campaign that "foreshadowed" the later women's and civil rights movements.[39]

From the beginning, the Wallace campaign took a stand against US military proliferation. In Wallace's policy statement on militarization, he wrote that "military fascism [in] service to monopoly capitalism" was one of the dominant issues of the 1948 campaign. He argued that the Democratic and Republican Parties were nearly indistinguishable in their support for military proliferation and attempts to outbid one another in anti-communist sentiment. Wallace instead feared the union of the military and civilian economies and that "military requirements" would integrate foreign policy into national policy and subsume the civilian economy. This was something that war industries were eagerly advocating. As proof, he quoted Charles Wilson, CEO of General Electric, who suggested that the US economy integrate military considerations permanently and abandon a "peace economy." The 1947 National Security Act embodied this commitment and became the foundation for US militarization and the creation of the permanent national security state. The bill created the Central Intelligence Agency (CIA) and the National Security Agency (NSA), merged military departments into one called the Department of Defense, and created a Secretary of Defense position. The bill formalized a permanent military and intelligence structure that prioritized military proliferation over social welfare.[40]

Wallace instead advocated disbanding war industries and putting them under public ownership. He feared that for weapons manufacturers, war meant profit and therefore profit meant war. He believed that the hawks advocating military buildup and shutting down the relationship with the Soviets were only acting on behalf of corporations and reminded people that military proliferation meant that the American taxpayer was subsidizing war profiteers. This kind of foreign policy was "using the public treasury, the armed forces, and the good name of the American people to support international big business." He also reminded anti-communists that US military intervention in other countries would effectively make the US the "greatest salesmen communism ever had." If, as others seemed to be advocating, the US became a global police force, he warned that it could mean the oppression of people across the world. Instead, he counseled standing up to corporate profiteering as a "patriotic duty of national defense." [41]

Wallace's stand against military profiteering was appealing to radicals, but his position on civil rights made him even more popular. The PP's position on it started with attacking the notion that the Constitution protected all Americans. It said that the nation had been "far too smug" in the assumption that the freedoms enjoyed by some were enjoyed by all. Graham Du Bois introduced the civil rights plank at the PP's founding convention in Philadelphia on July 23, 1948. She served as the Vice Chair of the New York Wallace for President committee, and she agreed to give a speech at the convention. In her speech, she discussed how US racism impacted her own family and other Black families. She discussed how her son, ill from tuberculosis, was refused service at a hospital because he was Black. She also spoke about her other son who had served in the war fighting for freedom but could not enjoy it at home.[42]

Castledine has pointed to this speech as evidence of Graham-Du Bois's and the peace movement's maternalism, but Graham Du Bois was articulating her desire for peace with justice. She told the audience that what she wanted was "Peace without battleships, atomic bombs, and lynch ropes; peace without murderers marked as statesmen; peace without military conscription and mangled, torn bodies lingering on in veteran's hospitals; peace in which to work and build." She continued saying that "we want peace which, by saving in the next years all that has been squandered in the hell of war, will mean health to our sick, homes to our homeless, education for our children, food for the hungry of the world and clothes to the naked." The peace she envisioned would mean housing people, providing healthcare, funding schools, and preventing hunger and she argued that the Progressive Party vision of peace and justice was possible in the United States.

Her speech ended with the PP's civil rights platform which called for anti-lynching legislation, voting rights, an end to the poll tax, a permanent FEPC, and the end of discrimination. The platform also included the abolition of Truman's loyalty oaths and dismantling the House Un-American Activities Committee (HUAC).[43]

On the West Coast, Charlotta Bass was organizing for Wallace. She had been a registered Republican for decades until 1936 when she voted for Franklin Roosevelt. In that election, her newspaper endorsed his Republican opponent, Al Landon. The political tides were shifting, and the "party of Lincoln" was starting to lose its traditional Black support. Bass worked for and with the Republican party for thirty years; this changed in the 1940 election. During the election, she was the Western Regional Director of the Wendell Wilkie campaign for president. When she traveled to Chicago for a party convention, she noted that despite Wilkie's promise to stand for one world, there at the segregated GOP headquarters she saw two worlds—one for white America upstairs, and one for Black America downstairs. She likened the moment to the awakening of the "children of Israel" who realized that they would have no place under the Pharaoh's rule in Egypt, so they built a monument out of stones to commemorate the "rolling away of the burdens of their bondage." She claimed she could no longer see a future for herself or Black America in the "Great Elephant party."[44]

As some scholars have speculated, it was her nephew John Kinloch who moved Bass gradually to the left, and his death pushed her further. Kinloch had come to live and work with Bass on her newspaper, and he was engaged in many left-wing organizations and campaigns. Then during WWII, he was deployed to Europe where he died in battle. This event devastated Bass whose commitment to peace and opposition to anti-communism grew. Kinloch had written a column for Bass's paper titled "Kinloch's Corner." After his death, the column continued and was "Dedicated to the memory of John Kinloch, who died in the struggle to destroy fascism." In 1945, she ran for city council on the Democratic ticket, an election she lost. By 1947, she formally broke with both political parties.[45]

That year she attended a convention of California labor and civil rights organizations that called for a third-party candidate. The attendees noted their frustration with the two political parties and their nearly identical anti-communist positions, positions that increased the precarity of labor and civil rights organizing. This group formed the California branch of the Progressive Party and appointed Hugh Bryson, president of the San Francisco National Union of Marine Cooks and Stewards as president. On January 8, 1948, *The California Eagle* announced Wallace's candidacy and noted that he sought to end discrimination and segregation and that he was devoted to peace. Bass discussed the Wallace campaign in her weekly column "On the Sidewalk," emphasizing that it was a challenge to the old parties that had courted the Black vote but failed to make measurable progress for Black Americans. She challenged Black voters to think about their allegiance to the Republican party and highlighted that big business supported the GOP, which, she believed, should make any voter question its principles. She believed that the Democratic party was no better and she wrote that "the only benefits granted to Negroes by President Truman are on paper; where I opine they will remain until the end of time." She insisted that there was no measurable difference between the two parties when it came to Black America, and she hoped that a third party could finally make needed change. Wallace wanted "world peace, to prevent a depression, to break the power of the private monopoly system over the lives of the American people." She asked her readers: "Who will listen to the clarion call, and take up arms to fight for this glorious cause?"[46]

Bass reported that Walter White of the NAACP claimed that whoever won the Black vote would win the presidency. She therefore called for a coalition of Black voters along with "Mexicans and Jews" across Los Angeles to support Wallace. She wanted a coalition that could not be "shattered by unfounded anti-communist propaganda." Her newspaper ran several editorials in support, and she stationed a registrar in the newspaper office to sign up new voters. These new voters were encouraged to mobilize under the Progressive Party banner.[47] One of the biggest challenges was getting Wallace on the California ballot. To get Wallace on the ballot, the group was told they needed over 275,000 signatures by February 1948; this gave them little over a month to organize. Over 4,000 volunteers mobilized to collect the needed signatures, Bass assisted and encouraged people in her newspaper and those who came to register to vote to sign. The group was successful.[48]

Wallace traveled to Los Angeles in May of that year and spoke to a crowd of over 30,000 Los Angelenos. He also marched downtown where he spoke to a group of Mexican Americans that had organized themselves in the group "Amigos de Wallace." Christina Pérez Jiménez has argued that this group was one of the earliest attempts to organize Latinx into a bloc in US elections. Significantly Wallace urged Spanish speakers to see the election, and the position of president, as something that belonged to them too. It was their country as well, he told the audience, and it was their children's future that was in the balance. Jiménez has argued that this early attempt at creating a Latinx coalition was significant for its inclusivity and that Wallace's campaign principles were progressive for the time and remain so now. This progressive coalition was precisely what Bass was hoping to create.[49]

The California Progressive Party organized a conference to be held in Fresno to formally endorse Wallace. The group, however, faced resistance. The hotel where it was supposed to be held refused to allow Black members in. Bass and the others protested until the hotel management finally relented. Bass was elected to serve as a delegate to the national convention in Philadelphia where Graham Du Bois gave her speech and introduced the PP's civil rights platform. She described the convention for her readers celebrating the growth of the "people's movement" and the diversity of the crowd which included Japanese Americans, Mexican Americans, Chinese Americans, and Black Americans, all excited to organize not just a political party but a movement. Most important to Bass was that this group was committed to peace. She wrote that both the Democratic and Republican party conventions claimed to want to secure a peaceful future, but neither did anything to secure it. Since they were the parties in charge, she noted that it was in their power to secure peace; but when Congress returned to session after the conventions, neither moved on any of the issues that would achieve peace or social security. The keynote speaker at the PP convention, Charles Howard, a progressive attorney, said that the White House reported it was "tired of talking over differences" at the negotiation's tables, but Howard noted that "we are tired of dying over them." In an article after the convention, *The California Eagle* editors wrote: "It's everybody's job, who believes in freedom, to work for the election of Henry Wallace and the defeat of our betrayers. Get on the Wallace train! It's headed for Freedom Land!"[50]

Bass returned from the national convention energized, she continued to organize other events including another state-wide convention in August, and an event in September that featured an appearance by Paul Robeson to rally voters and raise money. Wallace returned to Los Angeles in October rallying voters across the city. *The California Eagle* featured an article that said despite claims to the contrary, the Wallace campaign was still energetic and still gaining supporters in the weeks before the election. It noted that Wallace's crowds were larger than Truman's and larger than GOP candidate Thomas Dewey's.[51]

In the Midwest, a very young and increasingly radicalized Lorraine Hansberry cut her independent political teeth in the Wallace campaign. She attended the University of Wisconsin. There she watched the Sean O'Casey play *Juno and the Paycock* about war-torn Dublin which, according to Robbie Lieberman, influenced her understanding of "what theatre could accomplish." She was also involved in efforts to integrate campus, but it was the Wallace campaign that drew her further to the left. She joined the Young Progressives of America and became the local president; it was the youth group devoted to the Wallace campaign and the PP. She wrote to a friend that one inspiration for becoming "100% Progressive" was that a local police chief declared that "any [racially] mixed meetings" would be considered Communist. She would eventually (though briefly) join the Communist Party.[52]

Eslanda Robeson was one of the cofounders of the Progressive Party, and she and her husband attended its convention in Philadelphia and gave their vocal and visible support to the campaign. Barbara Ransby argues that Eslanda and Paul were attracted to both the Wallace campaign and the candidate as he was a devoutly religious man devoted to anti-racism and anti-war. Eslanda was an important "advocate for internationalizing the Black Freedom Struggle" and "drawing parallels with socialist, Communist, and anti-colonial movements abroad."[53]

Eslanda helped to draft the campaign platform, she also pushed others on the committee to recognize self-determination in South Africa, as well as in the US colony of Puerto Rico. She traveled with Wallace on his 1948 Peace Tour where she spoke out against increased US militarism and growing tensions in Korea. Robeson focused her campaign speeches on anti-racism and anti-war noting that the PP "stands for freedom," while mainstream politicians focused on war. She also organized "rallies, meetings, and forums" near the Robeson home in Connecticut. She advocated a third-party alternative because the mainstream political parties were focused on war and, she insisted, "we can't stand for peace on one foot and war on the other."[54]

Wallace's loss was no great surprise, but the extent of the loss was. His campaign only captured 2 percent of the vote and no electoral votes. He and his supporters were regularly red-baited by the other political candidates, he was often denied airtime on the radio, and newspapers dismissed the campaign as Communist-inspired. Like the California PP's issue with securing a hotel, Wallace supporters regularly found themselves scrambling to secure a location for rallies. In two cities, the group faced rioters organized by veterans' groups and in an early case of anti-communist job loss, at least one professor lost his job after he appeared on stage with Wallace. While many scholars have focused on anti-communism as the downfall of the Wallace campaign, Thomas Devine instead argues that it was racism. Wallace attempted to court the labor vote, and several unions, especially in the South, resented his anti-racism.[55]

In the end, Truman would secure the labor vote leading to his surprise upset. Truman held on despite the third-party challenges, he gained just under 50 percent of the popular vote, and Dewey received 45 percent. The other third-party challenger, Strom Thurmond, and his States' Rights party, also known as Dixiecrats, secured only 2 percent of the popular vote, but 39 electoral votes. Thurmond, a lifelong Democrat, had broken with Truman over civil rights. The states' rights he was trying to secure were the right to discriminate against Black Americans, and many voters agreed with him. That he gained electoral votes while a progressive coalition failed to get any was both humiliating and disturbing.[56]

Despite the loss, Bass was determined to hold the other political parties accountable. She argued that the PP proved that there was an important progressive element in the United States that wanted a positive peace. The PP coalition would continue to organize behind peace and equity, and she hoped for progressive victories in 1950 and 1952. *The California Eagle* kept an eye on the Democrat's campaign promises; but was ultimately disappointed when its military appropriations increased but not its social welfare spending. Additionally, the demands for a permanent FEPC went unfulfilled.[57]

Claudia Jones supported the Wallace campaign, though she did not take up a forward role in it; perhaps because of her visibility in the CPUSA. What Jones liked about Wallace's platform, something that would influence her theories about peace was his idea of the "common man." The common man came from a May 1942 speech Wallace gave in which he outlined his support for World War II but also his devotion to Franklin Roosevelt's four freedoms—freedom of speech and religion, and freedom from fear and want. For Wallace and Jones, this was what positive peace was, a peace grounded in justice and freedom from those who would "enslave" others. Wallace's common man was someone who wanted a world that could "enhance his well-being" and use technology to extend freedom to all. While this idea would stay with Jones and the others who would soldier on after the failed campaign, Wallace himself largely disappeared after the devastating loss.[58]

When the US entered the Korean War, Wallace disappointed his supporters by releasing a statement that reiterated his commitment to the common man, but also stated that when "Russia, the US and the UN appeal to force, I am on the side of the US and UN." He noted his commitment to peace and to finding a solution that was beneficial to the Korean people, the US, and the Soviet Union, but he said that as a former vice president and cabinet member, he would always side with his country. In contrast, the PP's statement on the war noted that it was created in opposition to the "bi-partisan policy of the Cold War," and that the Korean War was a product of that policy. It sought a peaceful resolution and the strengthening of the UN as well as an immediate end to the war and the creation of an independent and unified Korea, and it condemned the possible use of the atomic bomb. While the

PP's coalition around Wallace collapsed, the PP continued to seek peace and opposed anti-communism, and it inspired others to remain committed to peace and equity.[59]

PEACE CONFERENCES

Peace conferences were the primary organizing center for the Cold War peace movement. At these conferences, people from around the globe made connections with other radicals and with leaders and participants in liberation movements, often individuals fighting against the US military. There was no single organizing body behind them, but what they shared was opposition to US anti-communism. Lieberman argues that while the "Soviet-inspired peace movement" included Communists, non-Communists attended and participated in the conferences which were largely made up of intellectuals, artists, and scientists who "rested on the hope [they] might lead popular resistance to Western government measures." This included the Marshall Plan and NATO. Opposition to the Marshall Plan and NATO centered on both as escalations of conflict between the US and USSR and antithetical to peaceful coexistence.[60]

The Marshall Plan followed the Truman Doctrine and was also announced in a speech. In June 1947, Secretary of State George Marshall detailed the plan in a commencement address at Harvard University. In his speech, he acknowledged that Europe's reconstruction left it vulnerable to communism and therefore, the US planned to commit billions of dollars to help rebuild. The US had been aiding Europe since the war's end, but this was the "most dedicated effort to reduce Communist influence in Europe." US policymakers like George Kennan and Dean Acheson recognized that the plan was more than just aid for reconstruction, it was a means to bolster Europe, especially the countries in the Eastern Bloc, against Soviet influence.[61]

In March 1949, Shirley Graham Du Bois was part of the National Council of the Arts, Sciences, and Professions (NCASP) peace conference organizing committee. It was the first in a series of conferences announced at a meeting held in Wroclaw, Poland, in 1948. In February 1949, a committee from the Polish conference "announced a series of meetings" starting with the one in New York. Graham Du Bois was one of the New York organizers, and the group secured the Waldorf Astoria and invited peace activists from around the world to attend; it became pejoratively known as the Waldorf Conference.[62] Graham Du Bois and the organizers wrote in the conference program about their fears that the Cold War prevented the expression of all opinions and viewpoints and international cooperation and exchange. The conference program noted that the Cold War was expensive, half of the allotted US military budget for 1949 ($15–18 billion) could address housing issues, fund education, and provide healthcare. More concerning to the organizers was that the Cold War allowed for active intervention on behalf of conservative governments and that all that money failed to bring "economic recovery or stability."[63]

Harlow Shapley, a scientist, was the conference organizer. There were over 3,000 attendees including radical leaders like W. E. B. Du Bois and Howard Fast. Entertainers Paul Robeson and a "very young" Marlon Brando were also present. There were prominent liberals like Norman Mailer, Arthur Miller, Norman Cousins, and Albert Einstein. Several people traveling to the conference had their visas denied including Pablo Picasso; three Canadians who tried to travel to New York were deported. Inexplicably, the visas that were issued were from Soviet sphere states. According to British sources, this was because they "had the backing of their governments." The State Department publicly dismissed the conference as Communist propaganda, and the press largely treated it as such, though there was criticism of the visa denials.[64]

Graham Du Bois gave a talk highlighting the desire for peace among the "darker people" of the US. She articulated the concern of Black Americans and others who understood that violent repression was the US government's most effective tool to silence its critics. While the US claimed to be a beacon of democracy in the world, many Americans did not enjoy that democracy. There was no bipolar order between the Communist world and the capitalist/democratic world because the US was not a democracy and capitalism ensured oppression. These criticisms of US policy heightened the concern of intelligence agencies. Graham Du Bois wrote that during the conference FBI agents were "thicker than baked Alaska" among the crowd.[65]

As Gerald Horne argues, while Jim Crow segregation and racist violence were embarrassing to the US on the global stage during the Cold War, intelligence officials continued to target those most outspoken in the Black freedom struggle. This had the effect of pushing several Black activists, like Graham Du Bois, to the political left. The targeting of the peace conference and its organizers was one example. The federal government interpreted calls for peace as allegiance to a foreign power and a desire to disarm the US, ostensibly to allow for a takeover. Federal officials had a choice between democracy as guaranteed in the Constitution, or oppression; Communist containment facilitated the decision and officials chose oppression. The peace conferences were of particular concern to the federal government as

Black activists worked actively with others in the Soviet sphere states and they were united in their condemnation of US resistance to civil rights. Graham Du Bois saw the conferences as an opportunity to discuss the Black freedom struggle and its connection to liberation movements abroad. It was at these conferences that she would create relationships with others who were outspoken against US militarism.[66]

Phillip Deery has written that the Waldorf conference's "ostensible, if naïve, intention was to ease the growing tensions between the Soviet Union and the United States." For some of the attendees, for intelligence agencies like the CIA, and later for historians looking back on it, the conference marked an important change in the relationship between liberals and Communists. There were tensions during the meeting; for example, in Norman Cousins' speech he affirmed that "Americans are anti-Communist but not anti-humanitarian." He was booed. Deery wrote about the Soviet composer Dimitri Shostakovich who was questioned directly by Josef Stalin because he rejected an invitation to travel to the Waldorf conference. He told Stalin that he would have to answer questions about why his compositions were banned in the Soviet Union. Stalin feigned surprise that his compositions were censored and lifted the ban the next day. Deery has described Stalin's surprise as disingenuous.[67]

The conference was protested and outside the Waldorf "chanting picketeers and kneeling nuns" were spotted as were members of the Veterans of Foreign Wars, a group whose members often protested progressive events. Historians have disagreed about the catalyst behind the conference, whether it was the NCASP or the Soviet Union, but the press response after the conference saw it as a farcical attempt to influence foreign policy. It was also the inspiration for the American Committee for Cultural Freedom, an anticommunist organization funded by the CIA with many former Marxists in its ranks who would take up combating Communist influence.[68]

The HUAC dismissed the Waldorf Conference as part of a Communist-inspired "three-ring circus." In 1951, HUAC released a report on what it called the "Communist 'Peace' Offensive," putting quotation marks around peace, according to Lieberman, to signal that it did not represent "any serious concern for peace." In it, the report claimed that the Waldorf Conference was "staged" and "was actually a supermobilization of the inveterate supporters of the Communist party and its auxiliary organizations." It claimed that the meeting's purpose was to issue propaganda in support of Soviet policy and against US policies like the Marshall Plan, to "mobilize intellectuals" to take part in civil disobedience against the US government, to attack US culture and praise the Soviets, and to plan other peace conferences. The committee's language was overwrought and concluded the meeting, and its attendees were part of a worldwide Communist conspiracy.[69]

Despite the challenges, Graham Du Bois declared the conference a success and she noted her pride in those who came knowing that federal officials and protestors were there. More important was that the conference demonstrated the international efforts to challenge US containment. She and the other NCASP organizers and sponsors were invited to the World Congress of the Partisans of Peace to be held in Paris the following month. Graham Du Bois wanted to go to Paris to see "the larger world picture." Her plans to attend were nearly foiled because of financial difficulty, but she managed to complete a manuscript which allowed her to afford the trip. This meant she had to leave later than her American comrades and she arrived after the meetings had started on April 20, 1949.[70]

She missed Paul Robeson's speech, which famously set off an explosive controversy in the United States. In the speech, Robeson claimed that Black Americans should not be asked to sacrifice their lives in US wars while being denied their rights at home. This was the crux of Black radical opposition to the Cold War; therefore, Robeson was not saying anything new that had not been said by other activists. His comments echoed Graham Du Bois's statement at the New York peace conference pointing to the hypocrisy of claiming to deliver democracy to other countries while it did not exist in the US. But Robeson was a popular and public figure, and his comments were made on a global stage. The reaction was swift and volatile. US audiences and the press interpreted his comments as un-American and proof of Robeson's allegiance to the USSR. Former Communist Manning Johnson claimed that Robeson's goal was to become a "Black Stalin," and Robeson's one-time friend turned red-baiter Max Yergan denounced him. The US press misquoted him making his comments appear more damning.[71]

Graham Du Bois later defended Robeson claiming that he argued Black workers would not take up arms against white workers, even Russians; it was a message of unity, not division. The comments led to denunciations of Robeson as treasonous and HUAC hearings, but Graham Du Bois argued that what he said was a message of peace, a message that was increasingly criminalized in the US. As Burden-Stelly argues, the US commitment to war and anti-communism during the Cold War "transmuted . . . seemingly universal ideas like peace and progress" into crimes. Graham Du Bois insisted that Robeson's comments were not treasonous, they were about solidarity, anti-communists instead saw him as a traitor.[72]

While heated controversy emerged in the US, the conference continued. Two thousand delegates representing "700 million" people and seventy-two countries attended the Paris Peace Conference. The conference pushed for solidarity across national lines against imperialism, both from the old empires and the new militarized US empire. Graham Du Bois noted, for example, that Vietnamese delegates denounced French intervention, but still sought solidarity with French workers.[73] The attendees produced a manifesto that articulated this vision of peace. Graham Du Bois noted that the preamble to the manifesto said that it represented people from "every creed, philosophy, color, and type of civilization" and that it declared that peace was the "concern of all peoples." The goal was to resist war in even the smallest villages and towns. They called for trade unions to organize shop floors for peace, they called on women's organizations and other progressive groups to spread the message, and they resisted the dismissal of their movement as simply an attempt at Communist revolution. They wanted to "face the plotters of war" with a permanent "popular force" committed to peace. The group declared they were ready to "win the battle for peace" which they equated to the "battle for life."[74]

The manifesto had six points that were all unanimously agreed upon. The first was to publicize the decisions made at the conference. The second was to develop relationships between peace groups across national lines and to nurture peace actions in other countries. The third was to denounce all attacks on the peace movement and encourage national independence movements; it also included aid to the victims of war and oppression. The fourth point was to encourage cultural expressions for peace by establishing financial prizes, and the fifth was to plan future congresses. The final and sixth point called for creating the "means of propaganda" to spread news about the movement in multiple languages.[75]

Graham Du Bois wrote that she found the conference "breath-taking" and she felt she was at the "crossroads" of many nations and many people coming together. Volunteers were requested to take the manifesto across Europe, Graham Du Bois volunteered and during her travels, she noted that the devastation of World War II was still visible and the desire for peace among those she met there was palpable. The US did not have a similar experience in the war and was not engaged in postwar reconstruction, thus war remained an abstraction to Americans. Graham Du Bois noted that this devastation compelled Europeans to seek peace and only Americans were eager for more conflict. War was becoming a unique US export to newly decolonized states, to secure capitalist interests. She argued that containment was a justification that conveniently hid that US taxpayer dollars were funding military incursions to secure capitalist resources.[76]

From Paris, Graham Du Bois planned to take a bus to Denmark to celebrate the birthday of artist Martin Andersen Nexo. It was meant to be a "leisurely five-day trip" that stopped in Belgium, Holland, and Germany. It turned out to be an "illuminating journey" as she witnessed the aftermath of war in these countries. She wrote about one incident in Hamburg where she had to stay on a yacht anchored in the Elbe River; there was simply no place to stay in the city since it had been nearly leveled. She described the city as a "massive pile of rubble" dealing with "a vast level of desolation." A woman confronted her asking what an American was doing there. When Graham Du Bois explained she was coming from a peace conference, the woman described how Hamburg was destroyed by US and British planes and that Hitler dismissed the city as "Red Hamburg" which meant it held little value to him; thus, the bombings were unnecessary. In highlighting this interaction, Graham Du Bois pointed out to her reading audience that US foreign policy shared something important with Hitler's fascism: an overzealous anti-communism.[77]

In the aftermath of the Paris Peace conference and Robeson's comments, accusations of communism against the activists were becoming louder. Graham Du Bois wrote an open letter about US anti-communism in response to a Soviet attendee worried about US redbaiting. She wrote that American women were "keeping the faith" and organizing despite the anti-communist witch hunts. She noted that when she returned home from the conference, the manifesto had been denounced and the word peace was held in contempt. Americans were being warned to prepare for war; politicians talked openly about war's inevitability, while those who were critical were considered Communist agents. She was critical of the US occupation government in Korea likening it to segregation and noted that those who claimed to protect democracy were the same people trying to censor people and books.[78]

But Graham Du Bois was not naïve, she knew that the harassment would continue. She noted the continued attacks on her friend Paul Robeson. In August 1949, Robeson was scheduled to appear in Peekskill, New York, to perform at a fundraiser for the Civil Rights Congress, an organization devoted to the legal defense of the oppressed. A violent local mob organized by and made up of local veterans broke up the concert. At the rescheduled event in September, the group was attacked again. Graham Du Bois described it as a fascist attack on the liberties of the radicals. Anti-communism at the legislative and law enforcement levels was only part of what the activists faced. Samuel White has described "popular anti-communism" as that which was practiced on the local and individual levels. Graham Du Bois and others faced legal repercussions for their beliefs and activism, but they also faced harassment and persecution from their fellow Americans. Civilians operated outside of legal infrastructure and engaged in surveillance of those suspected of being Communists. For example, the American Legion claimed that Graham Du Bois was a leading Communist organizer in one of its publications. Despite the harassment, both official and unofficial, Graham Du Bois believed that justice could only be secured with peace.[79]

HUAC's 1951 report included the Paris conference and described the World Congress of Partisans of Peace as militant. Graham Du Bois was listed as one of its US sponsors. The committee reported that the Chinese Communist victory was celebrated and that the Soviet delegation, "as is customary at these gatherings" took the "vanguard position." It was made plain during the conference that the US "was the chief target" of the attacks. The report mentioned Paul Robeson's "treasonous statements" which had been denounced by "prominent members of his own race" including Jackie Robinson and Walter White. The report dismissed peace as a cover for Soviet aggression and an attempt to weaken the US to create an opportunity for a Communist takeover.[80]

Despite the harassment, the peace movement still had momentum. In September 1949, Graham Du Bois traveled to Havana, Cuba as the US Representative for the Continental Congress for World Peace. She was interested in seeing the peace movement outside of Europe and was happy to note that the original venue for the conference had to be abandoned for another one to accommodate all the attendees. The FBI followed her movements there and noted that at the conference she spoke about her attendance at the Paris conference and that while in France she marched with French workers. She returned home "filled with enthusiasm" and with the message that there was a global movement committed to peace. She was also prepared to take up the task given to American peace activists in Paris, which was to create an organization that would stay in touch with the World Peace Council, a global peace organization, and distribute information about the peace movement.[81]

Even before the summer of 1950, when the US entered the Korean War, radical women were theorizing and agitating for peace in opposition to anti-communist foreign and domestic policy. Opposition to the Korean War was grounded in their objections to anti-communist-focused foreign policy, and this activism was forged in the years leading up to the war. In some ways, they predicted the war knowing that the US containment policy and its military commitments made war its primary diplomatic measure. While politicians and the US public believed that anti-communism and the Cold War were a commitment to democracy, Black radicals saw it as imperialism. They believed that US capitalism, supported by the US military was committed to upholding white supremacy by interfering in nations of color to prevent sovereignty and self-determination and to secure capitalist resources. Anti-Korean War activism sought to end aggression abroad and secure justice within the US. But increasingly peace was interpreted by US authorities as a foreign-inspired criminal enterprise.

CHAPTER TWO

Sojourning for Peace

A year after the outbreak of war in Korea and US intervention there, Claudia Jones wrote an article insisting that "Warmakers fear women." Her evidence was that so many women outspoken against the Korean War, including herself, had been arrested and indicted under the Smith Act. She described the arrest of Loretta Starvus Stack, a mother of two whose door was broken down by the FBI when she refused to open it after they could not produce a warrant. She was seized in front of her children and was prevented from planning for their care. The same happened to other women, including Dorothy Healey, a well-known California Communist, and mother who was taken into custody without a warrant or the right to phone family members to take her children. Jones called it "the Hitler technique," and it was being reproduced around the country. She included her arrest barely two months before, in the early morning hours of June 20, 1951.[1]

More concerning was that some women had lost custody of their children because of their political views. She mentioned the case of Jean Field, whose husband had abandoned her and her two children in 1940 but had been given custody in 1950 because of Field's association with the Communist Party and opposition to the war. Custody was never returned to her. Another woman in New York was allowed to keep custody of her child because a judge agreed political affiliation could not be considered; the fact that it became an issue demonstrated to Jones the precarity of peace advocacy and the bravery of women. Jones wrote that "this is a planned brutality—it stems from a policy of government—an imperialist racist policy of war and fascism. These attacks on Communist women leaders, on wives and children of the . . . Communist leaders, and also on their organizations are reminiscent of the Hitler decrees on home and family." Jones believed the women presented a threat because they were vocal advocates of a just peace grounded in social justice and the state was deploying all measures to punish them, including family law.[2]

Despite the costs to themselves and their families, the perseverance of radical women in the face of state oppression inspired Jones to conclude that women were essential in the fight against the war state. She believed that "This reactionary drive against women daring to act for peace will be defeated by an aroused united people."[3] This chapter explores the efforts orchestrated and led by Black radical women to highlight the dangers of nuclear proliferation and US militarism and to secure a just peace. In 1950, the global peace movement centered its peace campaigns around the Stockholm Peace Appeal. Written in reaction to Harry Truman's announcement that the US was committed to creating a thermonuclear weapon and issued months before the start of the Korean War, the petition became an effort to stymie the nuclear tide that had radicals on alert. The appeal called for a total ban on nuclear weapons and suggested that any country responsible for using these weapons should be indicted for crimes against humanity. Pejoratively called the Ban the Bomb petition, once the Korean War began, US intelligence viewed it as an arm of the North Korean and Soviet militaries and claimed any efforts to secure signatures or rally for the petition were treasonous. W. E. B. and Shirley Graham DuBois and their organization the Peace Information Center (PIC) publicized the petition and, as a result, became immediate targets of law enforcement. Graham DuBois was instrumental in Du Bois's defense and rallying support for the petition. The CPUSA officially endorsed it, and its members (including Claudia Jones) began organizing signature drives. These activists were driven by the fear that war in the nuclear age could mean global annihilation.

Some radicals felt that Soviet nuclear capabilities provided a necessary balance against the US including Black radical activists. They cited their fear that the US would use it against another nation of color as it had in World War II. This made the petition more urgent. They also felt that the escalating conflict in Korea, and the refusal of US political and military leaders to pledge not to use nuclear weapons there meant that the US was committed to using its full armory against independence movements. As anti-communist tensions escalated abroad and within the country, activists became more convinced that the US was the greatest threat to democracy in the world; the petition was one way to demonstrate these concerns. The US government's reaction to the petition was to surveil and harass the signers and promoters which only proved the US commitment to stifle democracy.

During the Korean War, the women continued theorizing and propagating an expansive notion of peace committed to the liberation of the oppressed in formerly colonized places, including Korea. Nuclear fears and the outbreak of the war made US radicals eager to collaborate with comrades overseas, particularly the Women's International Democratic Federation. The WIDF conducted an unprecedented observational study on US war crimes in North Korea and US activists circulated its findings. The study concluded that the Truman administration obfuscated the reality of the war behind claims it was spreading democracy. The reality was that the US brutally targeted civilians and claimed that its war crimes were Communist propaganda, and those that publicized its actions were Communists, or Communist collaborators.

Increased pressure at home failed to intimidate Black radical activists. Instead, their response to US militarism was the formation of the short-lived Sojourners for Truth and Justice. The Sojourners, organized by Beulah Richardson and Louise Thompson Patterson, has rightfully been seen as an organization that called attention to Black women's oppression and activism; its commitment to peace and anti-war in Korea was part of that mission. The Sojourners called for an immediate end to the war and argued for an expansive peace that included economic security, the end of segregation, federally funded public schools and childcare, and an end to racist violence. The STJ asserted that social justice could not be realized in a militarized state that prioritized war over its citizens.

Together the efforts to publicize and collect signatures on the Ban the Bomb petition and the STJ's creation and activity demonstrate Jones's belief that women were essential to the peace movement. For Jones and the others, peace had to be revolutionary, it had to commit to the liberation and self-determination of the oppressed, and it had to be accompanied by the end of militarism. None of this could be accomplished without women's radical leadership, nor without dismantling the capitalist war state.

COMMITTING TO WAR

On June 25, 1950, Democratic People's Republic of Korea troops crossed the 38th parallel in an offensive against the Republic of Korea (ROK). The demarcation line between what became known as North and South Korea had been arbitrarily chosen by US policymakers five years earlier, and it had long been the site of skirmishes between the two militaries. The line marked the post–World War II occupation zones of the Soviet Union in the North, and the United States in the South after the Japanese were defeated and forced to surrender their Korean colony. The line also marked the divide between two radically different governments.[4]

In the Soviet zone, Kim Il Sung became the leader. Kim had forged a heroic reputation in anti-Japanese resistance and a strong connection to the Chinese Communist Party. In the 1930s, he commanded a division of the Sino-Korean army that garnered a formidable reputation for its anti-Japanese guerrilla resistance. The Japanese military created a "Special Kim Detachment," which launched a massive campaign against Kim and those he commanded in 1939. The Japanese killed a woman suspected of being Kim's first wife to try and lure him out but never managed to stop him. Bruce Cumings argues that Kim's experience in the resistance and knowledge that Korean collaborators worked with the Japanese against independence led him to commit to a "totalized politics" that garnered "no dissent, [and] no political alternatives." The government that emerged in the North was populated by Kim and other anti-Japanese guerrilla leaders who led and whose descendants have led North Korea ever since.[5]

US intelligence and the American public assumed that Kim was a Moscow puppet, and anti-communist propaganda promoted this view. US leaders' failure to understand East Asian history and their single-minded pursuit of anti-communism let these assumptions influence policy. However, Kim's and other Korean Communists' relationship with the Soviet Union was complex. During Stalin's purges in the 1930s, Korean agents in the Communist International were executed, and "200,000 Koreans from the Soviet Far East" were deported on the assumption, driven by racism, that they were Japanese agents. Despite US beliefs, Cumings argues that the Soviets did not pick Kim to lead the North, and later research has shown that he became leader, "almost by accident" and not by some Soviet design. As early as 1945, the US State Department worried about the Korean guerrilla fighters returning to the peninsula and as a result installed collaborators in important positions in the South's government. Many of the Department planners were "Japanophiles" who had "never challenged Japanese colonial claims" in Korea and were more concerned about crafting a deal with postwar Japan than with liberating Korea.[6]

As Cumings describes it, to secure its influence in postwar Korea, the US "employed every last hireling of the Japanese they could find" for the occupation government in the South, some of whom had been educated in the US. While ostensibly there to secure democracy, the US government aided by the media concealed its activities. Oliver Elliott has shown that the US media, which had "restructured itself around the ideology of anti-communism" by the end of WWII, obscured that the US was backing its own handpicked authoritarian leader in the ROK. Rhee Syngman, a Korean Nationalist who had been held prisoner by the Japanese after participating in a March 1919 uprising against Japan's rule, lived in exile in the United States for thirty-five years where he ran a Korean government in exile which "never governed any Koreans." Rhee Syngman made some influential friends in the US including media mogul Henry Luce. During the postwar occupation, the US was looking for someone not linked to the Japanese collaborationist government who could take over as leader. The State Department did not like Rhee, but the Office of Strategic Services decided he would be the right man and it spirited him into Korea where he made American "reflexive, unthinking, and uniformed anti-communism" his "stock-in-trade."[7]

Elliot demonstrates that in the early occupation government, there were some media reports critical of the Rhee Syngman regime and its authoritarianism. Some criticism lasted into the war years, but by 1953 "few observers bothered to comment on the authoritarianism" in South Korea. Before 1950, the Rhee Syngman government conducted arrests of his critics, mass anti-leftist campaigns under the cloak of anti-communism, and censored the media. When the US occupation forces left in 1948, "there was an orgy of state violence against anyone . . . associated with the left or with communism." Historians have estimated that before the war began the Rhee regime killed up to 200,000 people and after the outbreak of war "300,000 people were detained and executed or simply disappeared." In 1952, in the midst of the war, Rhee had his opponents in the governing National Assembly arrested and detained. He used intimidation and violence to consolidate his power. Some US media outlets accused him of being a dictator but still the US backed his government and claimed its anti-communist mission was a democratic one.[8]

The South Korean military was led by a former officer of the Japanese army named Kim Sok-Won who had been one of the officers tasked with tracking "Kim Il Sung at Japan's behest." He also conducted border raids into the North after the Americans left, and the North Korean military, which was outnumbered, responded in kind. However, the US refused to arm the South Korean military with weaponry to launch a full-scale invasion, and UN military observers were left there to "watch *both* the North and the South." The two sides fought one another throughout 1949 and into 1950 as Kim sought Soviet support for a full-scale invasion. Stalin eventually gave reluctant support to Kim and offered equipment and advisers, but he distanced the Soviet Union from the cross-border attack to avoid provoking the US. Meanwhile, Rhee wanted the US to support an invasion, which it refused to do, but it did commit to come to the South's aid if it were attacked. When the North launched its invasion on June 25, 1950, President Truman committed the US to aid the South even before the UN agreed and without congressional approval. The US was now committed to war.[9]

BAN THE BOMB

The months before the outbreak of war were already tense as the Soviets became the world's second atomic power in September 1949, and it was US monitoring that revealed the Soviet's success. At the start of the new year in 1950, Truman announced that the US was going to pursue research into creating a hydrogen bomb. The US remained the only country (then and now) that had ever used a nuclear weapon against another population of people, and as Shirley Graham Du Bois and others would point out, it was deployed against a nation of color. In the summer of 1950, when the US intervened in the Korean Civil War, military leaders and Truman himself did not dismiss using nuclear weapons. The peace movement was on high alert.

The nuclear age heightened the anxieties of a world emerging from the devastations of World War II. Vincent Intondi has argued that Black America was particularly conscious of the dangers of arming white supremacist nations with weapons of mass destruction, and many in the Black freedom struggle were outspoken against its use. White America "differentiated between Nazis, Germans, fascists, and Italians, when it came to Japan, the entire country was responsible for Pearl Harbor" and was implicated in that nation's war efforts. This was clear in the racist imagery deployed in wartime propaganda. When Gallup polled Americans on the use of the atomic bomb in Japan, it found that 85 percent supported it.[10]

But, as Intondi argues, there were people opposed to its use, and many of them were concentrated in some of the older peace organizations. A.J. Muste, a deeply committed Christian, had taken the unpopular position of opposing World War II. Leilah Danielson argues that when the US bombed the Japanese cities, Muste saw it as a moral crisis and "the culmination of the existential crisis wrought by modernity." He argued that the US "could either become a 'savior nation,'" if it gave up its nuclear weapons or it could "usher in the 'apocalypse.'" He was not alone in his thinking as other pacifists refused to celebrate the bombings as an end to the war; rather, many saw it as the beginning of an immoral age. Catholic pacifist Dorothy Day wrote that now that two Japanese cities had been "vaporized . . . we will breathe their dust into our nostrils, feel them in the fog of New York on our faces." Scientists became some of the most outspoken critics of the bomb— some of whom had worked on it. Those concerned about atomic power organized in the Federation of American Scientists with a cohort in the Federation of British Scientists. The group produced the *Bulletin of Atomic Scientists*, which "became the definitive source for antinuclear information." It is also the organization that operates the famous Doomsday clock that warns citizens about our proximity to our own self-destruction, and it still operates today.¹¹ Famously, Albert Einstein issued a warning about pursuing the hydrogen bomb in the March 1950 issue. Einstein called the belief that security could be achieved through military superiority a "disastrous illusion." He warned that the hydrogen bomb "brought within the range of possibilities" the ability to annihilate all living beings on the planet. He feared that it would be impossible to secure peace if all the US did was prepare for war.¹²

Black activists were not just worried about the threat of constant war. Intondi argues, leaders and activists in the Black freedom struggle saw the bomb, along with "colonialism [and] racism" as "links in the same chain." This sentiment did not fall along partisan lines, as conservatives were often as critical of the bombings as liberals and leftists. Conservative George Schuyler warned that the atomic bomb "puts the Anglo-Saxons definitely on top where they will remain for decades." Religious leaders were some of the most vociferous critics of the bombings and in 1946, the NAACP "called for nuclear disarmament." Many saw it as arming white supremacist imperialism against the diasporic world.¹³

Robbie Lieberman argues that Lorraine Hansberry's response to the dropping of the atomic bomb while she was still a high school student provides an understanding of how she would approach war and militarism in the future. After the bombings, she wrote poetry and stories about "beautiful things" while also writing letters to government officials about her concerns for peace and equality. Charlotta Bass's *The California Eagle* featured several stories in the year afterward about opposition to the bombing. It also reprinted an article from the *Chicago Defender* in September 1945 highlighting how white newspapers viewed the attacks. It cited a poll taken in the Pacific Northwest, among white, "ultra-civilized people," that showed not only support for the bombing, but recommendations to use it more. The article questioned how, after witnessing its destruction, people could still recommend and embrace it. The poll, the newspaper assumed, was an indication that the white residents in the Pacific Northwest had the "same prejudices against the Japanese" as they did against Black Americans. The article expressed skepticism that those same people would have supported its use against the white people of Germany. It recommended that its further use be outlawed and any support for using it again would be "barbaric and stupid." Bass believed that the use of the bombs was a grave threat to people of color everywhere.¹⁴

Graham Du Bois remembered feeling "uneasiness and fear" after the attacks on Hiroshima and Nagasaki. This fear reemerged in the wake of

Truman's announcement. That spring of 1950, Graham Du Bois was part of the founding of the Peace Information Center (PIC)—a task she and others took up as part of the Paris Peace Conference initiative to organize in each country and propagandize the peace movement. W. E. B. Du Bois became the chairman of the organization, and the Du Bois' friend Elizabeth Moos became one of its leaders. While Graham Du Bois was not an officer, she was essential in the everyday administration of the organization.[15]

The idea for the PIC centered on the notion that they could circulate information about peace activity, and to do that, they decided to publish "Peace-grams," newsletters that shared information about the global peace movement. Graham Du Bois wrote that the PIC was created to mollify US intelligence by staying within the boundaries of US laws that had linked peace activists to foreign powers. They were not allowed to circulate foreign propaganda, but the group wanted to keep others abreast of the global peace movement, so they had to find a delicate balance between circulating news while not offending intelligence agencies poised to see a Communist conspiracy in their every action. The founding group included lawyers who helped to guide them around any legal troubles that might get the PIC into legal trouble. Even while the founders sought to stay within the stranglehold of US anti-communist laws, the federal apparatus would eventually find a way to silence them.[16]

In March 1950 the Permanent Committee of the Partisans of Peace, a group associated with the Soviet-backed World Peace Congress, met in Stockholm, Sweden, and created the Stockholm Peace Appeal known as the Ban the Bomb petition. The petition was a reaction to Truman's announcement and the tensions in Korea. The text read:

> By—the Committee of the World Congress of Defenders of Peace
> To—All men and women of good will
> Call for the absolute banning of atomic weapons and of all terror weapons of mass destruction.
> Call for the establishment of strict international control to insure that this ban is rigorously observed.
> Declare that any government which first uses atomic weapons, against no matter which other country, shall be branded as guilty of a crime against humanity and shall be treated as a war criminal.

American activists began collecting signatures for the petition and the PIC's first "Peace-gram" featured the text of it, calls for signatures, and lists of peace conferences.[17]

The 1950 International Women's Day celebration was devoted to organizing for peace and collecting signatures. Claudia Jones wrote an analysis of women's participation in the Ban the Bomb signature campaign in the party's *Worker* magazine. Women in Boston collected 2,500 signatures, and women in other cities like Cleveland, Gary, and Chicago were taking to the streets to rally support. Boston organizers claimed that women were eager but timid. They supported peace but were sometimes intimidated by outsiders. Jones noted that the success of the petition drive led the Boston women to create a permanent peace organization and to plan future events.[18]

Jones believed that this campaign helped US women realize that nuclear weapons were "instruments of civilian annihilation." She noted that even liberal peace organizations like the Women's International League for Peace and Freedom were urging the Truman administration to articulate a commitment to peace. But she retained skepticism about liberal leaders and organizers that sided with the Cold War state. She warned that "reactionary labor leaders" were effectively in league with anti-communists in the Catholic Church and US fascists. Jones emphasized that war and anti-communism were the truest bipartisan effort in the US and that Truman, and the GOP worked together, not necessarily in harmony, but not at cross purposes either, to "offer a perspective of death." These "warmongering agents of imperialism" worked to convince Americans that the US and USSR could not coexist and that the "land of socialism" was totalitarian. This meant that organizing for peace had to include freeing women from the "influence of the agents of imperialism" and arouse their solidarity with women globally.[19]

This global solidarity was perhaps the most important part of the signature campaign for Jones because it linked US women to an international resistance to the US war machine. Across Europe, Latin America, Asia, and Africa, peace activists were organizing around the Ban the Bomb petition; many of them women who not only opposed nuclear weapons but also opposed US Cold War policies like the Marshall Plan. Jones wrote that women in Greece, Spain, and Argentina feared for their lives as anti-fascist and anti-war activists were killed. She noted that French women faced violence because of their resistance to their country's war in Indochina, and across Africa, women were fighting for their liberation against imperialist militaries.[20]

That same year, Jones began a weekly column titled "Half the World." She used the column to address issues relevant to women, and much of it focused on the peace movement. Christina Mislán has analyzed Jones's column and argues that her "alternative journalism has played a key role in helping shape a gendered nation through its criticism of persecution, war politics, and US imperialism," long before the feminist journalism of the 1960s. Additionally, many of her columns focused on the Korean War as it was written simultaneously with US intervention there. Jones contextualized the war in the "McCarthyite era of surveillance and political persecution." The war and anti-communist persecution were conterminous, one could not have existed without the other. While anti-communist arrests predated the war, the war allowed for an escalation in the harassment of radical anti-war activists. It also silenced critics and allies who might have spoken out against the persecution and guaranteed public acquiescence.[21]

In April, as the petition was being circulated in the United States, Jones devoted her column to "what women do to ban the H-bomb." She wrote about her speaking tour in the Midwest dedicated to organizing signatures. In Michigan, she spoke to a gathering of labor union women. She claimed that the women were interested in peace but unclear on what started the war. She saw it as an opportunity to articulate how US Cold War policy and the wedding of government and capitalist interests had made war an inevitability. She warned her readers not to organize without education because so many Americans were unaware that the US had made war central to its foreign policy. She also concluded that the "anti-Communist, anti-socialist" hysteria was used to "paralyze the will of the people to fight." President Truman and Dean Acheson, who she described as red-baiters, claimed that it was the Soviet Union that was the aggressor, thus US policy was reacting to the danger it posed. This, she argued, was a falsehood which prevented real mass action and guaranteed American war support. Jones insisted that the unity of the working class was needed to focus on outlawing the atomic bomb and urging peaceful coexistence with the Soviet Union. Anything else was an escalation toward war.[22]

Jones told an audience in Chicago that politicians were presenting the American people with choices based on a "false premise." That premise was that the US was threatened by an alleged foreign conspiracy, and its preparations for war masked its imperialist intent. She told those in attendance that it was the United States that was the real threat to world peace and that they had to protest the "Atlantic war pact," (NATO). In her May column, she wrote about the government's "cynical contempt for life" as it prioritized spending billions of dollars to develop the hydrogen bomb, while a polio vaccine had not been completed and therefore, children's well-being was not prioritized. Children across the US "die and suffer insecurity because Wall Street financiers and their representatives place war appropriations against appropriations for the social well-being of children, basing their policies on war, not peace." This she described as the "disease of capitalist economic crises."[23]

Jones and the party were not the only ones organizing against the hydrogen bomb. The Peacemakers, the Fellowship of Reconciliation, and the Catholic Workers Organization planned a week-long fast leading up to Easter Sunday in April 1950 to protest its construction. Muste, along with his friend Bayard Rustin, felt a "sense of urgency" to draw attention to Truman's plans and demonstrate their "willingness to give life itself if necessary, in the cause of peace." They along with other members refused any food for the week. Even though they had similar concerns as the Communist Party, many peace activists rejected both working with party members and the Ban the Bomb petition. The American and British Federation of Atomic Scientists rejected the petition as an "effective piece of propaganda," and criticized the appeal in the pages of the *Bulletin*. The American Federation of Labor and the War Resister's League both dismissed it and the "Communist-led peace offensive." George Schuyler called it a "Moscow Hustle" and A. Phillip Randolph rejected it even while he acknowledged concerns for peace. The power of anti-communist politics meant that pacifists and peace liberals distanced themselves from their radical allies. The red-baiting within these organizations prevented a unified opposition to growing US militarism and arguably acted as *carte blanche* for the US government to ignore peace overtures and continue dismissing them as part of a Communist coup. Liberal anti-communism enabled US militarism because it prevented unity within the movement and a strong coalition against US war power.[24]

Meanwhile, Graham Du Bois and the PIC were busy producing "Peacegrams" and active in collecting signatures. By June, the American Communist Party started a campaign to try and secure 5 million signatures. The FBI reported that Graham Du Bois was at the campaign's opening ceremony, and she was joined by Paul Robeson and the artist Rockwell Kent. The CPUSA reported that the PIC would make the petition available for wide circulation among its members and had already printed 250,000 copies of it. Later that month, the fears of activists were heightened when the US intervened in the Korean War. From the beginning, politicians and military leaders did not dismiss the use of nuclear weapons, raising alarms among peace advocates.[25]

Graham Du Bois was part of a group that took a public stand against US actions. In July, 100 Black leaders issued a formal anti-war protest. The protest letter noted that neither "might of wealth nor military power" could settle the problems in Asia. It urged Black Americans to stand up against the war as they had yet to enjoy the promises of democracy, the very promises the US military was allegedly going to bring to Korea. But peace and democracy could not be achieved with weaponry. The letter also alleged that if the US was concerned about democracy, then it should be looking to the undemocratic apartheid system in South Africa, a major US ally. It accused the US of being on the path to replacing the old empires in "enslaving" the people of Asia and Africa, not liberating them, and it challenged the idea that you could settle conflict with force. Peace in places like Korea and other theaters of conflict in Indonesia and Malaya would mean that the Western nations could no longer force their policies on others. The group was especially concerned about the potential use of the atomic bomb and urged support for the Ban the Bomb petition. The signers wanted the United Nations to help settle disputes.[26]

US Cold War policy obscured its colonial ambitions as a moral crusade against communism. As David Vine has argued, the US used forts and bases to secure its claim over territory and resources from the nation's beginning. During World War II, the US negotiated bases even before it entered the war, as a belligerent in the conflict the US base construction spanned the globe. While there was a slight contraction of territory in the early postwar years, the Korean War allowed the US to justify its territorial expansion, and base construction increased by 40 percent. US anti-communism was not qualitatively different from how the old empires justified their expansion. As Vine argues, the invasion of other nation's lands, either through colonialism or military presence, is rooted in the belief in "white, male, Christian" superiority. Bases and interference in "classic imperial style" were used to "stabilize conditions to protect US corporate investments" or to open new markets and appeared value neutral even as the US displaced local populations and claimed sovereign territory in other nations' borders. Americans were infected with national pride that its government could bring democracy to others; this was enabled by propaganda that constructed nationalist movements as Communist and the freedom struggle in the US as threats to the status quo.[27]

This propaganda also convinced Americans that the US was in a fight against Soviet communism and the outbreak of the Korean War had little to do with Korea or Koreans. As Masuda Hajimu argues, many Americans saw it as the US's first confrontation with the Soviets and federal officials were happy to perpetuate that belief.[28] Officials hoped Americans would see the conflict as one between the free capitalist world and totalitarian communism. For radical opponents of the war and anti-communism, it demonstrated that US policymakers took a position firmly on the side of capitalism and capitalists. Activists who opposed US policy understood that anti-communism was used to secure capitalist interests and that capitalist interests did not often align with democratic interests. The Korean War, the hydrogen bomb, the increasing military budget, and the US military presence around the globe were not to fend off totalitarianism, nor was it to secure democracy. Cold War policy intertwined the military and civilian economies to secure the wealth of a few. This translated into violating the rights of people on the "darker side of the color line."[29]

The Ban the Bomb petition became the centerpiece of the peace movement, and the US's rejection of it demonstrated both its commitment to militarization and to maintain the threat of nuclear deterrence—thus, holding the world hostage. In August 1950, the World Partisans of Peace held another conference, this time in Prague. Graham Du Bois did not attend, but W. E. B. Du Bois and their friend Charlotta Bass did, and their experiences were harbingers of things to come as the Korean War empowered US officials to restrain the free speech and expression of citizens. Du Bois's application for a passport to enter Czechoslovakia was no simple task. The New York passport office wanted a letter from him confirming he knew about the "unsettled conditions" in that country. He was essentially meant to denounce the Soviet influence there, which he was unwilling to do. Eventually, Du Bois conceded to write a note that he wanted to make the trip, no matter the conditions. It took ten days and two phone calls before he was given his passport. But it was only good for sixty days and only for certain places.[30]

Charlotta Bass had no such travel restrictions, though she was denied the right to travel to China the year before for a conference that was meant to encourage the US to recognize the newly created People's Republic of China. On her way to Prague, she stopped in New York where she spent her few hours with Graham Du Bois, who she described as someone using her pen and voice to speak out for peace. She wrote that Graham Du Bois thought that fears of a nuclear war were hanging over everyone's heads, but even that was not the greatest threat; the biggest threat was coming from those in power who were constantly threatening war while using the state to silence peace activists. Once in Europe, the CIA followed Bass's movements.[31]

The Ban the Bomb petition became the focus of the Prague conference. W. E. B. Du Bois noted that the group wanted to expand the petition to include calls for disarmament. Bass reported that the conference decided that the Ban the Bomb petition would be an essential tool for the peace movement. Other countries were reportedly collecting millions of signatures, and the Soviet Union alleged that every adult in the country had signed. The goal was to increase the number of signatures to demonstrate the global desire for peace. Later that month, Bass, W. E. B. Du Bois, and Graham Du Bois were on a list of "prominent Americans" who endorsed the petition.[32]

After the US entered the war, US intelligence targeted the petition as subversive. Wartime allows politicians, law enforcement, and anti-communist civilians to deploy existing anti-radical tools to violate radical activists' civil liberties ostensibly in the interest of national security. It also allows the shifting of resources away from social programs and provides a false sense of national unity.[33] This was especially true during the Korean War and evidenced in the government's reaction to the petition. On July 12, 1950, Acheson dismissed it as a "propaganda trick" of the Soviets. The *Information Bulletin*, a monthly magazine out of the Office of the US High Commissioner of Germany, reiterated Acheson's claims calling the petition a propaganda trick to cover Communist's actions in Korea. The *Bulletin* claimed that newspapers across the United States were reporting that the petition was Communist-inspired, Communist-driven, and part of a Communist conspiracy. Days after Acheson's original statements, Du Bois wrote a statement attacking the Secretary of State for failing to note whether he had any interest in peace at all. The *Information Bulletin*, in contrast, painted Communists and communism more generally as aggressors and the US as the ones that sought peace. It was, in the end, a piece of propaganda itself given the US's rapid militarization. But peace to the US and Americans was increasingly seen as something the US forced on others, on its terms. Peace was no longer the absence of war; it was following US anti-communist policy or risking US intervention.[34]

In August 1950, the PIC was ordered to register as a foreign agent under the Foreign Agents Registration Act. The Act required those acting on behalf of a foreign agent to register and report their financial compensation as said agent. The use of the act during the Cold War was to link organizations to the Soviet Union. Registering placed not just a stigma on the organization but also a bureaucratic burden requiring paperwork and financial and membership disclosures. Du Bois and the other officers sought to meet with State Department officials to appeal the decision but were rebuffed. Eventually, the group decided to disband.[35]

This did not dissuade the federal government, which decided to indict W. E. B. Du Bois and three other officers, including Elizabeth Moos and a secretary who had organizational paperwork in her name. Shirley Graham and W. E. B. Du Bois were married amid the legal troubles and Graham Du Bois took up her new husband's and his colleagues' defense. The Du Boises traveled the country twice to raise defense funds and awareness about the silencing of the peace movement. They were followed by agents across the country who reported on speeches, followed their itinerary, and noted who they socialized with. The defendants were all exonerated, but not before paying thousands of dollars for defense and having their names associated with an alleged Communist conspiracy thus scaring others away.[36]

W. E. B. Du Bois chronicled this harassment, the arrests, and the trial in his book *In Battle for Peace* published in August 1952. Chronicling the government's attempts to prove he was a spy for a foreign power, Du Bois's text offers insight into his later years of intellectual production when he became increasingly radical and turned toward the CPUSA, which he would officially join in 1961 as a protest against anti-communist harassment. Graham Du Bois also contributed to the text, and in it the two attacked the US war state and its capitalist imperialist sponsors. The Du Boises confirmed their commitment to a social justice-based peace that necessitated the dismantling of the capitalist war machine. Even in the face of continued state harassment, neither were cowed and continued their outspoken anti-war advocacy.[37]

In the 1951 HUAC report on the peace movement, it included the Stockholm conference and the petition, calling it the "boldest and most far-reaching maneuver of the Communist peace movement." It described the petition as "psychological warfare" that was "shrewdly contrived and carefully timed." HUAC claimed that the petition would become a huge "red mailing list," an opportunity for recruitment into the Communist Party. In perhaps the committee's boldest claim in the report, it stated that the petition was maneuvered as a smoke screen to cover North Korea's assault on the South. The petition demands had behind them the hope that it would "weaken American defenses," which it concluded were needed against Soviet aggression. The committee was essentially accusing the American peace activists of being an arm of the Soviet and North Korean militaries, usurpers of the worst order, and enemies of democracy. Serious charges against people hoping to put an end to US militarism for the sake of social justice.[38]

Though Graham Du Bois's work in the PIC seemed to fly under the radar and not merit the same level of harassment, she remained the focus of FBI investigation and noted the harm it was doing to her career. She found that absent legal ramifications, the mere suggestion of being a Communist could make life difficult. She claimed that by 1950, she and her husband had both been blacklisted by publishers. She believed that one of her books had been rejected because of anti-communism and that libraries were no longer carrying her books. She felt that it was her attendance at the peace conferences and her membership in the World Peace Council that imperiled her career.[39]

Graham Du Bois had earlier noted that the peace movement recognized something that was becoming lost in the anti-communist hysteria and the individualism nurtured by capitalism—that humans were one community. She believed that peace held the key to the liberation of all, specifically the most exploited people on the planet. In the new global age with weapons of mass destruction being built around the world, Graham Du Bois argued that the key to survival was cooperation not competition, and that people could either begin to unite or they would die together. Hers was a vision of peace that encompassed all communities and entailed recognizing the dignity of every human. She shared that belief with her comrades.[40]

THEORIZING PEACE AT A TIME OF WAR

In 1952, Communist journalist John Pittman released an influential pamphlet on the Communist peace movement. Titled "The Negro and America's Wars: The Long Struggle for Peace," in the pamphlet, he wrote that Black liberals were not representative of Black America in their acquiescence to US war policy in Korea. Instead, Black Americans were some of the most outspoken and influential leaders and thinkers in the peace movement. He argued that they were standing in the "vanguard" of those who opposed the "predatory, unjust war waged by the imperialist rulers of our country." One need only look to history, he counseled, to understand that Black Americans have participated in all US wars, but that many had also been critical of those wars.[41] Pittman cited leading historians of Black America, including Carter G. Woodson and Herbert Aptheker, noting that they had explicated the voices of those opposed to US wars. He argued that Black Americans were not pacifists. War opposition was instead measured by whether it was "just or unjust." He argued that the US was using oppressed Black Americans in its military machinery to oppress others.[42]

Pittman's analysis foregrounded a concern that Claudia Jones had been articulating throughout the Korean War and even during World War II: Black Americans were expected to participate in the instruments of US oppression even while they could not enjoy the democratic commitments the country claimed to hold. Erik McDuffie has argued that Jones "simplified the political complexities" of the Korean War. She saw the US as "rogue aggressors" against a "defenseless North Korea." As he writes, both sides were guilty of war crimes, and there was more nuance behind the escalation of the war. But he argues she was correct in noting the higher death toll among Black troops and racism in the military. Korean women and children were a "higher proportion of civilian deaths" than in WWII; thus, she correctly pointed to their disproportionate suffering. He also argues that writing against the Korean War was dangerous, and Jones would have known it would lead to consequences. Jones had already been arrested and detained by this point, and many of her comrades were facing prosecution and jail time. She nevertheless continued to write and theorize about her radical commitment to peace.[43]

Her article and speech on International Women's Day and her "Women Crusade for Peace" article, both released in March 1950, highlighted the basic premise of Jones's peace commitment: that justice and war cannot coexist. She continued to articulate that in her "Half the World" columns and her other publications during the war. Like Pittman, Jones aimed much of her criticism at liberals who aligned themselves with federal policy. They were effectively collaborators in their own oppression. While the US government might have made small concessions to the Black freedom struggle, in the end, it remained committed to maintaining white supremacist infrastructure. This was especially true of the US military which became a weapon against liberation struggles and resisted integrating its ranks.

On Mother's Day in 1951, Jones devoted her column to a discussion on the war. She argued that Mother's Day should be a "tribute to the peaceful desires of women." The CPUSA had long commemorated Mother's Day as a political holiday. Rather than see it as a nostalgic recognition of mothers, the party believed it should be marked with efforts to provide women and families political rights like publicly funded childcare, maternity leave, birth control, and more. Jones's commemoration criticized a radio address she heard in honor of the day that claimed women had to "nurse the wounds of life." She asked why they should nurse wounds rather than live in peace and reasoned that it would be the "greatest tribute to motherhood" for women to be able to raise their children to adulthood without the threat of war. The radio tribute was just another example of "bourgeois idealists" who wanted to make women "accept the Truman-Mac Arthur plan for World War III." She insisted that women had a right to be considered in what she called the "Wall Street Korean adventure" because it could cost the lives of the men they loved.[44]

She continued by arguing that peace meant gender equality, but an "A-bomb psychology" was being taught in schools where youth were learning that war was for democracy; the reality was that the US was a "sham bourgeois democracy" that prevented women from "participation in social and public life." The continued belief in women's inferiority in the US perpetuated "their exclusion from elementary human and social rights." She concluded by calling for the 1951 Mother's Day celebration to be devoted to recognizing women's activism for peace and for the need to secure equality and end the war.[45]

In another column, she claimed that General Douglas MacArthur's removal from the leadership of the war was celebrated by women activists. MacArthur had been removed in April 1951 after he publicly disagreed with Truman's policy in Korea. Truman claimed that he was committed to subduing the Communist threat in a limited war. He told the American people that MacArthur disagreed with that strategy and thus had to be removed. Jones emphasized that women's desire for peace meant celebrations that MacArthur was gone; the war threat, however, was not. She articulated that it was especially poignant for Black mothers as they were witnessing their son's unfair treatment in the military. She worried that others might use the firing as political capital and urged women to unite against the war.[46]

Jones had been invited to speak to students at Roosevelt College in Chicago. Her appearance there was controversial as what she described as "pro-fascist-influenced youth" protested, and the protests made national news. Though Communists had spoken at the school in the past, her speech was different because "reactionary minded" students objected to a speech by a Black woman Communist. She saw the whole episode as an example of the anti-communist hysteria gripping the nation and evidence that "the fight for peace is connected with the fight for freedom." Jones argued that these divisions were wrought by "Wall Street aided by its Social Democratic lackeys" that saw war as profit-making. Upon her return home, she faced the FBI who took her into custody for the third time. This time she was charged under the Smith Act which meant she was accused of trying to overthrow the US government. The arrest did not disrupt her writing and only informed her analysis of the war's anti-democratic nature.[47]

After she secured bail, Jones took up her pen again to rail against anti-communism. In an August column she described the Smith Act cases as a "nullification of the Bill of Rights," specifically aimed at women peace activists. In one of her columns the month after the war began, Jones linked the war and anti-communist harassment in the US. She wrote that people seemed surprised that people who had historically been "ground under their heels" were willing to fight back. They were surprised in "Formosa, Viet Nam, and South Korea" when there was resistance to leaders like Chiang Kai-shek (China), Bao Dai (Vietnam), and Rhee Syngman (South Korea) who were effectively doing the US's "dirty work." That included "perpetuating exploitation, slavery, division and starvation" and using the colonized to help prop up corrupt and unpopular governments. Meanwhile, in the US, Black jurors in the Smith Act trials are "built up in the reactionary press" as evidence that the trials are just and democratic. She likened it to the use of "house slaves for their masters." For Jones, the war in Korea and US support for colonial regimes elsewhere was the same as using Black people to oppress others. Jones believed that she and the other women arrested and charged under the Smith Act were only guilty of calling for solidarity with women around the globe, including Korean women who desired the "right of our children and children's children" to live in peace.[48]

As an internationalist, Jones linked her activism with the global resistance to imperialism. The Korean War had ultimately dashed the hopes of so many in the post-World War II world that as the great empires continued their decline, independence, and sovereignty could finally be achieved in the former colonies. Instead, US Cold War policy stepped into the breach, facilitated by its power expansion during the war. One effort that Jones and her comrades became committed to was women's international organizing, and the organization that most embodied that was the Women's International Democratic Federation founded in France in 1945. The organization was rooted in anti-fascism with some of its founding members Holocaust survivors, while others had been widowed by the war or lost family members, some of the women had also been involved in anti-Nazi resistance.[49]

Suzy Kim argues that the Korean War emboldened the international women's movement centered in the WIDF. Socialist feminism emerged from these women's peace efforts as they "facilitated a productive understanding of difference" among women. The group was a pioneer in analyzing the structural differences that women faced, and it integrated the concerns of Western women with their comrades in the former colonies and the Global South, recognizing that liberal feminism was insufficient because it universalized women's experiences. The group articulated an intersectional socialist feminism forged in its opposition to the Korean War that Kim argues remains relevant today.[50]

Taewoo Kim outlines the WIDF's "five guiding principles": starting with (1) peace, (2) a commitment to women's progress and (3) equality, (4) children's health, and (5) the eradication of fascism. It organized with the World Congresses, including the one that Bass attended in Prague, and it worked to circulate the Ban the Bomb petition. As the Cold War took root, the group's anti-fascist commitments were lost on outsiders as they began to be accused of being allied with Communists. This cost the organization as it was forced to relocate from Paris to East Germany after its leader Eugenie Cotton came under French government scrutiny when she counseled French men to resist the draft to fight in France's war in Indochina.[51]

In 1946, radical American women, including Communists, organized the Congress of American Women as a WIDF affiliate. As Kate Weigand argues, the group emerged from the many disappointments US women faced in the aftermath of World War II, including the end of job opportunities and childcare subsidies. The CAW, however, was also committed to peace and was an early opponent of US militarism. Its members testified against several bills before Congress that authorized the use of military personnel in other countries as well as appropriations for providing weapons to other nations. It opposed the Truman Doctrine, and the Marshall Plan arguing that they only escalated conflict with the Soviet Union and prevented coexistence. The organization urged the nation to focus on social welfare; it called for women's equality, a focus on children's welfare, securing women's economic prospects, and an interested federal government that would fund health and well-being and not war.[52]

For International Women's Day in 1949, the CAW called for action against the Cold War. It urged women "of all races, creeds, and political persuasion" to take up leadership in the peace movement and petition the Truman administration to end its conflicts with the USSR. They feared a "third world war" and hoped US leaders would end the "grip of a relentless cold war" that threatened a "war of world destruction." It also called on American women who were "spared the horrors" of wartime destruction, to stand with other women globally against more war.[53]

Jones had become an active member of the CAW and it in turn defended people like her under legal anti-communist assault. This led to unwanted attention from authorities that soon claimed the organization was Communist-inspired and linked. In May 1948, it was put on a list of subversive organizations. In 1949, HUAC issued a report accusing the CAW of being a Communist front, Jones was featured throughout. She and her friend and fellow Communist Elizabeth Gurley Flynn were both central to the CAW, which strengthened the government's case that it was Communist. Association with Communists was enough to link it to communism, and the organization was ordered to register as a foreign agent in January 1950, but the group voted to disband instead. This did not stop Jones and others from working with and reporting on the WIDF.[54]

In her "Women Crusade for Peace" article, Jones praised the work of the WIDF and its membership. For International Women's Day in 1950, the WIDF issued a "clarion call" that called for women's unity against war. The call read: "Women of all countries: We bear a great responsibility to our children, to our peoples, to mankind, to history—and if all of us—and we comprise half of humanity—go forward with closed ranks against the instigators of war, there will be no war." Jones described WIDF members' efforts to oppose war in their countries and to oppose mobilization. This, for Jones, had become part of another anti-fascist effort after World War II, but now the fascists were her own country.[55]

In 1951, as secretary of the CPUSA's National Women's Work Commission, Jones reported on the WIDF's work for the national convention. In it she praised the WIDF as the leader in the women's global movement for peace. The WIDF was an important supporter of the Ban the Bomb petition and called for its member groups to work to secure signatures. They viewed the petition as an opportunity to "isolate the warmakers" and enable women to take up their duty to "assure the future of the young generations." The group was also a leader in the international anti-Korean War movement and had a Korean affiliate—the Korean Democratic Women's Union (DUKW). The month the US intervened in the war; Eugenie Cotton sent a telegram to the DUKW stating the WIDF's "profound solidarity in their struggle for defence." She called US involvement a "criminal military intervention" on the part of American imperialists against the rights and wishes of the Koreans and she hoped for a "prompt liberation victory."[56]

Jones agreed with Cotton's sentiment and noted that American women had a particular responsibility to work with WIDF women because it was the "imperialists of our land" within the United States that compromised peace and security around the world. She wrote that women across the globe had appealed to American women to urge the US government to stop its support of authoritarians in places like Greece and Spain. American women, she noted, bore a responsibility to the world to resist the militarization of the US government and to stand for "peace and anti-fascism" in the places that the US sought only war and conflict.[57]

Charlotta Bass featured news of the WIDF in the *California Eagle*. She recognized the potential of women's organizing for peace, and in one editorial, she included a letter from the WIDF addressed to American women from their global sisters. It was a plea for American women to join in the global struggle against war, armaments, and nuclear weapons. The article cited the Stockholm Peace Appeal and insisted that nuclear weapons as deterrents were as dangerous as using them because it meant nuclear powers could hold non-nuclear nations hostage. These weapons could also discipline liberation movements and prevent them from securing sovereignty. This did not require the use of the bombs, just the threat of using them. The WIDF feared that the war in Korea, where women and children were already dying from US bombs, made nuclear war more likely. The letter reminded its readers that these bombs were being dropped by "sons of American mothers" who were now engaged in "terrible deeds." The letter told American mothers that their sons were dying needlessly. More importantly, the Korean people did not want them there, and no Russians had been found, contrary to US propaganda. The letter was an appeal and an accusation, Bass insisted that American mothers had to be responsible for preventing their sons from being both murderers and cannon fodder.[58]

The WIDF organized an anti-Korean War campaign and sought to expose US brutality after reports emerged that civilian casualties were high. In May 1951, it responded to a request from its Korean affiliate and sent an all-female delegation, with twenty-one women representing sixteen countries to North Korea to investigate. In the early months of the war, the US gained significant ground; then in October 1950, the Chinese entered the war after the US ignored a warning not to lead its forces to the Yalu River, which marks the border between China and Korea. The US advance ended, and the war reached a stalemate. In response, the US turned to an "aggressive and prolonged air campaign" that did not discriminate between civilian or military targets and led to significant casualties among the civilian population and the destruction of cities. The bombings were so widespread and indiscriminate that by 1953, the US effectively destroyed North Korean cities and towns and the Air Force ran out of targets. It turned to targeting dams, destroying even more infrastructure, and killing more civilians. So extensive was the bombing that as of 2017, experts estimate it will take another one hundred years to remove the remaining unexploded ordinance from the country.[59]

The WIDF observed, filmed, and wrote about the devastation and published their findings in a report titled *We Accuse!* which concluded that the Korean people were living under a brutal US occupation that was intent on extermination. It listed four ways the US-led forces violated the Geneva Convention and were thus guilty of crimes against humanity. The first was dooming the Korean people to starvation through the destruction of crops, the killing of farmers in bombing campaigns, and destroying food stores. The second was the "systematic destruction" of towns and villages, again with bombing, but also other artillery; this was linked to the third, which was the use of weapons "banned by international convention." These included "incendiaries, petrol bombs, napalm-bombs, time-bombs" and "machine-gunning" from low-flying planes. The final was the killing of civilians in US and South Korean-occupied territories. It called for an immediate ceasefire and withdrawal of US troops and the organization of international aid for the Korean people.[60]

Jones reported on the WIDF's investigation and its findings in an August 1951 "Half the World" column. She described tears of "unrepressed anger" reading about rape, pillage, and murder. She wrote that the report was also an allegation against the same people who put her and her comrades in jail, who she described as the "imperialist jailers" of those who sought only peace. The document accused the "interventionists" of a "vast waste of life," and it described mass graves with men, women, and children. She noted that it filled her with shame to read about the children left dead and it led to the question "how [could] decent boys become Barbarians."[61]

Jones discussed another WIDF pamphlet titled "The Children of Korea Call to the Women of the World," in which the WIDF discussed how war made soldiers behave in brutal ways. Jones's friend Elizabeth Gurley Flynn wrote a guest column for "Half the World" discussing the same pamphlet in detail. In it she wrote that "the Korean people are not being liberated but annihilated" by occupation forces led by US troops. She accused the US military of pursuing the "total devastation" of the nation and its people. The pamphlet quoted a WIDF Executive Council meeting report given by the Minister of Education in North Korea. Her report quoted a US Press dispatch from January 1951 that described the annihilation of Wanju, where homes and bridges were destroyed as were food stores. She claimed that the chairman of the Korean branch of the WIDF and the organization that helped the WIDF during its investigation was burned alive, and her body was left hanging in public for a month. Flynn called for an American women's delegation to travel to Korea to investigate the claims and she wrote that "American women have a great responsibility not to allow our youth to become brutalized Nazi-like white supremacists, wreaking vengeance on helpless civilians." Both she and Jones likened the activities to Hitler's Germany and warned against letting American soldiers descend into barbarity.[62]

Jones provided a lengthier analysis of both the war and the WIDF's report in a December column. She took issue with Acheson's claims that the North Korean and Chinese militaries were barbarians and she accused him of ignoring and belittling the WIDF reports. She noted that the definition of barbarian described a foreign invader and reminded her readers that it was the US troops that were the foreigners. She asked whether Koreans were foreigners in their own country after over a year of a "murderous war" that was taking its toll on the nation's people, infrastructure, and environment. This, she argued would only be true for "mad-imperialist minded men" that are "driven by greed [and] crave world domination." She saw this as an "arrogant white supremacist characterization" of the Koreans and Chinese in the "same spirit of contempt" held against Black Americans at home. For Jones, the war and racist brutality were both part of a "white supremacist lynch mob passion" that was fomented against the "darker peoples of Korea and Asia" and in the United States.[63]

She urged Acheson to look at the WIDF's report and its findings of brutality by the UN forces there. She emphasized that the committee that traveled to Korea represented "various political beliefs." The WIDF delegation was made up of women from different political backgrounds, including some women who had been associated with the US coalition in WWII. Jones reiterated many of the delegates' findings including the devastation left in the wake of aerial attacks, the destruction of food supplies and other infrastructure, and the large number of civilian deaths. She also noted that thousands of US soldiers had been injured and killed in the process, but the US continued to pursue policies that left massive destruction and death.[64]

Jones was also concerned that, under US influence, the UN and the international community at large were not taking the report seriously. The WIDF presented its report to the UN and the United States immediately dismissed it as Communist propaganda and put pressure on the UN to ignore it. It also put the WIDF under CIA surveillance. The US attempted to counter the claims that it was using illegal weapons by holding congressional investigations. Jones noted that the US delegate to the UN, Warren Austin, denied the report's accuracy and resisted WIDF representation at discussions about atrocities in Korea. Jones warned that it was the "Trumans, Mac Arthurs, and Austins" that wanted to cover up US activity there.[65]

Paul Robeson's newspaper *Freedom* also reported on the UN's intransigence regarding the brutality against Koreans. In one article, it noted that Austin worked to "block every effort" for a peaceful settlement of the war. The Korean Democratic Women's League (DWL) sent a "passionate message" to the "women of the world" demanding peace and accusing the US of war crimes. The letter specifically described the destruction from the aerial war against the North. The indiscriminate bombings, the letter charged, were destroying old age homes, schools, as well as roads, and crops. The DWL claimed that the "morality of the American imperialists" was not "the morality of human beings." The group argued that the US military "Hate what is honest; steal what is precious; trample upon what is beautiful [and] demolish what is defenseless." The letter accused Americans of rape, destruction, and murder. It appealed to "women of the whole world" and asked for support against US-led troops, and for the Korean fight for "liberty and justice, for peace, and against the fomenters of a new war."[66]

Because it was the radical press reporting on US war crimes, this made it easy for officials to dismiss it as Communist propaganda. Kim argues that the presence of radicals and Communists in the WIDF commission allowed the US and its allies to ignore the accusations within the report. However, documentary evidence shows that the US and its allied forces engaged in massacres and caused widespread suffering and death from its aerial bombardments. Later evidence would uncover other atrocities at the hands of US troops in Korea, including the July 1950 No Gun Ri massacre in which US troops killed hundreds of civilians. US officials, in their attempts to paint

Communist nations as barbaric, put North Korean atrocities in the foreground, while ignoring their own and those of its South Korean allies.[67]

Many of the women in the WIDF delegation faced legal harassment in their respective countries after the trip to Korea. Jones wrote about the harassment of Lilly Wachter, a West German delegate. Because she lived under US occupation, she was subject to US occupation laws. She was arrested after speaking publicly about the group's findings; the crime she was accused of breaking "Allied Control Council Law No. 14" made it illegal to make "statements harmful to Allied prestige in Germany." Wachter, a German Jew, who watched her family die in a Nazi ghetto, was not a Communist, but she found herself censored in much the same way Jones and other Communists were. Wachter was sentenced to eight months in prison for her reports on US war crimes. Jones likened the US anti-communist laws to the same laws used in the Korean and German occupation. In the wake of Japan's defeat and efforts within Korea to secure its independence, the US occupation government passed a series of ordinances that, as Monica Kim argues, set itself up as a "Benevolent Sovereign" that did not believe Koreans were capable of self-government and would eventually be given independence from the US. These laws made it illegal, and punishable by death, to denounce the occupation government and military. US officials silenced dissent within the US and its allied territories, which Jones argued was fascist.[68]

The WIDF delegation members never retracted their claims even in the face of punishment, harassment, and marginalization, which Taewoo Kim believes lends credibility to them. As she contends, this along with new sources suggests that a "more nuanced" analysis of the report is warranted. For one thing, the WIDF had concerned itself with women's conditions in postcolonial states before and had sent its members on other research missions to places like Brazil and Malaysia; thus, the Korean delegation was not "unprecedented." But in an era when anti-communism became ascendant, attacking the capitalist states was akin to subversion. The WIDF would survive as an organization but by 1954, it lost its consultative status with the UN because of US pressure. [69]

Elizabeth Armstrong shows that the report inspired more international resistance to the US-led war. Anti-war posters across Eastern Europe depicted the US and UK as brutal aggressors. American Communist and Jones friend, Betty Millard launched the "Save Our Sons" campaign to protest the war, and there was a "letter writing campaign to President Truman" to release *We Accuse!* to the public. Armstrong argues that anti-Korean War activism demonstrates that internationalism "was a praxis that had two terrains . . . one imperialist," the other "under imperialist domination," and activists had to choose which side they were on. The WIDF report forced liberals to confront whether they supported imperialism and they chose to ally themselves with anti-communists, and thus with imperialist brutality.[70]

But government machinations also made public support almost irrelevant. Marilyn Young has argued that the Korean War was not popular, and that the Truman administration put little effort into selling it to the American people. Instead, it found a way to prosecute war "without public enthusiasm or understanding." Anti-communism obfuscated the reality of the war, meaning, Americans saw it as a battle against communism, while the war's critics, like Jones, saw it as an imperialist venture. For Young, "public acquiescence" to the death and suffering the US inflicted in Korea offered a lesson to subsequent administrations; brutal neocolonial wars could be waged without permission and just as often without knowledge of the war.[71]

This did not change the fact that it remained an unpopular war. At the start, the public was "less than enthused" and "more than a little confused" about it. Young called it the "Ford Pinto of war," it was hard to sell to the public then and remains a hard sell. Significantly, because Americans believed the war was about the Soviets they barely understood the role of Koreans. This reflected both racism and a limited understanding of the geopolitics involved. After a while "only those engaged in fighting it, and their families" were even aware the war was still being fought. It was in the government's interest not to draw attention to it, and thus silencing the peace movement was important.[72]

Jones saw the Korean War, the anti-communist arrests and trials, and the perpetuation of inequality at home as part of the country's war effort. In other words, bringing democracy abroad was a cover for the maintenance of white supremacist capitalism. The "legal violence" against herself, and the others "presaged an onslaught against the rights of all Americans." Jones insisted that the war was unpopular, but to wage said war, the government had to silence its more vocal and vociferous critics. She cited a Gallup poll that found 74 percent of Americans wanted a ceasefire in Korea and a peaceful conclusion to relationships between the US and the Soviet Union. But this did not serve the interests of the "Truman bi-partisan administration" and its allies on Wall Street. Hostilities continued against the will of the American people.[73] In the end, Jones's call for an immediate ceasefire and a peaceful negotiation was not totally out of line with public sentiment, but her CPUSA membership made her, and her comrades seem to be allied with the enemy and thus easy targets.

Jones was especially critical of the two political parties for their bipartisan commitment to anti-communism. In a 1952 article titled "The Struggle for

Peace in the United States," she critiqued the "sabre-rattling" of the Truman administration and its commitment to war for capitalist interests. Jones argued that Truman's State of the Union that year was an example of the obfuscation deployed to convince Americans the war was necessary. She claimed that "in his pose as 'savior' of the 'American way of life,' Truman invokes the divine right to impose war's 'blessings' on the Korean people and on the rising national liberation movements of the colonial and dependent countries." His goal was to convince Americans to "rally behind Wall Street on the basis of a 'peril' which he dares term 'internal aggression.'" Truman invoked a Communist conspiracy to convince Americans that capitalism was the only true guarantee of democracy. Effectively he conflated democracy and capitalism, a still present mythology.[74]

This for Jones was a "vicious hoax" perpetuated against Americans. The US was not in any peril, instead, the "Truman war program ... dooms our nation to endless war in which the rich become richer and the poor poorer." The war was not for democracy, instead, she argued, it was for the "glory of Wall Street profiteers." She wrote that the Chinese and Koreans sought sovereignty and self-government, that in other arenas of Cold War conflict like Egypt and Iran, the people "want to control their own natural resources" and the right to determine their government. In Indochina, Burma, Greece, and Spain, the masses sought a "free, democratic existence."[75] Instead of supporting democratic liberation, the Korean War served as a warning to the world that liberation struggles could face the same US intervention. Truman and others were committed to "looting the national wealth" and destroying the "national aspirations" of liberation struggles. The "Korean adventure" could lead to a world war in which the US continued its warpath to secure capitalist access to the natural resources of other nations. This "bi-partisan war coalition" committed the US budget to war and endangered the American people. Jones concluded that the struggle for peace had to focus on undermining anti-communism and ending capitalism's grip on the US government.[76]

Graham Du Bois later wrote that Cold War policy necessitated the silencing of the peace movement. The entire premise of the Cold War was that the US faced both external and internal threats and it had to secure its future by preemptively engaging in conflict to contain the spread of communism. This policy ensured constant warfare which was supported by a "monopoly capitalist" class that benefited from military incursion overseas. Graham Du Bois argued that the threats US officials claimed were at its doorsteps were just "shrill cries" drowning out reasonable voices that did not want to see the militarization of the country. The reality was that other countries desperately wanted to avoid war and only in the US were people experiencing the fever dreams that led them to think Communists were coming for them. This illusion served the capitalist class as it was able to rally people behind a patriotic war effort while simultaneously concealing their motivations. As Jones described it, she sought "peace, equality, freedom, and Socialism" and this struggle would have to be an international one.[77]

SOJOURNERS FOR TRUTH AND JUSTICE

In the summer of 1951, Beulah Richardson read her poem "A Black Woman Speaks . . . of White Womanhood of White Supremacy of Peace," at the American People's Peace Congress during a woman's workshop. The poem began with a description of white women's investment and participation in white supremacy. She wrote that white women's embrace of white supremacy was also an acceptance of their oppression: "White womanhood stands in bloodied skirt and willing slavery." She urged them to recognize that even as men claimed racial superiority, they engaged in sex oppression. Richardson described Black women's enslaved status as literal, while white women were also in chains; though their chains might be gilded, they were still chains. Women's oppression was a matter of degrees, she wrote, but white women had embraced it while simultaneously acting as enslavers and racial tyrants. She wrote that:

> Because your necklace was of gold
> you did not notice that it throttled speech.
> Because diamond rings bedecked your hands
> you did not regret their dictated idleness.
> Nor could you see that the platinum bracelets
> which graced your wrists were chains
> Binding you fast to economic slavery.
> and though you claimed your husband's name
> still could not command his fidelity.

Richardson argued that white women had accepted a "pink slavery."[78]

The poem described how white men forcibly impregnated enslaved women, and white mistresses had taken their anger out on the enslaved and not their husbands. They reveled in selling off Black women's children while turning a blind eye to their husband's infidelities. She noted that while some women allied themselves with the movements to liberate the enslaved, more had taken the wrong side. Richardson hoped that poor women would ally themselves with the oppressed and reject the attentions of the KKK which had committed itself to preserving white womanhood. Richardson's lyrics articulated an important part of the socialist feminism that she and her colleagues believed in; that women were just as often aligned with oppressors as they were with the oppressed and that gender (or sex to a 1951 audience) were no guarantee of unity. Though Richardson and Jones rejected the word feminism as bourgeois, they were creating a framework for women's emancipation. Even while Richardson and others often described what some might see as a universal woman, they recognized that sex alone was not enough to rally behind. As Jones had described two years earlier in her article "An End to the Neglect of the Problems of the Negro Woman!" Black women were superexploited. Richardson's poem was an artistic expression of that.[79]

The poem also outlined the emancipatory promise of peace. In it, Richardson urged white women to recognize that the Black woman's struggle was her struggle too, and that white supremacy kept all oppressed, including white men. In another poem that likened US racism to genocide written in support of the 1951 *"We Charge Genocide"* petition compiled by William Patterson and accusing the US government of genocide against Black America, Richardson asked, "has white supremacy ended your poverty, your pain, your misery?" The reality, she wrote, was that racism brought "Injustice and death for us," and "money for our rulers." Richardson asked the hard questions about who benefited from white supremacy, and she concluded that while it provided a sense of superiority, it did not provide food for one's children, nor safety from war or capitalist exploitation. It was the most effective tool in dividing working people and ensuring a future of war and conflict.[80]

McDuffie argues that it was this poem and Jones's writings that inspired the creation of the STJ. It was Thompson Patterson and Richardson who would organize the group along with their friends Lorraine Hansberry, Charlotta Bass, Eslanda Robeson, and Graham Du Bois, among others. The organization was devoted to organizing among and for Black women and it helped to formulate a "Black Left Feminism" which combined Communist Party "positions on race, gender, and class with black nationalism and Black radical women's lived experiences." The group was significant as the only Cold War organization that engaged with a precursor to what today we call an intersectional analysis of Black women's oppression. As James Smethurst has written about Claudia Jones, this generation's feminism was not intersectional because it remained grounded in Marxist Leninism. But he argues that Jones could be remembered as the "Black Marxist feminist ancestor of intersectionality." In other words, their feminism is part of Black feminism's genealogy, and influential for later generations. As Richardson's poem demonstrates, the STJ sought to address Black women's triple oppression in its critiques of not only Cold War politics and US racism but also in its engagement with the white left. The STJ "invented unique understandings of liberation and human rights" at a time of extreme duress. Dayo Gore argues that the group challenged the Communist Party on Black nationalism and its priority to promote interracial unity.[81]

For both McDuffie and Gore, the STJ was an essential, though short-lived, organization for articulating a broader conception of Black women in the Marxist canon. Black women party members were interested in expanding the party's theoretical scope regarding race, gender, and class. Its membership included the same women that had been pushing to promote the peace movement. While some of its members were Communists, many women were not but had been involved in other radical organizations including the Civil Rights Congress, the National Negro Congress (NNC), and the Council on African Affairs. In "keeping with the Popular Front," the organization included many non-Communists in its membership and leadership. They also drew in what they often referred to as lynch widows, the wives, mothers, and families of Black men murdered in the criminal legal system.[82]

Much of the scholarship written on the STJ has focused on its important contributions to the expression of Black Left Feminism, a feminism that would influence later organizations and individuals. But the organization was also an important voice in the opposition to the Korean War and for a social justice-based peace. The Sojourners recognized that Cold War policy and its first hot conflict in Korea, endangered Korean lives, and the lives of American soldiers, but perhaps more significantly, committed the country to a state of permanent war that threatened the lives of freedom-seeking people globally. The group actively organized against anti-communism by supporting their comrades who had been indicted by the Cold War state for speaking out against the war. The STJ's work challenged both the domestic and international Cold War as a detriment to its social justice goals.[83]

In September 1951, Richardson and Patterson, along with a committee that included Eslanda Robeson, Vicki Garvin, Marvel Cooke, Alice Childress, and others issued "A Call to Negro Women," to attend a march in Washington. The group sought an audience with government officials, specifically the President and his Secretary of State, to address concerns facing Black Americans. They also wanted to speak to the Attorney General and individuals in the Department of Justice to address their concerns with lynch law, a phrase that described the use of the criminal legal system as a tool of oppression. The call demanded that the government address racist violence, segregation, and disenfranchisement. It stated that they were tired of being treated as "second-class citizens" as their children faced "starvation and disease" and their husbands, brothers, and fathers were killed or maimed from racist violence, often at the hands of law enforcement. The group noted that the government already had the tools in place to protect Black Americans, namely the Reconstruction amendments (13th, 14th, and 15th), but that its unwillingness to uphold the law and insistence on states' rights allowed states to continue their racist practices. The women also demanded the "full dignity of Negro Womanhood."[84]

The group took its name from Sojourner Truth and the call included images of her and Harriet Tubman linking it to a long tradition of Black women's resistance. It listed specific demands that included an anti-lynching law, "indemnity" for the "widows and orphans . . . left behind after lynchings," an anti-poll tax law, and guaranteed Black representation in government. The group called for a permanent FEPC and security for Black women who defended themselves against sexual assault.[85] It also included in its language, opposition to Cold War anti-communism and militarism. It wanted:

> The coming together of our government with the other great nations to work out the guarantees for permanent world peace, so that we, along with all other women everywhere, may live and rear our children in a free, secure, and peaceful world.

Included was their opposition to Black men's service in a Jim Crow army. It read that the group opposed the conscription of their "sons, husbands, sweethearts, and brothers" to fight in a segregated army "in the name of democracy," when they did not enjoy democracy at home. The group's opposition to the Smith Act trials was part of their critique of the Cold War, and the document included a demand to end the Smith Act prosecutions that their friends, husbands, and comrades were facing. The Sojourner's goal was to become a voice for the Black woman and to organize the masses in the struggle for "full dignity." But it also theorized a vision of equality rooted in a just peace and a vision of themselves as global citizens; thus, the organization offered an anti-imperialist, internationalist concept of social justice.[86]

Lorraine Hansberry described the group's sojourn to Washington in the October 1951 issue of *Freedom*. The first day, the group had gathered at Frederick Douglass's home where they read out a proclamation. The next day, they gathered at a church where the attendees discussed their experiences that brought them to the Sojourners. Hansberry described the mothers and wives of men who had been shot and killed by police or framed in the courts to take the fall for a crime they did not commit. She also described women whose sons and other family members had been shipped off to war and come back in caskets. Mrs. Pauline Taylor described how her son had returned from the "senseless war in Korea" but her nephew had been killed there. Taylor faced government harassment after she attended a peace meeting in Poland. In the church, they left seats empty for people like Claudia Jones who was unable to attend because she was not legally permitted to travel to DC. They left other spots empty for those imprisoned and for those who had been killed.[87]

They marched to the capital and demanded meetings with Justice Department officials, the Attorney General, and the President. At the Justice Department, they met with Mateo Hubbard, a Black lawyer in the Civil Rights Division. This was significant as other white employees watched the confrontation. Angie Dickerson, the STJ spokesperson urged the white onlookers to stay as surely they too had mothers and must value the concerns of women. Dickerson told the officials that they were there to protest the lynching of Black men, capitalist exploitation, and the humiliation of segregation. But they were also there to protest the conscription of Black men into the Jim Crow army. Some of the women who had lost family to racist violence confronted an uncomfortable Hubbard. A "housewife from N.Y." asked him what he was going to do because: "We Negroes are always proud to have our people put in high places, but we like for it to mean something."[88]

The committee sent a letter to Alexander Pace, in the Defense Department, to arrange a meeting and protest Black men's war service. It accused the military of taking away "our Negro sons and brothers . . . to fight against the colored peoples of Asia" allegedly for democracy and to assure "freedom to all people in a free world." The letter asked how the US could bring peace and freedom to any other nation when "our government has never and does not now protect the lives and liberties of fifteen million of its own citizens." The letter also asked why the confederate flag was flown on bases, on battleships, and in other locations and why bases continued segregation. It went on to protest the cases of soldiers court-martialed in unfair military courts and the lynching of Black men at home, again at a time when the US claimed to be spreading democracy. A similar sentiment was in the letter to the President which protested that Black men's blood was "vainly spilled in Korea" during a war "whose stake is questionable" and fought against other people of color, "while the color bar robs them of freedom." The women were not given an audience.[89]

The women were also not able to meet with the Attorney General, but their first gathering was declared a success. If official attention is any indication of success, the Sojourners garnered the notice of the FBI, Secret Service, the Counterintelligence Corps of the US Army, and later Naval Intelligence. The monitoring began within days of the group's founding after an informant told the FBI about the organization. The fact that four intelligence agencies began surveillance upon its formation and continued it well after the organization folded, indicates that the federal government considered the advocacy of social justice a criminal act. Also noted in its FBI file is the organization's opposition to the Korean War and its support of individuals under investigation or on trial for alleged treasonous behavior.[90]

Claudia Jones was one such individual the organization supported during her arrests, detention, and trials. Carole Boyce Davies argues that it is noteworthy that Jones was not among the "initiating committee" of the STJ, because the organization championed the causes that she had been writing about. Boyce Davies argues that her role was of a "champion and supporter" and a "philosophical ally." In her November 1951 "Half the World" article, Jones celebrated its founding and its goals. She saw the group as the culmination of so many of her aspirations to see Black women lead the working-class and peace movements. She called the group a significant step in the struggle for peace and the women as the best alternative to the "passive and pro-war sellout" leaders among Black liberals.[91]

Jones attended an STJ New York "Report Back" meeting which was meant to report back to the national organization. During the meeting, she observed newly minted activists and longtime organizers that came together to launch the "powerful organized movement of Negro women."[92] Jones wrote a much lengthier article on the STJ in the February 1952 issue of *The Woman Today* for Negro History Week. The article outlined the organization's many goals and campaigns and included its concerns for Black men serving in the Jim Crow army, and the growing war economy that benefited Wall Street and not Black workers. Jones's hope for the organization was to see it as a leader not just in the US movement against war and racism, but also as a global leader in anti-imperialist struggles against the US military. She wanted to see the women promoting and working with "colonial women's movements in Korea, the Far East, in Latin America and in Africa," and she wanted to see it affiliated with the WIDF. She hoped that the Black freedom struggle would be a leader in the international "peace and freedom movement."[93]

While the group was committed to peace, part of that movement included resistance to anti-communist repression and advocacy for peace leaders like Jones. In its letter to Dean Acheson, the STJ included a list of demands. The demands began with a list of grievances that included objections to Black men serving in Korea "to fight for freedoms which they themselves are denied" and a call to drop the indictment against W. E. B. Du Bois, and the return of Paul Robeson's passport and the passports of Pauline Taylor, Laura Leak, and Theresa Robinson, other Black radical peace activists. The State Department had begun using anti-communist legislation to prevent the international travel of radicals, which in the case of Paul Robeson, damaged his career.[94]

The STJ was particularly interested in Jones's case because she was the only Black woman indicted under the Smith Act and the government had further endangered her because as an immigrant she was denied the right to naturalize because of her Communist leadership. Charlotta Bass was the STJ chairman, and a leading organizer in the National Defense Committee for Claudia Jones. Rosa Lee Gray, the Manhattan STJ president was also part of the organization. Louise Jeffries, who served as the acting secretary of a Jones defense organization argued that Jones was targeted as a Black woman, and because "she has fought so staunchly for world peace." She claimed this was proven by the indictment itself which listed Jones's articles advocating peace.[95] The STJ issued a brochure in Jones's defense that reasoned she was charged not because she was guilty of any actual crimes, but because she "dedicated herself to the cause of peace and security." The brochure also indicated that for the three years before her last arrest, Jones had dedicated herself to criticism of the growing Cold War state and a commitment to the "peace and national liberation struggles of women" around the world and she was actively organizing women to fight for peace. The STJ urged those who "hold similar views for peace, equality, and security" even while not being a Communist, to stand up against the frame-up against Jones.[96]

Jones's case exemplified how the government deployed the excuse that national security during wartime allowed it to suspend American civil liberties. But what happens when war is being waged with no start or end date, a war against an enemy that changes according to the whims of the government, popular culture, or the media? The Sojourner's criticisms of the Cold War included that those seeking peace and social justice had suddenly become enemies of the state and the Korean War helped to convince others of that threat, but the Cold War existed in perpetuity, therefore, justifying regular state oppression.

Anti-communist repression was increasingly circumscribing the lives and activities of the Sojourners and their loved ones. Lorraine Hansberry, as journalist for Paul Robeson's newspaper *Freedom*, traveled to the Inter-Continental Peace Congress Conference in Montevideo, Uruguay, in March 1952 in Robeson's place after the State Department seized his passport. Hansberry described how the US State Department opposed the conference and had made every effort to prevent it from happening. Those who traveled to the country had their passports examined and they were questioned before entering the country; many were not allowed to enter. Even before the conference began the group struggled to find a country willing to allow them to meet as the US pressured each to bar the conference attendees. They tried Brazil first, then Chile. Even Uruguayan authorities claimed the meeting was not allowed because, as Hansberry wrote, they sought to "impose war on people." The sponsors decided to risk arrest and face the hostility of law enforcement since the people, Hansberry claimed, welcomed the peace activists.[97]

For Hansberry, the conference demonstrated the US military's reach into Latin America. She wrote that Paraguayans reported that their country had been asked to supply troops for the Korean War; meanwhile, Puerto Ricans complained that their country was being used as a military base. In Chile, peace representatives discussed the extraction of copper from their country, using their resources and labor for the US military machine without remuneration to the people. Leonor Aguilar Vasquez, an Argentinian woman who had participated in the WIDF delegation to Korea discussed the group's findings and its conclusion that the US was guilty of war crimes. She said that the people of Korea know better than to surrender to US and South Korean forces because they can expect no mercy from them.[98]

Hansberry read a statement by Paul Robeson at the conference and made a speech highlighting her concerns about her own country's growing power. She told audiences that to secure peace they had to work for it. But she was troubled by the symbols of US power across Montevideo and Latin America generally, from the US flag at the airport to the presence of US military officials. For her, this meant that the "fight for peace" was not separate from the "fight for national sovereignty." She questioned why Puerto Rico, with their language and flag, should have the US flag flying over it. She likened it to the US Black Freedom Struggle. She noted that at the conference, they discussed the link between national independence and peace; the "enemies of the liberation" of the colonized and formerly colonized were "the same enemies of peace." Anti-communism and imperialism were linked as the US used its growing military might to exert pressure in Latin America; she argued that to defeat US imperialism, peace had to be secured. That included freedom from US military presence and intervention. Though she traveled to the conference as a representative of *Freedom*, Hansberry remained a committed STJ member, and she spent time describing the work of women and creating relationships with other women activists. The conference proclaimed solidarity with the US movement against racist oppression.[99]

The State Department did not appreciate Hansberry's message at the conference and the FBI noted that she brought that message back to the US. She gave a talk to the American Peace Congress about her experience and that speech was reprinted in the CPUSA *The Worker* newspaper in June 1952. In it, she reiterated her impressions that the US military was effectively a neocolonial force ensuring that its interests and the interests of the government and capitalists remained at the forefront. She told the audience that "the 'monsters' that the people of the world are talking about are our own sons and brothers." She continued, "In 1952, the peoples of the world ask of the people of the United States what we asked the German people a few years ago." She concluded that peace activists had to inform the "American people what is going on in their name." That same month Hansberry's passport application for a trip to Europe was denied; her attendance at the Montevideo Conference and her alleged communism were cited as the reasons for the denial.[100]

The STJ and the women involved in it were devoted to addressing inequality and the oppression of Black women by racist forces and their progressive allies. They recognized that securing peace was integral to their liberation and the liberation of Black America and the colonized and that the Korean War was disruptive to a nation that had only been at peace for a handful of years. The war was a distraction from freedom struggles in the US and it shifted resources away from Americans in need. The Sojourners asserted that the US commitment to permanent war was a danger to the emancipatory aspirations of Black Americans and those whose liberation movements faced the threat of US intervention. They believed that the US had no business in Korea, had no interests in that country, and had committed US lives in the name of democracy when democracy would not be forthcoming. The persistence of segregation, capitalist exploitation, and racial discrimination evidenced the absence of democracy in the US and the racist US criminal legal system exemplified the failure of the state to uphold the constitutional rights of Black Americans. Radical activists described lynch law as the intentional use of the police and courts to maintain white supremacist control over Black America and they used it to demonstrate that the US government had little interest in democracy. This laid bare the falsehood undergirding the containment policy.

CHAPTER THREE

No Freedom Here

In May 1952, interned soldiers at the Koje Island POW camp in South Korea took US General Francis Dodd captive. Dodd, who Eslanda Robeson described as the "boss of the camp" was held for three days before being released unharmed. The prisoners made demands to improve camp conditions and end repatriation interviews. In January of that year, the US delegate to the United Nations Command proposed voluntary repatriation of Prisoners of War (POW). North Korean representatives argued that this was a violation of global agreements made in 1949 for mandatory repatriation. The US did not formally recognize North Korea and thus argued that mandatory repatriation was not required. US officials were effectively making POWs pawns in the greater Cold War contest; they hoped to demonstrate that given the choice, the POWs would choose capitalism over communism. According to Monica Kim, this delayed the armistice an additional eighteen months and made interrogation rooms where prisoners had to make their choice a site of "US liberal power."[1]

Robeson wrote that the Dodd abduction forced the US to explain why it was refusing to end the war over repatriation. The Defense Department "rushed into the full-time job of explanations and denials" claiming that POWs were being treated well and interrogations were not forced. She also pointed to the hypocrisy of administration officials who called Korean hostiles "barbarians" and now a year later were embracing and trying to protect them from being repatriated.[2] She analogized the repatriation interviews arguing that it was like taking 170,000 Black prisoners, having them interrogated by KKK members or Southern Sheriffs, and asking whether they would want to return to peonage labor in the South. The Korean and Chinese prisoners, she wrote, had insufficient interpreters and the US was holding them hostage insisting that few of them wanted to go home. US officials claimed that of the 170,000 POWs in its camps, only 70,000 wanted to return to either North Korea or China. This, like the POW interrogations, was putting individuals into dangerous situations. For Robeson, this was the barrier the US put up to ending the war. She insisted that the Truman administration explain why the war continued, why the US was holding up the armistice, and how the US was "defending freedom and democracy" by killing civilians and making unreasonable demands. She saw this as an abuse of POWs and likened it to the abuse of Black Americans; therefore, she was accusing the US war state of meting out undifferentiated racial violence against the colonized in Korea and at home.[3]

The Progressive Party (PP) issued a statement to Congress protesting the interviews, because they closed ceasefire negotiations. It also doubted the government's claims that troops did not want to return to the North since no evidence had been disclosed to prove it. It cited a Red Cross investigation at the Koje Island camp that accused the US of conducting "re-interrogations" of soldiers who wanted to return to the North; effectively it accused the US of failing to honor the wishes of the POWs and instead forcibly persuading them. The PP was accusing the government of surreptitiously engaging in torture to influence repatriation. The Red Cross investigation did indeed support the PP's claims that several Koreans indicated they wanted to be repatriated to the North and that they were then subject to re-interrogation.[4]

Repatriation was not the coup US officials had hoped and it was also more complicated than generally described. Many Koreans who fought with the North were from and had family in the South, which impacted their choices; the opposite was also true. Surprising officials, there were many Koreans who chose to be repatriated to the North. In a particularly troubling episode for US leadership, 21 US troops chose to stay in Korea, this sparked concerns about brainwashing and fed anti-communist hysteria about mind control. For Robeson and the PP, the voluntary repatriation issue was an attempt to make a political message about democracy and freedom, while compromising the actual freedom of those fighting in the war.[5]

Increasingly, critics of the war became concerned that war and Cold War anti-communism were fascist. The US military and political leaders, ostensibly tasked with spreading democracy, were deploying fascist methods to enforce their will. Even the military failed to be democratic because the war was meant to be the first that was integrated, but Black troops remained segregated, and discrimination persisted. The arrest and prosecution of Lieutenant Leon Gilbert highlighted the military's unfair treatment of Black soldiers and became a rallying cry for radicals opposed to Black participation in the war. The Black soldier personified inequality: US authorities claimed that the country was committed to ushering in democracy and sometimes imposing it by force in places like Korea. Black soldiers were part of that mission, neither integrated into the military nor at home, they faced injustice and violence, or what radicals called lynch law. Lynch law had at one time referred to the extralegal lynching of suspected criminals; radicals instead used the phrase to describe how legal institutions lynched Black Americans.

Meanwhile, inside the US racial fascism persisted. The Scottsboro Boys had made lynch law a central feature of radical anti-racism. During the Cold War, opposition to anti-Black violence was central to anti-war activism, some of that violence came in the form of disciplining Black soldiers. But anti-Black violence on the home front, particularly the cases of Willie McGee, the firebombing of Harry and Harriette Moore's home, and Rosa Lee Ingram's incarceration, demonstrated that the US was incapable of bringing freedom and democracy to its citizens, let alone the world. While lynch law persisted within the US and among US troops abroad, US capitalist democracy could not claim the moral high ground in the Cold War contest. For this reason, radical Black women argued that US Cold War policy was fascist and the justifications for the Korean War were morally bankrupt. They concluded that US fascism amounted to genocide against Black Americans.

Radical peace activism revolved around the concern that racist violence and its use to control and discipline Black Americans were being exported and deployed against people of color in decolonizing states like Korea. This was the crux of radical Black activism against the Korean War specifically, and Cold War anti-communism more generally. Truman had ordered the desegregation of the military in 1948, but the military continued to resist integration and deployed a segregated force to the Korean War. An integrated military was meant to demonstrate US democracy, radicals instead argued that Black men were being used as imperialist tools. While the government proclaimed its commitment to usher in democracy and resist Communist totalitarianism, it had never secured Black Americans' rights. Additionally, US anti-communism undergirded its marriage to monopoly capitalism and government officials parroted the superiority of capital in the quest to secure freedom. In other words, US officials admitted that the Cold War was waged to secure capitalism. But Black Americans had been exploited under US capitalism and continued to face racist violence that went unpunished. For anti-Korean War activists, peace required justice and justice required peace, a state invested in capitalist exploitation at home and abroad stood for neither nor could secure either.

LEON GILBERT

During World War II, the FBI conducted a study on Black soldiers and the supposed "Foreign-Inspired Agitation" among them. It produced a report called the Survey of Racial Conditions in the United States (RACON) which was not released to the public until 1980. As Christine Hong argues, the report described Black soldiers who were "excluded from the benefits of American democracy as enemies." The US treatment of Black soldiers in World War II showed that several soldiers "harbored 'implacable hatred for the Army." Rather than see this as a problem within the military or US culture, it was interpreted as disloyalty on the part of Black soldiers. Desegregation was meant as both the appearance of democracy and an attempt to placate Black soldiers and those making civil rights demands. After the war, the government focused on a "Cold War multiculturalism," because of its "anxiety about the threat Black demoralization posed to U.S. war power." This was not, as Hong argues, because the US wanted to end racist segregation; rather, it was part of the effort to ensure the "war machine's efficiency." Cold War anti-communism necessitated the "institutionalization of a permanent war posture" committed to battling internal and external enemies. Military desegregation made it appear that the federal government was committed to a multiracial democracy; meanwhile, it engaged in neocolonial projects.[6]

Charisse Burden-Stelly has shown that RACON demonstrates the "entanglement" of the Black Scare and Red Scare. The document included an analysis of the Communist Party's work in racial equality and specifically highlighted its Black Belt Thesis which recognized Black Americans in the South as a nation with the right to self-determination. But for Burden-Stelly, the FBI used it as evidence that the Black freedom struggle was an arm of a foreign power that sought to overthrow the US government. RACON justified FBI surveillance of Black radicals and liberals, and shifted the agencies focus on to civil rights advocates, many of whom were anti-communist themselves. This mattered little to an agency led by a director (J. Edgar Hoover) who believed that the Communists were in control, and his agents were ordered to find the evidence. It also demonstrates that the government prioritized militarization over committing to an inclusive multiracial democracy and expanded its punitive state against Black Americans in the interests of war.[7]

For US officials, the Korean War came at an important moment in its "domestic management of race." Since the war's mission was confused for an already war-weary nation, "the Korean War was heralded by the U.S.

government as a 'breakthrough on the color front' a 'successful racial revolution.'" Racial integration was celebrated by authorities who congratulated themselves on embracing Black soldiers, or as Hong calls it "militarized blackface." It put the US military "at the vanguard of civil rights reform." Indeed, even mainstream civil rights organizations like the NAACP celebrated military integration as a step in the right direction. But this image, questionable from the start, was necessary to "camouflaging the illiberalism" of a war waged to suppress the independence of Koreans. While the white and Black liberal press might have celebrated it as a momentous occasion, radicals were not so easily taken in.[8]

US officials were aware that racism was a liability as the nation tried to construct an image of democracy and freedom in contrast to Soviet totalitarianism, but radical Black activists argued that the country's Cold War containment policy only affirmed its fascist tendencies. Truman's desegregation order was meant to make the Korean War the first US war fought with integrated troops, but barely two months into the war, incidents of discrimination against Black troops prompted Roy Wilkins of the NAACP to request a formal investigation. The investigation was precipitated by the treatment of Black soldiers at military installations in Japan. Wilkins noted in his request to Frank Pace, the Secretary of the Army, that as the US was trying to "disabuse the minds of the Koreans and others that this is a racial war," abuse of Black Americans by their fellow soldiers persisted.[9]

The case of Leon Gilbert exposed the reality that Black soldiers could not expect democracy within the ranks of the US military. Only a month into the war on July 31, 1950, at Sangju, Gilbert, a WWII veteran, and career military man, had fled from battle and refused to lead men back because of "poor equipment" and the "heavy loss of men." Gilbert was ill from dysentery, and his troops had not had sleep in six days. A commissioned officer had ordered a retreat, but during the retreat "a newly arrived major ordered him to advance. Lt. Gilbert, pleading incapacity, did not carry out the order." Gilbert was arrested for "violation of Article of War, No. 75: 'Misbehaving himself before the enemy by refusing to advance with his command.'"[10]

At his court-martial, he was found guilty by an all-white jury, though Gilbert served in an all-Black regiment, the Twenty-Fourth Infantry Regiment which was part of the Twenty-Fifth Division attached to the Eighth Army. He was sentenced to death. Truman and the media claimed Gilbert was a coward while civil rights leaders saw him as emblematic of a "racial double standard." His wife Kay asked Truman to commute his sentence, which rallied people to his cause. Activists did not claim that he was innocent, instead, they focused on the fact that white deserters rarely received death sentences.

As Mitchell Lerner has argued, there were others that emphasized that his case represented a double standard because of "structural racism within the Army, which, because of his race failed to provide him with satisfactory training and weapons, denied him adequate food and sleep in the nights before the incident, and placed him under the command of inexperienced and often racist officers."[11]

In November 1950, the PP issued a statement demanding Gilbert's release. The statement described Gilbert as an injured veteran carrying a metal plate in his head from his WWII service, father of two, and devoted husband with another child on the way. Gilbert's refusal in the field of battle came after six days under heavy fire; he was ordered to lead his troops to "certain death" by a major that had not been in battle. The PP argued that Gilbert's story was one of "discrimination in our U.S. Army," where underequipped and segregated Black soldiers were intentionally put in harm's way.[12]

For Lerner, the compelling part of Gilbert's case was that he had an "inadequate defense," and because of this, he faced a harsher punishment than similarly charged white soldiers. The Civil Rights Congress founded in 1946 with Louise Thompson Patterson's husband William Patterson as the "heart and soul" of the group, took up legal cases involving working-class and oppressed defendants like Gilbert. The CRC took up the work previously done by the International Labor Defense and became the central organization behind lynch law cases. Gilbert's wife dismissed the family's original attorney and turned to the CRC. The STJ and the CRC worked together to organize and rally around the accused and many of the women in the STJ, like Thompson Patterson, Bass, and Richardson, were also members and activists in the CRC.[13]

The CRC showed that an Army Medical Report found Gilbert "emotionally disturbed" and plagued with anxiety which made following orders more difficult. This report was not allowed in evidence during his court-martial. Prosecution witnesses were relieved from combat duty so that they could testify against him; in contrast, defense witnesses were not given the same consideration. Some officers testified that he and his regiment were put in an untenable position to hold a forward position that was under extreme attack. Gilbert's original defense attorney refused to put him on the stand and did not deliver a final summation to the court. The CRC challenged the legality of his trial because of the inadequate defense, and that he was tried by an all-white jury. But it also argued that because Congress had never declared war, Gilbert could not be charged with a crime that was only used during wartime and it questioned the legality of the court-martial on the same basis.[14]

Gilbert's case garnered national attention and NAACP attorney Thurgood Marshall requested permission to travel to Tokyo, Japan, where the trial took place, to investigate military tribunals. General MacArthur responded that there was "not the slightest evidence of discrimination . . . as alleged." He claimed that all soldiers were treated according to the same rules and therefore, there was no bias against any one soldier. MacArthur told Marshall that he was welcome to travel to Japan to represent soldiers who were given the right to choose their counsel, but he said nothing about the trials that had already taken place. Another request was forwarded to MacArthur to investigate all the cases, and Marshall was allowed to travel to Japan where he worked with the Inspector General to investigate.[15]

Marshall's five-week investigation found that Black soldiers were charged more often than white soldiers, trials were shorter, defense attorneys were deficient, and they were given little to no time to meet with clients. He also noted that General MacArthur had made no effort to uphold integration and that segregation perpetuated "low morale." Marshall concluded that the entire military court system was bad, but that it was far worse for Black soldiers.[16] Over eighty Black men were being held in a Tokyo stockade after their trials. Marshall spent three weeks in Japan investigating their trials and speaking to the condemned, including Gilbert. Some of the convicted Black soldiers told Marshall that they were unable to meet with their attorney, defense witnesses were barred from testifying, some were sent to the front as punishment, and some had "jurors that slept through the trial." Marshall collected as much information as he could in Tokyo and then asked if he could travel to Korea to speak to some of the witnesses and the defense attorneys and access the records that were not available in Japan. He was granted permission and was assigned a Deputy Inspector General as escort.[17]

The Twenty-Fourth Infantry had been in battle for ninety-three days, along with two other white divisions that saw an equal amount of time at the front line. Marshall noted, however, that the ratio of Black troops fighting was one Black man to every 3.6 white men; Black troops were being sent to battle at higher rates than white troops. He found that complaints filed by officers, all of whom were white, against soldiers disproportionately targeted Black men. Black troops were 28 percent of the unit but they were "88 percent of those charged and received 97 percent of the convictions." Racism was crucial in the excessive sentencing of Black soldiers and created a "hostile atmosphere" that made it "impossible for jurors to be impartial." Of the thirty-two that were convicted, two had trials that were less than an hour and both were sentenced to death. Marshall highlighted the case of a Black soldier who was accused of disrespect toward a white officer, he was sentenced to "25 years of hard labor," while a white soldier accused of manslaughter was sentenced to just three years. The military rejected Marshall's conclusions and though he did manage to get a reduction in sentences for some of the convicted, systemic change was needed. As Lerner argues, some movement leaders initially supported the war effort hoping Black participation would encourage full integration into the body politic; Marshall's report and the Gilbert case led to liberal doubts about the war.[18]

While liberal civil rights leaders were beginning to question the war, radicals continued to voice their opposition. Charlotta Bass described Gilbert as a "victim of Jim Crow" who was being punished because he refused to lead twelve men to their deaths. Claudia Jones wrote about Gilbert's case in several "Half the World" columns. In one she compared his supposed crime to that of Douglas MacArthur who famously disobeyed Truman's order and urged full combat in Korea rather than a limited war. Gilbert's "frame-up" and his death sentence were more unjust since MacArthur, who she called Mac, had only lost his position and not faced death or imprisonment. Jones argued that the service of Black men in Korea was a "growing genocide" occurring during the "aggressive and vitriolic war of extermination against the colored peoples of Korea." Gilbert was saved only because women, like his wife, had insisted on bringing his case before the public.[19]

In Beulah Richardson's letter on behalf of the STJ seeking a meeting with the Secretary of War, she wrote that Gilbert's wife gave birth to a stillborn baby because of the family's stress, which the letter described as a "direct result of the segregated frame-up." The Communist *Daily Worker* printed a letter Gilbert sent to CRC attorneys about the death of his third child. He described how the death brought him "great grief, adding more injury to my unfair trial and sentence." His wife, who had been working tirelessly to secure his "just exoneration, being with child throughout her flight from Japan to aid me at home, seeking help, constantly working under the shadow of death" worried her husband would be executed. He wrote that the "mental and physical exertion took its toll," and their baby "lived but a few minutes and then took its eternal rest."[20]

The *Daily Worker* printed a letter from William Patterson back to Kay about Gilbert's case and the CRC's stand on the war. In it, Patterson likened the war to Black oppression, it was to "bring the Korean peoples under the form of terror and oppression" to which "16 million negroes are subjected in America." Black troops, he continued, were used as an instrument of the US military to bring Koreans under the US heel and to distract them from organizing for their freedom. This was what concerned the STJ, the US could not commit Black troops to a foreign theatre of conflict when the real battle was at home. As Communist leader Ben Davis argued, "Truman could 'cook up a red-baiting pretext to send Negroes 10,000 miles away to die, but he can't find a single way to get the anti-lynch, anti-poll tax or FEPC bills passed."[21]

International pressure from activists, both radical and liberal, led to Truman commuting Gilbert's death sentence to seventeen years, he would serve five. Even his imprisonment worried activists; Black troops, many argued, should not be committed to war when lynch law reigned in the United States. Radicals argued that the Korean War was only a different chapter in the US's long history of racial fascism and government officials pursued it in the quest to secure capitalist domination.[22]

WILLIE MCGEE

In a CRC pamphlet on Gilbert, the organization likened his case to the ongoing legal battle to save the life of Willie McGee. While Gilbert's refusal to follow orders in Korea might appear disconnected from a death penalty case in the United States; for activists, McGee and Gilbert personified the reality of the US criminal legal system's lynch law. As Burden-Stelly has argued, peace to Claudia Jones and her comrades was an "antidote to anti-Blackness, labor exploitation, and perpetual war." The war state, both at home and abroad "played out" its violence on Black Americans; it also deployed Black men to engage in that violence against the colonized. What Burden-Stelly calls radical Black peace activism, linked anti-Black violence, anti-communist policy, and the US commitment to perpetual war and formulated a vision of peace that necessitated an anti-capitalist movement.[23]

The movement to free Willie McGee demonstrates the peace visions of radical Black women and inspired their increasing commitment to radical activism. In November 1945, McGee, a World War II veteran was accused of raping Wiletta Hawkins in Laurel, Mississippi. Hawkins, who it was later revealed had sexually harassed McGee and who had accused other men in the days before settling on McGee as her alleged assailant, claimed that he snuck into her home and sexually assaulted her while her husband slept in the next room. McGee said that he and Hawkins once had a consensual affair, but her interest became too intense, and he left the state to avoid her. After he returned to Mississippi, he tried to avoid Hawkins, but she continued to harass him.[24]

Rosalie McGee described this in *The California Eagle*. When she learned about her husband's affair with Hawkins she left him, but eventually, the two reconciled and hoped that Hawkins would leave them alone. But then

Wiletta's husband Troy beat her "almost to death" and as was "Southern custom," Wiletta claimed that her injuries were from a Black man that had raped her. A mob of white men took McGee from his workplace, beat him, and then handed him over to the authorities. That the mob turned McGee over to law enforcement indicates that they knew the state would ensure his punishment, regardless of guilt.[25]

Law enforcement did not entertain McGee's accusations against Hawkins. The trials, imprisonment and eventual execution alarmed activists and profoundly influenced radicals. The CRC became instrumental in the McGee defense and issued a fact sheet on the case that highlighted the injustices of McGee's arrest, trial, conviction, and subsequent failed appeals. McGee confessed to the assault after police officers drove him to Hawkins's hometown and threatened to release him to a lynch mob. He was defended by court-appointed attorneys at the first trial. The jury took only two minutes before it returned a guilty verdict. McGee was then sentenced to die in the electric chair. This decision was overturned on the basis that there should have been a change of venue. At the second trial, McGee's conviction and death sentence was upheld but thrown out on appeal. This time because there were no Black jurors. During his third trial, he was represented by attorney and future Congresswoman Bella Abzug. The defense attorneys asked the judge for protection because of threats against their safety; protection was denied. McGee was found guilty again and his execution date was set for three months later. The CRC went to work to secure a stay.[26] Activists, meanwhile, rallied to commute his death sentence. An execution date was set for the summer of 1950, just as the US committed troops to Korea.[27]

Defense Attorneys argued that McGee's confession was secured under duress and the threat of violence. They argued that his treatment throughout the entire process demonstrated racial discrimination that was "enforced by State officials," in violation of the Fourteenth Amendment. This the attorneys described as "purposeful discrimination" by people acting under the guise of the law. This was an important argument made by activists who insisted that the federal government was guilty because it failed to uphold the constitutional rights of Black Americans. The federal government could have upheld McGee's rights by intervening in his case and the cases of hundreds of other Black Americans who faced unjust local courts, instead it cited the state's right to police citizens. McGee's defense emphasized the unjust trials in Mississippi and pointed out that white men never received death sentences for rape in the state.[28]

Because the CRC became involved, locals dismissed McGee's defense as Communist-inspired. The *Jackson Daily News* printed a threat against the attorneys during the commutation appeal. It described the Civil Rights Congress as "Communistic" and claimed that it had planned an invasion of Jackson, Mississippi. The newspaper described McGee as a "thrice-convicted rapist," and noted that Mississippi residents probably had never seen a Communist. Nevertheless, it warned that it was "closed season on varmints," but that the locals could be "impetuous and act quickly" if a Communist was mistaken for an animal. It noted that a local might ask the question: "Why the hell go to Korea to shoot Communists when the hunting is good on home grounds?" The paper did not realize that it had made the same connection radicals themselves had, independence fighters in Korea and the US were confused for treasonous Communists regardless of political affiliation; therefore, they were all threatened with racist violence. Appeals continued until midnight on May 8, 1951, when McGee was executed in the electric chair.[29]

It was the McGee case that inspired Beulah Richardson to write her poem "A Black Woman Speaks . . . of White Womanhood, of White Supremacy, of Peace." She wrote the poem after speaking with Louise Thompson Patterson and Rosalee McGee. Claudia Jones regularly cited the case as exemplary of lynch law and the kind of "frame-up" cases that Black Americans faced in the legal system, and Charlotta Bass featured the case in *The California Eagle* and organized delegates to travel to Mississippi to protest the execution. Imani Perry, Lorraine Hansberry's biographer, argues that McGee's execution "haunted her pen." Hansberry had traveled to Mississippi to organize McGee's defense, and she wrote about it in *Freedom*. McGee was executed before the STJ was created but his state-sanctioned death was one inspiration for the group's founding and remained an inspiration long after. For these radicals, McGee's murder as the US committed resources to the Korean War confirmed that the US's democratic commitments were illusory.[30]

Bass and *The California Eagle* used the case to highlight the paradox of fighting for democracy while a Black man faced legal execution on flimsy evidence that pivoted on a white woman's questionable testimony. In a July 28, 1950, column Bass published a letter from a reader who argued that McGee would have been eligible for the Korean draft, as other young Black men were, while "being denied democracy in their homeland." The same issue featured an article titled "Koreans vs. Willie McGee" that stated even if the US won in Korea, it would not have gained "territory in the struggle for democracy in a free world" while executing a Black man only on a white woman's words.[31]

Jones compared McGee's and Gilbert's cases describing them both as "frame-ups." She believed that Cold War anti-communism positioned US political and military leaders as virtual dictators and their abuse of power was clear in the abuse of Black men. Jones articulated another paradox in the government's efforts in Korea and the McGee case, the US claimed to be avoiding another genocide, this one orchestrated by Communist forces. Instead, it was engaging in genocide against the Korean people while its policies, and more importantly its indifference to constitutional rights, perpetuated the legal lynching of Black Americans. This, Jones argued, was itself the continuation of genocide that had a long history dating to slavery. She noted that even "bourgeois organizations" were realizing that the Cold War encouraged teaching children the bible, then making "killers of them." In the era of atomic bombs, all wars had the potential to be genocidal. Jones therefore rejected the notion that "peace was appeasement"; rather, it was a concerted effort to end the "killings on a worldwide scale."[32]

One of the concerns both Jones and Beulah Richardson articulated in their writing on McGee was the desire to make white women aware of their role in perpetuating lynch law. Richardson wrote in her poem that white women accepted their sex oppression in exchange for the benefits of white supremacy. In the poem, Wiletta Hawkins represented the "depraved, enslaved, adulterous woman" whose lies "killed what she could not possess." White women making false accusations of rape "upheld" the "bloody deeds" of US officials but also sealed their fate. Richardson addressed white women warning that:

> This is what they plan for you.
> This is the depravity they would reduce you to.
> Death for me
> And worse than death for you.

Richardson argued that white supremacy would not and could not emancipate white women, all it guaranteed was their inequality, poverty, and war. She urged them to ally with Black women: ". . . take my hand; and the hand of . . . Rosalee McGee" and work together for "PEACE IN A WORLD WHERE THERE IS EQUALITY."[33]

Both Jones and Richardson described white women's complicity in white supremacy as hiding behind skirts; Richardson described them as "bloodied skirts." She concluded her poem on an optimistic note, hoping that they would recognize their collusion and begin to ally with Black women. Jones believed there was a "necessary initiative" on the part of white women to recognize their complicity and challenge white supremacy. She felt that the McGee case had begun to break down some of those barriers. She described the work white women did organizing food for the picketers outside the prison where McGee was held. This was a first step in "disassociating themselves from white supremacist ideology" and recognizing that the fight for Black equality was their fight too as it would advance their interests.[34]

Jones knew there was a long way to go to secure interracial unity, but participation in the McGee case was an important sign of the unity of all women. She wrote about white women who organized in Mississippi against McGee's execution and demonstrated that "disassociation of themselves from white supremacist ideology is tribute not only to their recognition of the self-interest nature of their struggle for negro rights, but to the detriment of the warmakers in America who threaten peace at home and abroad." She also praised the work and leadership of Black women, including McGee's wife, in organizing against lynch law. These women "give the lie to those who speak of women's innate weakness, for they compose a strength born of struggle" which was "consecrated in hatred and indignity" in the violence meted out to Black Americans. She described the "hypocritical white supremacy system which operates against Negro men doubly, and triply for Negro women."[35]

During McGee's incarceration, Rosalee McGee was left to raise four children on her own, two of whom had to be sent to relatives out of state because she did not have the funds to care for them, another was no longer attending school so she could work. The CRC encouraged Rosalee to be involved in the defense writing letters to officials asking for clemency, and highlighting that without him, she was left to her own devices to care for her family. In 1950, Rosalee wrote a letter detailing Wiletta Hawkins's interest in her husband. She claimed that because he was going to die in the electric chair and was out of reach of any lynch mobs, she could finally describe how Hawkins had pursued a sexual relationship with McGee. She alleged that Hawkins asked Willie for a date and "People who don't know the South don't know what would have happened to Willie if he told her no. Down South you tell a woman like that no, and she'll cry rape." This led to an affair that lasted until McGee served in the military during World War II. After the war, Hawkins pursued him again. To escape Hawkins, McGee left the state; he eventually returned to be with his family, and Hawkins began pursuing him again. This continued until she accused McGee of rape. Rosalee wrote that outsiders could not understand the power Hawkins had over their family and speaking out for a Black man meant your life was not worth anything to others anymore. She claimed that sexual manipulation was happening "all over the south," and neither Black men nor women were safe from the abuse nor false accusations of assault.[36]

This was one of the concerns Jones had warned about in her writings, white men sexually assaulted and harassed Black women without repercussions. White women, however, were as guilty of sexual manipulation, which demonstrated their collaboration in upholding white supremacy. Jones argued that white women should be interested in the McGee case as part of the liberatory hopes to emancipate all women. Lynch law was justified as protection of white womanhood, and it perpetuated the control and manipulation of Black Americans and by extension the colonized and formerly colonized world. To achieve peace, there had to be a unity of purpose behind liberating the Black woman; this struggle required the destruction of the war state which had made clear that it sought the continued subjugation of the non-European world (both inside and outside of US borders). To emancipate the most exploited was to emancipate the world.[37]

Lorraine Hansberry called the case one of the "greatest antilynching struggles" in the country. Hansberry's poem "Lynchsong" was inspired by McGee. In it she described her mother warning her about racist violence:

> I can hear Rosalee
> See the eyes of Willie McGee
> My mother told me about
> Lynchings
> My mother told me about
> The dark nights
> And dirt roads
> And torch lights
> And lynch robes
>
> The
> Faces of men
> Laughing white
> Faces of men
> Dead in the night
> Sorrow night
> Sorrow night
> And a
> Sorrow night

The poem narrated the elements associated with lynching and extralegal violence by lynch mobs in the dark of the night. But in the "eyes of Willie McGee," the lynch mob was the legal system. He was killed by the state, but the agents of the state were no different from those in the mob. As Soyica Diggs Colbert argues, the poem "mourns systematic killing by depicting a spectrum of violence from vigilante justice to state-sanctioned execution." This state violence was not confined to the criminal legal system, the state put weapons in the hands of Black men like Leon Gilbert to force them into acting as its agents killing Koreans. The violent killing of McGee was akin to the state's war-making.[38]

Shirley Graham Du Bois's article "Oh No Brother, No One is Going to Forget about Willie McGee" summarized how many of the radical activists felt about the execution. The article written the month after McGee's death insisted that he was not dead, rather he was "planted in the good, black soil of Mississippi." Graham Du Bois described how McGee had cost the "sovereign state of Mississippi" very little during his life since the state did not, as a policy, invest in the schooling of Black children or the infrastructure of Black neighborhoods. Even as an adult, McGee was called a boy, though he had fathered four children and served in the military. Graham Du Bois wrote about Hawkins's harassment of McGee and the power she had as a white woman to manipulate him by accusing him of rape.[39]

She described the anger and frustration of so many activists who understood the McGee case as just one of many that prevented democracy in the US. Graham Du Bois described McGee's quiet and calm demeanor in the moments before his execution. She wrote that though he was gone, he was not going to be forgotten. McGee's execution became central to radical resistance to lynch law and ultimately to the Korean War; it was a moment that proved the state had not only failed in securing democracy but that it was an accomplice in upholding white supremacy.[40] The focus on the McGee case was because it had garnered media coverage and activist interest, but it was only one of many cases in which a Black American died at the state's behest. Lynch law focused on the use of the courts against Black Americans, but it was also used to describe the impunity of white vigilantes who faced no punishment for killing Black people, this included the killers of Harry and Harriette Moore.

HARRIETTE AND HARRY MOORE

On Christmas night in 1951, a bomb that had been placed underneath the bedroom of Florida NAACP secretary Harry Moore exploded. The bomb killed Moore that night, and his wife Harriette died from her injuries on January 4. The Moores lived in Mims, Florida, where they had both worked in anti-segregation campaigns. Harry Moore was a leader in voter registration campaigns, and he and Harriette were outspoken against police violence and segregation.[41]

The NAACP believed that it was Moore's work on the Groveland case that led to the killings. In 1949, in Groveland, Florida, Willie Padgett claimed that four Black men raped her. In response, the white residents of the community attacked Black sections of town, burning down three homes and displacing hundreds. Samuel Shepherd and Walter Lee Irvin, both twenty-two years old, and Charles Greenlee, sixteen years old, were arrested and charged with her rape. The fourth, Ernest Thomas ran away before the police arrested him; he was killed by a "sheriff's posse" in the swamps. Not unlike the McGee case, the white residents rallied behind a white woman making an unfounded accusation of rape against Black men. The NAACP provided attorneys for the men while Moore led the campaign to free the accused. In November 1951, Sheriff Willis McCall shot and killed Shepherd and wounded Irvin while he was transporting them. Moore urged for McCall's arrest and prosecution, and one month later, he and his wife were assassinated.[42]

The NAACP President Walter White wrote a tribute to Moore in the organization's annual report. He began by noting that while the murder was horrendous, there had been civil rights progress. Evidence of this progress was that the US military had been integrated and that the NAACP was successful in defeating the Winstead amendment, an amendment to the Universal Military Training Bill that would have allowed inductees to choose to serve in segregated units. In contrast, Claudia Jones saw the murder as evidence of violence and inequality perpetrated by the war state. The murder indicated to Jones that the state remained unwilling to uphold the rights of people while instead focusing on war abroad to ensure capitalist power. This difference of opinion highlights the divide between liberal civil rights activists in the NAACP and the radicals in the STJ and the CRC. For White and other liberals, equality included acceptance into the US military machinery; for Jones, the war enabled the state's oppression and recruited Black men as agents of imperialism.[43]

She argued that "Wall Street boasts that American working women possess the 'greatest equality' stops at the water's edge." Jones compared the Moore case to that of a Baltimore Black woman, wife of a soldier, raped by white soldiers who were "let off with light sentences." These "daily indignities" were made worse in the "worsening economic conditions in the war economy." The capitalist boast about equality was hollow in the face of the mounting deaths of Black soldiers abroad. She cited the Leon Gilbert case as further evidence of the injustices faced by Black men in Korea, while their wives, mothers, and sisters faced brutality in the US. She wrote about the importance of the STJ in the campaigns against lynch law because women "increasingly question what stake the Negro soldiers have in a war against the colored peoples of Asia when we have freedoms yet to win at home." This "outraged humanity" showed the paradox of claiming a "free America" committed to freedom abroad.[44]

On New Year's Eve, a delegation that included union representatives, CRC members, and one STJ member, Rosa Graham, traveled to Mims, Florida to attend Harry Moore's funeral. Graham, one of the founding STJ members, was part of the group's original sojourn to Washington D.C., and she served as its representative in Florida to attend Moore's funeral and to protest the murder. It was the first time she had been to the South since moving from New Orleans to New York twenty-five years before. During the drive from the airport, Graham described trees covered in moss like those in Louisiana where her family had made a practice of "mossing"—collecting and drying moss to use as stuffing for mattresses. She remembered these trees fondly but seeing them again in Florida, she wrote, reminded her of lynchings: "I saw that same moss hanging from the tall trees-and it didn't seem as beautiful as when I was a child. I came to hate it, because to me it took the shapes of broken bodies swinging from the branches." It was the same in the citrus groves the group passed. Black workers labored to harvest the fruit, were paid poverty wages, and lived with the constant threat of white violence. Graham said she felt the overwhelming "strength and devotion" of Black people, but also "hatred of the southern ruling class and their stooges."[45]

Graham traveled in an integrated group, and she claimed that the white people in it were perhaps hated more by white Floridians than she and the other Black delegates. The Black delegates were expected to conform to Jim Crow; their white compatriots were so "enraged by the taboos and discrimination that they would overstep the line." This meant they would talk to their Black comrades, try to eat with them, or ride in the same vehicle. The problem was that while segregation upset them, their flagrant violations endangered everyone's lives. Local Black men created a phalanx around the mourners during and after the funeral given how tense the atmosphere was.[46]

The delegation met with Democratic Governor Fuller Warren to urge the prosecution of the murderers. Communist journalist Albert Kahn reportedly told him that the case made him "ashamed to be white." The delegates urged Warren to act against the Ku Klux Klan and to recognize that the state's segregation laws put them all at risk. Graham noted that while the delegation was only in the state temporarily, Black Floridians had to live with the terror daily. But she was clear that it was not just a southern phenomenon, in New York Black residents faced violent police, and discrimination in housing, employment, and medical care. She concluded that "white supremacy in the North is really no different from what it is in the South," and she argued that her fellow radicals had to "fight white supremacy here, every day of our lives, even in the progressive movement."[47]

A week later, Charlotta Bass, acting as chairman of the STJ, joined Kenneth Ripley Forbes (a Philadelphia Episcopal minister) and Rabbi Max Felship in issuing an appeal to encourage people to travel to Florida for Harriette Moore's funeral. Harriette had initially survived and even attended her husband's funeral but died from her injuries days later. The appeal stated that the murders "showed a pattern that must be stopped now." The pattern was an attack on social justice-minded activists and leaders who faced legal harassment, violence, and in Moore's case, death for their work. Bass was among the delegates to make this second sojourn.[48]

The delegation represented several organizations; Bass went as an STJ representative and was joined by leaders of the Progressive Party, CRC, Parent Teacher's Association, the Emma Lazarus Foundation, and others, including church and union leaders. Bass wrote that the group traveled to Florida to prevent it from becoming "America's first Dachau. For it has already gone far on that road." Moore's funeral was short, and Bass noted that though she had been a schoolteacher, "very few school children came to the funeral . . . the parents kept them home for fear of possible Klan violence at the funeral itself."[49]

The group went to see the Moores' ruined home. Bass described it as an utter ruin: "after the bomb had done its work we could see nothing but a shambles." She described how they could see where the bomb had been placed so that it would do maximum damage. There were remnants of the couple's curtains and book pages strewn all over the damaged area. It was "a wreck, destroyed by a devilish machine in the dead of night." She claimed that the neighbors were afraid as was the local NAACP because they received threats against their own lives in the wake of the murders.[50]

This second delegation also met with Governor Warren the next day. Bass listed the demands the group made starting with taking "extraordinary measures" to bring the killers to justice, "conduct public hearings for the purpose of investigating and ending the intimidation and destruction" of Black Floridians. And finally they asked the governor to "Issue a public statement condemning in the sharpest terms of all persecution, intimidation, and murderous attacks upon the Negro people, and all minorities, and outlawing the Ku Klux Klan." They managed to get a tepid agreement from him that he would "go beyond ordinary measures" to locate, arrest, and prosecute the killers. He also agreed to hold hearings to investigate the violence. Bass gave a press statement and said that the murders which she described as "acts of genocide," not only "bring ruinous disgrace to the state itself, but also shame and discredit to our beloved nation in the eyes of the world." She urged federal action against the killers arguing that the government was complicit because it allowed the state's jurisdiction over voting rights, segregation, and racist violence and thus failed to uphold constitutional rights. For the STJ, the lack of federal action is what perpetuated racist violence.[51]

The governor invited the delegation to lunch which was "precedent shattering" because they were an integrated group. However, Bass warned about seeing this as a sign of his goodwill. He had recently issued a pardon for a white man imprisoned for murder because he had reported a "supposed 'escape plot'" engineered by Black prisoners. He also told the delegation that Sheriff McCall was "not a bad man." And he "not once . . . use[d] the correct mode of address speaking of Mr. and Mrs. Moore." Instead he called them by their first names "a disrespectful custom which is usual when Southern whites speak of and to Negroes." He never used Bass's name and instead called her "his 'friend from California.'"[52]

The STJ released a statement on Harriette Moore's death that likened it to the "daily violent assaults against Black womanhood." The group also called for thousands of women to wear mourning clothes and to join a march in Washington to protest the murders. The march never happened because, as Eric McDuffie argues, the "repressive political" atmosphere made it dangerous. Bass linked the Moore murders to the genocide of Black America and the US's violence in Korea. She called on the STJ and its allies to "serve notice that the Negro women of America, the wives, sweethearts, mothers, sisters, of the Negro men who are being discriminated against, framed, legally lynched in Korea, who are being dynamited and lynched on the home front, are sick and tired of giving our men to die." Black men, she said, had served in all US wars and had never been rewarded with their own rights. Harriette Moore's brother was serving in Korea when she was murdered and was given leave to return home to attend her funeral. She told an audience that he witnessed fighting and experienced deprivation in Korea, sacrificing for his country and "he was rewarded with the sight of the shattered, dynamited bodies of his relatives."[53]

Florida did invite the FBI to investigate the bombing, but the killers were never brought to justice. The FBI located and indicted Ku Klux Klan members for their participation, but no one was ever prosecuted. This failure was one among many by the federal government to protect the rights of Black

Americans. It was emblematic of a militarized white supremacist nation at war that armed its citizens to kill Koreans abroad and failed to protect Black Americans at home. The Moore case made national and international headlines, and the STJ and its members were active in the campaign to hold Florida accountable. But the case that consumed much of the STJ's time and energy was that of Rosa Lee Ingram and her sons.[54]

ROSA LEE INGRAM

Rosa Lee Ingram was a widowed sharecropper and mother of twelve children living and working in rural Georgia. Her white neighbor John Stratford had long been hostile to her and her children and had also made sexual advances toward Ingram. In a confrontation on November 4, 1947, Stratford attacked Ingram and two of her sons intervened to protect her. In the fight, the Ingrams managed to take Stratford's weapon and he was shot, he later died from his wounds. Ingram and four of her sons, Charles, Wallace, Sammy Lee, and James were arrested. During their incarceration, the family made conflicting statements coerced by the police; these statements were used against them in court. On January 26, Ingram and her sons Wallace, and Sammy Lee, 16 and 14 years old respectively, were tried, found guilty, and sentenced to death. Charles had been exonerated using the same evidence that was used to convict his brothers and mother, and James, only 12 years old, was released.[55]

Ingram's mother Amy Hunt made appeals for money to help the family's defense and the case appeared in the Black press which drew attention to it and the death penalty convictions. The NAACP provided attorneys for the family. In March of that year, Claudia Jones, Louise Thompson Patterson, and their comrade Audley Moore traveled with a delegation to Washington, DC, along with nearly 100 other individuals to speak with President Truman about the Ingrams. The delegates were unable to secure an audience with the President and instead were met by Phileo Nash, a Truman assistant who claimed to be sympathetic to the cause. The Department of Justice informed the group that it did not have jurisdiction and urged them to trust in the local courts. The delegates balked at this suggestion and pushed Nash to defend this stand given that it was those very courts that had already condemned the Ingrams. Moore made the point that the federal government could not help one of its citizens, meanwhile, it had recently committed aid to both Turkey and Greece (in the Truman Doctrine). The federal government's motivation to contain communism usurped any real commitment it had to democracy there or in Georgia. Thompson Patterson asked officials to protect the Ingrams from the Klan; no help was forthcoming.[56]

When the STJ was founded over three years later, the organization saw the Ingram case as emblematic of everything that plagued the American Black woman. As Dayo Gore argues, the campaign organized to free the Ingrams exhibited many of the tactics that were deployed to raise awareness of the racist criminal legal system and campaigns against legal lynching. But, as Gore describes it, the Ingram case was markedly different from the usual cases which featured Black men "wrongly convicted and sentenced to die" generally for the alleged rape of a white woman. The Ingram case made sexual assault of Black women central and, according to Gore, validated a "Black defendant's use of deadly force." The women involved in the campaign to free the Ingrams insisted that "sexualized racism and violence" against Black women "be taken up as core civil rights issues."[57]

As Jacqueline Castledine has argued, the Sojourners also saw the case as exemplary of US colonialism. Castledine, exploring the STJ's relationship with the anti-apartheid movement in South Africa, argues that the Sojourners saw Black wives and mothers as particularly vulnerable to the exigencies of empire building. Theirs became a commitment to protect Black women and girls from white supremacist violence and similar to South African women, the STJ highlighted that "sexual and racial violence made girls and women uniquely vulnerable" under colonial regimes. South African women and Black American women were attacked as a matter of course under white supremacist governments, their bodily autonomy was never secure, and even in the act of defending oneself, it escalated into state violence against them and their families.[58]

For McDuffie, no other issue "galvanized Black women in the Black left" as much as the Ingram case. This was in part because sexual harassment by white men was an experience that many of the activists could relate to, and it demonstrated that self-defense was not an option for them. The women involved in the campaign made Ingram a "household name" among Black Americans and "generated worldwide publicity." The mainstream press and the court case tried to downplay Stratford's harassment while the Black and Communist press featured stories that centered on his sexual advances, demonstrating that white Americans viewed Black Americans as sexual aggressors. Cheryl Higashida argues that the repeated sexual harassment and attempted sexual assault against Ingram and the court cases that followed became an inspiration for Jones to write her most famous text, "An End to the Neglect of the Problems of the Negro Woman!"[59]

Jones rejected universalizing women's experiences and argued that Black women were "superexploited." The Ingram attack emphasized the unique dangers that Black women faced, and the lack of protection they were given when assaulted or when defending themselves. She wrote that protecting white women was merely a pretense to exert total physical and social control over both Black men and women, a point important in Jones's writing on McGee. Stratford's behavior toward Ingram was not anomalous but exemplary of the daily harassment Black women faced; all Ingram was guilty of was rejecting "indecent advances" and protecting herself. White men were able to use false accusations of rape to exert sexual power over white women and Black men and women because the criminal legal system would punish those that challenged their control.[60]

Even while white men maintained control over white women, Black women faced regular sexual harassment and assault. Scholars like Danielle McGuire and Allison Berg have documented how the threat of and the act of sexual assault against Black women was a tool to limit civil rights gains and to punish the women involved in freedom struggles. This was something Jones was acutely conscious of as she theorized about Black women's triple oppression. It was in her "neglect" article that she outlined Black women's oppression, and it was during her discussion of Ingram that it was articulated. Jones had long counseled her fellow left-progressives to recognize that Black women were triply oppressed and that they had to take up leadership in class struggles. As she expressed in the article, the "Negro Question" was "prior to" the issue of sex oppression. It was not enough to address sex oppression; rather, she urged her fellow progressives to understand that to emancipate Black women was to emancipate all.[61]

She wrote that the Ingram case was an opportunity for progressives to confront racism within their ranks and to recognize that it was a "dastardly crime" against all women and all Black Americans. She noted the work activists had been doing on Ingram's behalf. Before the STJ founding, liberal and radical civil rights activists rallied around the family in the National Committee for the Defense of the Ingram Family (NCDIF) led by Mary Church Terrell and Maude White Katz. The group included STJ founding members Eslanda Robeson, Shirley Graham Du Bois, and Charlotta Bass. It organized funds for Ingram's other children and sent a delegation to visit her in prison.[62]

Louis Thompson Patterson led a mutual aid society called the International Workers Order which worked alongside the NCDIF to raise funds and awareness. The NCDIF also circulated a petition that urged Truman to pardon Ingram and her sons, they hoped to collect a million signatures. Jones believed that justice would not be forthcoming in the US criminal system so she counseled activists to seek help from the international community and petition the UN, which would make it impossible for President Truman to ignore the case. The NCDIF took up Jones's suggestion and petitioned the United Nations. Maude White Katz asked W. E. B. Du Bois to write the appeal. In the appeal, Du Bois wrote about the sexual double standard that led to Black men being legally lynched on mere rumors of attacks on white women, while Black women faced punishment for defending their bodily autonomy. While the UN took no action, this appeal to the international community became an important tool in exposing US racism. As Jones hoped, it would be a humiliation for the Truman administration and reveal its inadequacies in protecting citizens. It also presented a challenge to the US claim that it was a model democracy.[63]

The Congress of American Women also worked on the case and urged its "chapters and affiliates" to demand Ingram's "unconditional freedom." It included in its campaigns the demand for reprieve of those condemned in lynch law cases and it became devoted to advancing Black women's freedom. CAW colleagues in the Women's International Democratic Federation were also paying attention to US lynch law cases and used them to highlight US contradictions in its overseas incursions. At its 1953 meeting in Copenhagen, Dr. Andrea Andreen, the president of the Swedish WIDF presented a report on the struggle for women's rights. She wrote that within the US, a government that was "preparing for war" there was a "redoubled offensive" against the rights of the people; she cited a State Department list of 120 organizations that were labeled subversive, including the American Women for Peace. Within the report is an image of Rosa Lee Ingram with the caption "Black people have no rights that need be respected by white people." The case was cited in its 1953 report *For their Rights as Mothers, Workers, Citizens*; it specified that Black American women had no rights and featured the same image of Ingram with a caption that stated: "In the eyes of white supremacists, a Negro woman had no rights a white man is bound to respect." The same report featured an image of Claudia Jones with a caption explaining her indictment and linking it to her opposition to the Korean War.[64]

In the STJ founding documents, the Ingram case was one of the most significant campaigns for the group. In its constitution and by-laws, the group articulated its goals to "secure our freedom and full rights," and to ensure the protection of Black women against white sexual assault. The group committed "to pledge a fight to the death of genocide as it is directed against Negro people in the homeland." And to "wage a ceaseless war against the persecution of Negro women, such as the case of Mrs. Rosa Lee Ingram, wherein they are denied the protection of the courts and the justice of a democratic society." It also committed itself to "support, comfort and cheer" family members of "lynch victims," like McGee's widow. The group sent representatives to visit Ingram and had delegates attend her parole hearings.[65]

Claudia Jones celebrated the group's leadership in lynch law cases like the Ingrams. The organization's founding followed almost immediately on the heels of what Jones described as the "lynch murder" of Samuel Shepherd and the wounding of Walter Lee Irvin the month before the Moore's killings. These incidents confirmed for Jones and the other Sojourners the need for an organization of Black women to create "a powerful movement of their own." Jones noted that Ingram was a "living sacrifice" of the "degradation imposed on Negro women by the lynch system," and thus STJ leadership was necessary. She also noted that the freedom of Ingram and her two imprisoned sons was a "key demand" of the group.[66]

The FBI was especially concerned about the STJ's organization in the Ingram case. During the DC sojourn, which bureau agents called "Communist-inspired" Eslanda Robeson proposed a "Walk on Georgia" of Black women to protest Ingram's imprisonment and a picket at the prison where she was being held.[67] An informant claimed that during the march the group would try to break Rosa Lee Ingram out of prison and that it would be a "testing case" for launching a revolution. This plan would have the STJ mobilize Black women in several southern cities to provoke the revolution presuming that others would follow. The spark to this alleged uprising would be that the women would claim white racists were massacring Black women. The agent reporting on these claims felt that the informant "may have exaggerated the scope and extent of the program" that the "Walk on Georgia" planners were making, but he still asked for direction on whether to inform Georgia authorities and what precautions needed to be taken.[68]

That the agent could seriously entertain the claims speaks to the anticommunist hysteria that influenced law enforcement, especially in the bureau. His concern was that even if there was no uprising planned, the group was planning to cause "racial friction." Georgia authorities were informed of the alleged threat and in response, secured an injunction to prevent anyone from protesting within one mile of the prison where Rosa Lee Ingram was being held. It also increased security at the prison, required a more rigorous visitation policy, and stationed eighty additional police. The STJ did propose a march to the prison to be held on Mother's Day in 1952 and it advertised it in the CPUSA *Daily Worker*, but it was postponed several times and never happened.[69]

McDuffie argues that though the STJ was founded while its organization and its members were under government pressure, it faced "considerable hurdles in actualizing their goals" other than state-sanctioned harassment. These hurdles included imagining their emancipatory visions and those of women under colonial regimes as the same. Sojourners saw them all as an oppressed class; this ignored the complexities like "an appreciation of social location and of how systems of oppression (white supremacy, heterosexism, colonialism and patriarchy for instance) operated in more relational, historically specific terms." He argues that the group also tried to mobilize working-class women though many of its leaders were "relatively privileged." The STJ effectively ended operations around 1952 when the FBI described its work at a "low ebb." The organization around the imprisoned Ingrams continued, initially under the CRC aegis, until it too folded in 1956. Activists and NAACP lawyers pushed for parole, which was denied for several years until 1959 when the Ingrams were finally released after serving eleven years in prison.[70] The importance of the Ingram case, along with those of Gilbert, McGee, and the Moores, was that they evidenced the absence of US democracy for Black America. But more than that, radical activists argued that these cases were part of an ongoing genocide against Black people.

WE CHARGE GENOCIDE PETITION

In 1951, the CRC under William Patterson's leadership, compiled the *"We Charge Genocide"* petition to present to the United Nations. In the document, the CRC tallied thousands of cases of legal and illegal lynching that it argued amounted to genocide against Black America. It was the third attempt by an organization to appeal to the UN on behalf of Black Americans. The National Negro Congress tried first in 1946, then in 1947 W. E. B. Du Bois under the NAACP banner tried again. Patterson noted that his petition was different because he situated the genocide within US Cold War policy. He argued that the "criminal, racist policies" had a "destructive impact" on the nation and on peace. It was in the international community's interest to pay attention to the "flagrant injustices of racism" because "no quarter of the globe" would be safe from the US as its foreign policy was influenced by the same white supremacy it practiced within its borders. He stated in the preface that the US "racist theory of government" was not the "private affair of Americans, but the concern of mankind everywhere." This was especially true as the US took up the self-proclaimed mantle of global defender and enforcer of democracy. The petition, in contrast, protested US racism, colonialism, imperialism, and war and argued that the US was not democratic.[71]

As Hong argues, attempts to appeal to the UN embraced human rights rather than a civil rights perspective making Black American concerns, the "concerns of mankind everywhere." The goals were to expose to the world the "racist brutality of the world's foremost democracy" proving what radicals in the US had been arguing: "the falsity of its promises of full political participation through citizenship." The petition took on more significance during the Korean War because it was a time when US "unilateral violence on the global stage . . . was impossible to ignore." It also made a "structural correlation" between racism in the US and its imperialism. The petition revealed that the US democratizing mission was a cover for its imperialist ambitions and that racist violence at home was being exported as part of its foreign policy. Patterson made these connections explicit in the forward to the petition when he wrote that the "wantonly murderous and predatory racist attacks on Korea" were linked to the "equally criminal murders of rebellious black youths." The Korean and Black American liberation movements were the "crimes of a desperate class." Patterson accused those with power who believe in "aggressive wars" of trying to force their "moral bankruptcy, their ideological corruption" to uphold a white supremacist government. He predicted that "racism and predatory wars" are doomed to failure and that it will be "racists and neo-colonialists" that will be defeated.[72]

The petition was meticulously researched and included the McGee and Ingram cases among hundreds of others; it was an attempt to reveal the lie behind US democracy. Beulah Richardson wrote her performance poem titled "Genocide" in support. The three-part poem was staged as a dramatic reading with a chorus of children's voices. In it, Richardson confronts white America asking: "has white supremacy ended your poverty, your pain, your misery?" She claimed that the US was likely an inspiration for Hitler and pointed to the over 2000 unprosecuted deaths of Black citizens in the document, which she noted, meant that over 2000 killers were walking free, many of whom were state agents. She wrote about the hypocrisy of the nation claiming to be a democracy when it was built on the genocide of Indigenous people with enslaved labor; the poem invoked McGee and Ingram and many of the other cases that inspired the CRC and the STJ's work. She highlighted these cases to argue that the genocide continued and that the US government "exports armies across the sea to spill the blood of another colored nation . . . and yet another."[73]

Many of the Sojourners signed the petition and Richardson's poem was performed at the US introduction of it in December 1951. Paul Robeson led the group that introduced it in the US while William Patterson traveled to Paris to present it to the UN. One week later was the firebombing that killed the Moore family. US officials dismissed the petition as Communist propaganda and escalated legal cases against those involved, including Patterson. The Soviet Union used it as evidence of the paradox inherent in US policy.[74]

The *We Charge Genocide* petition was the culmination of the lynch law campaigns that radicals had been working on for years, but the US's outsized influence in the international community meant that no action would be taken. It and the cases above highlighted the contradictions inherent in US Cold War policy, a policy that was sold to the US public as a commitment to spreading democracy. The reality was that US policymakers conflated democracy and capitalism as an ideal and contrasted it with authoritarianism and communism. The women in the STJ pushed back arguing that US capitalism and militarism was genocidal, and US domestic policy enabled the mass disenfranchisement, abuse, and premature death of Black Americans.

Under anti-communist policy, war was becoming a US trademark and as Jones reasoned, war propaganda was uniquely capitalist as liberal democratic governments practiced and exported authoritarianism in service to capitalists. Jones, the most prolific writer of the women in this book, argued that socialism was the "final and full guarantee" of the emancipation of women; and for Jones, the emancipation of the most oppressed meant the freedom of all. Resistance to racist violence, embodied by lynch law and embedded in the state and the actions of non-state actors, was a natural part of war opposition as was pushing lawmakers to recognize that US policy more closely resembled racial fascism than democracy.[75]

FIGURE 1: W. E. B. Du Bois and Shirley Graham Du Bois on his 87th birthday, February 23, 1955. W. E. B. Du Bois Papers, Robert S. Cox Special Collections and University Archives Research Center, University of Massachusetts Amherst Libraries

FIGURE 2: Claudia Jones, Alamy Stock Photo

FIGURE 3: Charlotta Bass with Paul Robeson, Alamy Stock Photo

FIGURE 4: Beulah Richardson, known as the actress Beah Richards. Bill Cosby Show, 1970. UtCon Collection.

FIGURE 5: Lorraine Hansberry, ca. 1960. Courtesy: CSU Archives / Everett Collection.

FIGURE 6: Paul Robeson, his wife Eslanda Goode Robeson, and their son Paul Robeson Jr., at their house in Enfield, Connecticut, ca. 1940s. Everett Collection Inc.

FIGURE 7: Louise Thompson Patterson, ca. 1930s, Louise Thompson Patterson Papers, Stuart A. Rose Manuscript, Archives, and Rare Book Library, Emory University, with permission of family.

FIGURE 8: W. E. B. Du Bois with fellow defendants during trial in Washington, DC, November 1951. W. E. B. Du Bois Papers, Robert S. Cox Special Collections and University Archives Research Center, University of Massachusetts Amherst Libraries.

FIGURE 9: W. E. B. Du Bois and Shirley Graham Du Bois with Mao Zedong, 1959. W. E. B. Du Bois Papers, Robert S. Cox Special Collections and University Archives Research Center, University of Massachusetts Amherst Libraries.

FIGURE 10: Louise Thompson Patterson, ca. 1930s. Image provided by Daily Worker Photo Collection; PHOTOS223; Box 236; Folder 13505; Tamiment Library & Robert F. Wagner Labor Archives, NYU Special Collections, New York University—Courtesy of Longview Publishing / *People's World*.

FIGURE 11: Henry Wallace (far left) with Eslanda Robeson, Image provided by Daily Worker Photo Collection; PHOTOS223; Box 258; Folder 14706; Tamiment Library & Robert F. Wagner Labor Archives, NYU Special Collections, New York University—Courtesy of Longview Publishing / *People's World*.

FIGURE 12: Eslanda Robeson with a delegation of women to speak to a UN representative to urge a ceasefire in Korea, Image provided by Daily Worker Photo Collection; PHOTOS223; Box 258; Folder 14706; Tamiment Library & Robert F. Wagner Labor Archives, NYU Special Collections, New York University—Courtesy of Longview Publishing / *People's World*.

CHAPTER FOUR

Charlotta Bass for Vice President

On a hot summer day in Chicago in July 1952, Charlotta Bass took the stage at the Progressive Party (PP) convention to accept her nomination as vice president. She celebrated being the first Black woman on a political ticket for the second highest office in the land as a personal victory as well as a victory for the Black community. She claimed to be heartened by other pioneers in the fight for justice for women and Black Americans. But Bass wasted no time in addressing the principles on which the Progressive Party would be running its 1952 campaign—against war, imperialism, and the fascist Cold War policies that silenced dissent at home while launching war abroad.[1]

The party's campaign goals were like the 1948 campaign: opposition to Jim Crow, holding the government accountable to secure Black rights, addressing women's rights, ending military proliferation, and seeking peaceful coexistence with the Soviet Union. Unlike the 1948 campaign, however, this one was set during the Korean War, a war launched as a direct result of the US's Cold War policies, the very policies that Henry Wallace believed would lead to war. At the same time, the domestic Cold War had increased pressure on Bass and her colleagues. By 1952, Claudia Jones was on trial, Shirley Graham Du Bois had launched a nationwide campaign to defend her husband against charges he failed to follow the Foreign Agents Registration Act, the Robesons, Hansberry, and the Du Boises had their passports taken, and all the women were under regular surveillance by the FBI and, when overseas, the CIA. It is within this dynamic and embattled political atmosphere that Bass launched her vice presidential campaign with the Progressive Party. She was troubled by anti-communism and believed that it reflected the fascism the US fought to defeat in World War II. She also saw it as an attack on the Black freedom struggle, while simultaneously ensuring the continued oppression of newly decolonized states abroad. Bass' campaign thus had a dual purpose: to guarantee the exercise of liberty and justice for oppressed populations at home and to end the US neocolonialist ambitions abroad.

Both, she argued, perpetuated the oppression of the formerly colonized, and the ambitions of the Black freedom struggle.

While many Civil Rights advocates and activists felt pressure to mute their criticism of US foreign policy after World War II, Bass, and *The California Eagle* became more "internationalist" in outlook and linked the Black freedom struggle to anti-colonialist struggles abroad. Bass was fast becoming a recognized figure in the international peace movement. She was invited to travel abroad to attend peace conferences, and she used her newspaper to inform Los Angelenos about the global peace movement. She was also critical of the anti-communist purges and remained openly friendly to Communists and the party. This outspoken refusal to abide by Cold War mores that demanded obeisance to US militarism and anti-communism would lose Bass subscribers, but she did not relent. She became a leading voice for peace on the West Coast and in 1952, when she was nominated to run for vice president on the PP ticket, she became a recognized national leader. Bass used her platform to argue that anti-communism was detrimental to peaceful coexistence in the United States and abroad.[2]

The PP had been launched as a protest of Cold War anti-communism. Its 1952 election campaign formulated its platform as a continuation of its 1948 goals to end the policies that perpetuated conflict with the Soviet Union and as a challenge to the bipartisan commitment to anti-communism. The Korean War confirmed that anti-communism committed the US to war and violated the rights of those seeking liberation in former colonies. It also distracted attention from social problems in the United States. The PP did not advocate for the destruction of capitalism, but without Henry Wallace at its helm, the party openly questioned US democracy and put a Black radical woman in a leadership position. Once there, Bass pointed to monopoly capitalism as a villain and a barrier to democracy and she centered racial justice as essential to securing peace. The 1948 campaign was progressive, but the 1952 campaign was revolutionary because it put an outspoken radical Black woman on the ticket.

THE CALIFORNIA EAGLE AND PEACE

Black newspapers and Black Americans were deeply divided over the war and Black newspapers issued widely varying editorials at its advent. As Mitchell Lerner demonstrates, when US hostilities began, reactions were mixed. In the *Cleveland Call and Post*, one editor wrote that only "the most stupid American Negro" would question the government's motives in Korea, and many would sign up to advance the "American cause in the Korean adventure." But in the same issue, Charles Loeb, a veteran war correspondent, wrote a poem questioning the war and Black participation. In one stanza he wrote:

> "We cry to be full citizens,
> We grumble bout our civil rights,
> So in return we gotta join
> Ol' Uncle in his stupid fights.
> Korean may be colored folks
> And some may look like Cousin Fred,
> But looks or not, we gotta grab
> A gun and fill'em full of lead . . .

Lerner writes that these editorials on the same page from the same newspaper show the conflicts among Black Americans over the war and how to view US democratic commitments abroad. As with other wars, some hoped participation could lift Black Americans into full citizenship, while others questioned fighting a nation of color to uphold US white supremacy, knowing that in previous attempts to support US war efforts, Black sacrifices were not paid in kind.[3]

In the years before her 1952 vice presidential bid, Bass used her newspaper to articulate her objections to US Cold War policy and her advocacy of the peace movement. With the launch of hostilities in Korea, Bass focused on rallying Black Americans against the war. One primary concern was the discrimination Black soldiers faced in the military, and the paradox of the United States alleging to bring democracy to another country while continuing to fail to bring it to Black Americans. Only three weeks after hostilities began, the paper's July 16, 1950 headline read "Uncle Tom is Not Dead." The lead article, authored by Bass, argued that the US's insatiable appetite for colonialism was not satisfied with African territories or overseas bases. Both world wars "to all intents and purposes were white men's wars," but the Korean War, which she felt was likely to become World War III, demanded the loyalty of Black Americans. She wrote that "we, the American people carrying the fight to Korea, should be considered out of line as a powerful, dignified nation such as ours fighting a little country only about half the size of California." Bass believed that Black Americans should be loyal to the government and the Constitution, a document she had faith in; however, she attacked "Uncle Tom's" at liberal Black newspapers like the *Chicago*

Defender that insisted Black men should fight in the war to counter racist propaganda. She wrote that "To demand loyalty to the government by Negro Americans is a play on words."[4]

The article focused on the mistreatment of Black soldiers in training, the refusal of white troops to eat or train with them, and the military hierarchy's refusal to promote Black soldiers. Though Bass reaffirmed her loyalty and desire to fight for freedom and democracy, she did include serious questions about the rationale for US involvement in the war and attacked the belief that Russia was to blame. The article included a caveat that her newspaper did not hold "a brief" with communism, she insisted that the conflict could have and should have been settled by Koreans. She also feared that the unquestioned loyalty of "Uncle Toms" in the military would compromise Black America's goal for first-class citizenship. She argued that others in the Black community should use their energy to attack racist violence, rally for a permanent Fair Employment Practices Committee (FEPC), and not advocate war against "other men of darker hue" in Korea.[5]

The following week, Bass' weekly column, "On the Sidewalk," began "We can't outlaw Democracy in the United States and make it work in Korea." She included a letter from a reader who wrote "I question the fact that Black men are being sent to defend democratic principles in Korea and being denied democracy in their homeland." Bass highlighted the regular discrimination and poor treatment Black soldiers experienced at the hands of white soldiers in the most recent world wars and at training camps. Meanwhile, the Truman administration and Congress refused to protect the rights of its citizens and would not take seriously a permanent FEPC. The government, she wrote, "find ways of how not to do, but never a way to do the things that would outlaw discrimination against Negroes." Two years after Truman allegedly desegregated the military, Bass argued that "Jimcro" was alive and well in the armed forces. She pointed to the hypocrisy of sending troops abroad to secure democracy: "This commentator reminded the American people that these dark-complexioned people, not only of Korea but of all Asia, are wondering just how sincere Americans are in their loudly proclaiming desire to establish democracy."[6]

The North Korean army was aware of this conflict and used a tactic that would later be adopted by the Vietnamese, using US racism to its advantage. The Korean People's Army produced a pamphlet titled "Negro Soldiers! There's a letter for you inside, Read it!" It opened by asking if Black soldiers had ever "stopped to think why you should be in Korea, fighting other colored people, while lynchings, murders, and insults pile up." The North Koreans were paying close attention to internal US conflicts, it listed the killing of several Black men, some veterans, by white Americans. This included the firebombing that killed civil rights activists Harry and Harriette Moore in Florida. Interrogators in prisoner-of-war camps often engaged the American prisoners in conversation about W. E. B. Du Bois and Paul Robeson in a show of their own "third world internationalism" and an attempt to "decolonize" the American troops.[7]

One of Bass's staff writers, Raphael Konigsberg, an Austrian immigrant, used his weekly column to attack the containment policy and the war. Konigsberg was a trusted ally and was often left with editorial leadership when Bass traveled; he was also an activist and involved in the PP. Konigsberg's column was the most consistently outspoken against the containment policy and he denounced the country's investment in militarism as profiteering. In a September 1950 editorial, he wrote that the United States was both the most powerful nation in the world and the most "fear-ridden nation in the world. All its power seems to offer little comfort." The country emerged from WWII poised to enjoy "abundance and greater freedom." But "five short years later this great vision is maggot-ridden, destroyed. This most powerful nation, which promised so much, is afraid of its own shadow." Politicians, he wrote, were competing over who was the most anti-communist while ignoring the need for fair housing, jobs, and equitable salaries. During WWII, the people refused to collaborate with fascists abroad and now refused to collaborate with "American fascists." In another article, Konigsberg argued that it was the American people who were being contained and that anti-communism was the "domination of the economic and political resources of other nations."[8]

Konigsberg challenged the US mission in Korea and argued that it was only propping up ineffective and unpopular leaders. He wrote about concerns that Rhee Syngman, the US-backed South Korean leader, was unable to win support in that country. This suggested that the US efforts to support Rhee were not to benefit the Korean people but rather to maintain a leader that the US could manipulate. He argued that the war was not for democracy but to benefit US investors in Asia and that the war was deeply unpopular with the American public, but that policymakers were more interested in profit than the "vital interests of the people."[9]

Like Bass, Konigsberg argued that the war was fascist and that a fascist element had long existed in the United States in the form of anti-Black racism. In an article titled "Negroes know fascism," Konigsberg wrote that the US had a "longer and more violent preconditioning" in fascism than other countries, the evidence of it was its treatment of Black, Indigenous, and Latinx Americans. He wrote that "The Negro people don't have to have fascism defined to them. They know what it is. They live under it. Every significant feature of life under the Nazis is true and has been true of Negro life under American white supremacy." The Korean War accelerated poor treatment as the United States delivered violence to the Korean people and ignored the violence against Black Americans. He wrote that racial fascism gave Americans training and "We may ask whether the 'strange fruit' of this training isn't being harvested in Korea." Referring to the anti-lynching song "Strange Fruit" famously performed by Billie Holiday in 1939, Konigsberg argued that American soldiers were versed in violent racism and it was this they brought to Korea, not democracy.[10]

Konigsberg would pay a heavy price for his outspoken criticisms. In 1953, he passed the California Bar exam but was prevented from entrance to the bar because someone brought his writings in *The California Eagle* to the attention of the California Bar Association. The association argued that his articles demonstrated his failure to "meet the burden of proving his character" related to "nonadvocacy of violent overthrow." He appealed and his case was eventually heard before the Supreme Court. In 1958 the Court ruled against the bar association; however, he was not admitted until 1978 after several appeals and reviews. In 1955, he was called before a House Committee holding hearings on "Communist activities" in Los Angeles. He was questioned about his involvement as a teacher for a youth organization and again his writings were entered into evidence against him.[11]

The California Eagle would continue to feature articles denouncing the war and the containment policy, but Bass herself became in demand as an activist leader as well as a politician. She was invited to several overseas peace conferences and then in 1950 was asked to run for Congress to represent California. The newspaper became a way for her to report on the global peace movement as well as to rally around her Congressional campaign.

PEACE CONFERENCES

In 1949, Bass planned to travel to Beijing, China to represent American women at the Conference of the Women of Asia hosted by the Women's International Democratic Federation. As the US State Department frantically sought who to blame for the "loss" of China to the Communists led by Mao Zedong that same year, the international community did not know how to deal with the newly created People's Republic of China. The US's refusal to recognize the country led to China's marginalization in the international arena, this would be an issue discussed at the conference. Elizabeth

Armstrong has noted that this conference was the first significant event in "internationalist women's anti-imperialist solidarity." Predating the Bandung conference that inaugurated the non-aligned movement by eight years, WIDF leaders wanted to organize a meeting to "open a new chapter in Asian and African internationalist leadership."[12]

The WIDF was the primary organizing body for the conference, and the Congress of American Women was a cosponsor. The Alpha Kappa Lambda sorority, of which Bass was an honorary member, bought her luggage to take while her friends and colleagues raised travel funds. Her plane ticket was booked, and she was prepared to leave when her travel visa was denied. She had to travel through Hong Kong, a British colony, and sought permission at the British consulate. The British told her to go to the Philippine Consulate for permission where she was told because there was war in China, she would not be allowed to travel. However, the Filipino government operated with the blessing of the US government, and it prevented "dissidents to American-backed rule" from traveling in and out of the Philippines. Filipino officials likely prevented Bass's travel at the US's behest. Others faced similar barriers to attending. Thai and Japanese representatives were barred from traveling, and some foreign nationals were only able to attend because they were already in China.[13]

In August of the following year, Bass used the money raised for her China trip to travel to the World Committee of the Defenders of Peace meeting in Prague, Czechoslovakia. She was invited by Joliet Curie, the organizer and a leading scientist involved with the Defenders of the Peace, an affiliate of the Soviet-led World Peace Council. Bass wrote a series of observations that appeared in her weekly column, and she wrote an additional series titled "Europe as I saw it" about the conference. She wrote that fellow peace activists feared the threat of an atomic bomb, but also the containment of protests in the US. She linked the war fears to the greater fear that capitalist greed fueled US military might and kept workers enslaved, unable to speak out in support of the "Holy Grail" of world peace. Though Bass was leaning politically left, she retained faith in electoral politics arguing for progressives to take back Congress in the 1950 midterm elections and to check the power of the President, reign in capitalist greed, and stop the attacks on progressive change.[14]

Bass' first column on the conference likened it to a religious gathering. She wrote that she was reminded of the last supper of Jesus upon seeing the delegates seated at the table, all of whom traveled to Prague to "quell the war hysteria" plaguing the globe. Though there were some disagreements, they came together "in the great effort to discover a panacea for a war-torn world, and to establish a peace that will endure." The primary goal of the meeting was to "reach a working basis for securing signatures for the Stockholm Peace Appeal." She listed for her readers the number of signatures already obtained and wrote "Notice how those countries said to be 'Communist controlled' are overwhelmingly for peace." She reasoned that a nuclear weapons ban was in the interest of all working people because they were the ones who suffered most during wartime, they were the ones whose bodies were on the line, and they worked for the profit of war industries and not their own families.[15]

A Korean delegation led by Lieutenant Colonel Kan Puk made a statement that North Korea was celebrating its fifth anniversary as a liberated country after the Soviet Red Army expelled Japanese imperialists. Puk described South Korea as a US "colony and military base" under the regime of the "US-puppet" Rhee Syngman and accused the US military of being invaders and attacking civilians in towns and villages and trying to "submerge [the] country in blood." He claimed that the US military had "lost their human feelings" and were "murdering defenceless women and children." The North Korean delegation was met with applause and the conference passed a "Resolution of Solidarity with Korea."[16]

Also in Prague was the National Student Peace Conference attended by youth associated with radical peace organizations in their home countries. Bass reported on the Korean student's statement to the conference. He told his fellow students that: "During the five years from 1945 until the first six months of this year, American imperialists and their puppets in the S. M. Rhee government massacred in a barbaric way more than 200,000 of our patriots." Rather than support Korean independence, the US government chose to uphold the brutal Rhee regime. Meanwhile, he continued "The democratic national front of Korea emphasized in its appeal that our people do not want civil war. Our people do not want bloodshed in the interest of American imperialists and their reactionary lackeys." Instead, the Korean people wanted independence on their terms and not the US's. The speech suggested that without US anti-communism which necessitated Rhee Syngman's reactionary South Korean government, the war might not have happened.[17]

After the Prague conferences closed, Bass used her press credentials to travel to the Soviet Union where she hoped to "penetrate the Iron Curtain." She took a flight into Moscow and was greeted with a bouquet of flowers by women who had attended the Prague conference. Bass was taken on a tour of the city, and she noted massive housing construction. She had spent time organizing against restrictive covenants in Los Angeles and the United States experienced housing shortages after the war that impacted Black

Americans. She noted that the Soviets did not use restrictive covenants nor was there discrimination in obtaining housing; meanwhile, the US was in near crisis mode over the lack of housing and conflicts over who would have access to it. Bass told her newspaper audience that the US was a dream unfulfilled, she was increasingly interested in the Soviet system, something that US authorities made note of as they followed her movements.[18]

Bass, like many of her comrades, had idealized visions of the Soviet Union. She focused her observations on what she described as the lack of a "color bar" in the Soviet Union. There were some Black Americans who had settled there, and she wrote about their experiences without Jim Crow or restrictions on interracial marriage. She also noted that women were active participants in the country's growth, and she claimed they did not face discrimination. But as important to her was that while she visited, she never heard any "war talk." The country was busy rebuilding and engaging with economic development and was not concerned with the atomic bomb, containment, or anti-communist purges. While her observations were no doubt idealistic and her tour curated, it was not unusual for Black Americans to note the lack of racial restrictions there.[19]

For Bass, the contrast to the Cold War United States was stark as the US increasingly tied its well-being to militarism and overseas intervention. On her way home from the Soviet Union, she stopped in Paris, where the people were still rebuilding from the war. Poverty was widespread, housing was scarce and in poor condition, and food was in short supply. She wrote that in conversation with some French people about the Marshall Plan, some had denounced it as making things worse. The plan had driven wages down while driving prices up; meanwhile, the government was diverting funds toward the military as the country desperately tried to hold on to its colonies in Indochina.[20]

The Prague group planned another meeting to be held in Sheffield, England in November. The Korean War escalated global tensions which made travel difficult, but activists felt the war made their meetings even more important. One goal was to demonstrate the ability of people from around the world to work together, especially people from the Soviet bloc; and to point to the US's refusal to talk to the Soviets. Bass was listed as a sponsor of the conference, but she did not travel to England. Those who did try to enter the country faced resistance. British Prime Minister Clement Attlee called the planned conference "bogus" and an attempt to sabotage "national defense." Foreign attendees were kept out of the country, including Joliet Curie, and the group went from two thousand delegates to only five hundred.[21]

Bass's observations of the Soviet Union and the peace conferences reflected how closely she aligned with Communist Party policy. She opposed the Marshall Plan as US neo-colonialism, she praised the Soviet system and in particular its lack of formalized segregation, and she rejected the containment policy. She argued that US anti-communism abroad had prevented substantive progress for the newly decolonized and it prevented open relationships with the Soviet Union and the Soviet sphere states. As these countries sought peace, she argued that the US was compelled to wage war. She concluded that war was endemic to capitalism; profits required quelling dissent and securing resources and labor, this meant taking up arms against those that posed no threat.

1950 CONGRESSIONAL CAMPAIGN

When Bass arrived in Paris, she was greeted with a cablegram from the California State Executive Committee of the Independent Progressive Party asking her to run for Congress for the Fourteenth Congressional District in California. She wired back that she would accept the invitation, and she began preparations to take up the campaign which began only days after she returned. In the 1950 midterm elections, the PP sought to increase Black representation in Congress. Bass also saw it as an opportunity to highlight her criticisms of the two political parties' commitment to anti-communism and perpetual war. By the 1940 election and maybe even earlier in 1936, Bass began to dismiss the Republican party as the electoral voice for Black Americans. But she remained deeply skeptical that the Democratic party deserved Black America's vote. This was in part because both parties sounded the call to arms and attacked outspoken peace and social justice activists. But she failed to see any substantial difference in the party's policies.[22]

In the California PP's announcement of her candidacy, the group wrote that the Democratic and Republican Parties failed to provide "adequate representation" to Black Americans. As the only party to create a program for Black American equality it was active in "fighting Jim Crow" and the disenfranchisement of Black voters. The PP accused the political parties of being nearly indistinguishable in their anti-communist foreign policy and *The California Eagle* reported that people in the Fourteenth District were excited to have someone who would be the voice of Black and white soldiers in Korea who were needlessly dying in a colonial war.[23]

The party National Committee issued a statement on the Korean War noting that the "outbreak of hostilities ... marked a new more ominous stage in the transformation of our free nation into a militarized, garrison state, gearing for total war." The statement read that unless the war was ended it would "claim the lives of millions" and compromise the freedom and liberty of the Korean people. Military leaders were claiming that the war was a "preventative" war against China and the Soviet Union, but it was a "suppression of the liberation movements" that were spreading across Asia and Africa. It warned that "Unless halted by the people of America, the terrible adventure on which big business and big brass have embarked our nation will claim all mankind as its victim. But the cruelest blow will be struck at our own people." The statement was made in September, only a month before the Chinese became involved and US casualties increased substantially.[24]

The PP statement claimed that war and US intervention in other theaters of conflict was a new bipartisan policy of "arming fascist reaction throughout the world." This included not only the US intervention in the Korean War but the Truman Doctrine, US support of the fascist Franco government in Spain, and its funding of the French war in Indochina. In exchange, the US was asked to commit to a permanent standing army, a large portion of its budget to be given to reactionary governments, and the wholesale abandonment of equality and a higher standard of living for Americans. The PP accused Truman of demanding of Americans "harder work, longer hours, and heavier taxes," that benefited corporations. There would be no "fair deal" for Americans, instead it would be a "program of disaster." The PP argued that a vote for its candidates in the midterm elections would be a vote for "peace, security, and freedom."[25]

Across the country in New York, Socialist Representative Vito Marcantonio convinced W. E. B. Du Bois to run for Senator on the Labor Party ticket. The goal was to raise awareness of the issues peace activists were concerned with, and to make a visible effort to increase Black representation in Congress. Du Bois, eighty-two-years old at the time, found the idea of running for Senate ludicrous, but did agree because the campaign would "afford him a chance to speak for peace." A reluctant Du Bois took up the campaign and he included in his platform criticism of the existing political parties, and he argued for a third party to counter anti-communism.[26]

Eslanda Robeson ran as a Progressive Party candidate for congressman-at-large representing Hartford, Connecticut. In her acceptance speech she and her guest speaker Communist journalist Albert Kahn focused on anti-communist harassment. Her speech was titled "Peace and the Right to Work for Peace," and in it she attacked the anti-communist purges. In another speech, she told the audience, facetiously, that she looked for her loyalty but could not find it. She wondered if she had left it in England where she and her husband had lived, but instead she told the audience that her loyalty had only expanded there. While traveling in Africa she had extended her loyalty to include "my African people" and the "progressive Europeans in Africa." She did not leave it in Russia because she came home "more consciously loyal to the United States" than before, loyal to the promises within the Declaration of Independence and the Constitution. She claimed that in the Soviet Union she had seen the promises of these documents in action and thus became even more committed to them.[27]

It was a miracle, she noted, that Black Americans had any loyalty left after being abused and mistreated. In the recent past, hers had taken a "terrific beating" after the press misquoted her husband Paul at the 1949 Paris peace conference, described him as an enemy of the people, and stoked a controversy that led to further harassment. Her son Paul Robeson Jr. had been booed at his own wedding after he married a white woman. She noted that when people came out to greet her son and his wife in that manner "a great many things" had become clear for her, that those people had wished "evil" for the newlyweds, because the press had worked them up. Robeson raised a question that she and her compatriots would regularly confront during the harassment: were they being harassed for being radicals, or for being Black?[28]

The Connecticut PP had a total of six candidates in various elections in 1950 including Clyde Trudeau for Lieutenant Governor and Dorothy Haven for Secretary of State. Robeson's marriage to Paul brought a sense of celebrity that the PP tried to use to its advantage. Her marriage was invoked in articles and her image was used in campaign material. In one publication on its platform, the PP included an image of Eslanda and the instructions to "vote for peace" by pulling "the fourth lever" for the Progressive candidates. Its platform included the "cessation of hostilities in Korea" and opening "top level negotiations" with the USSR; recognition of China and the removal of the US fleet from waters near that country; the end of the "policy of preventive war"; the repeal of both the Taft-Hartley and McCarran Acts; rent controls, and among other major economic reforms, "Tax the greedy not the needy." Bass's campaign platform, and that of the PP more generally, included civil rights and "stressed world peace, world-wide neighborliness, jobs for all, civil liberties, and security." The Connecticut PP advertised that their civil rights plank included a permanent FEPC, anti-poll tax and anti-lynching laws, and laws to ensure Black Americans "equal access, without segregation, to all educational institutions and housing." The party effectively wanted to "Outlaw Racism."[29]

These policies were largely ignored by both the Democratic and Republican Parties. In an editorial, Bass described the parties as twins that manipulated token Black people to stand for them, when neither were concerned with civil rights. She accused each party of choosing a "representative negro" that would demonstrate how they believed Black people should behave "think and believe, especially politically." One such representative, William Dawson, an Illinois congressman, was brought to California to attack her campaign. Though he did not name her, he instead attacked the Progressive Party. But Bass pointed out that this same Mr. Dawson had supported repressive anti-communist legislation like the McCarran Act, which she argued endangered Black Americans, and he failed to support the FEPC. Meanwhile, Robeson attended a debate between the Republican and Democratic congressional candidates for Connecticut to press the candidates to "say what their parties would do for civil rights." Prescott Bush, the GOP candidate answered that he followed his party's 1948 platform; Democrat William Benton declared that he had voted for an FEPC but that his southern colleagues defeated it.[30]

In a radio address, Bass told the audience about her one-time allegiance to the Republican party and that she struggled with members of both the political parties for the rights guaranteed to all citizens and her struggle to get the parties to recognize "civil rights for all." But after thirty years of "broken promises," she abandoned hope that either party would be the voice for fairness and equality. The Progressive Party had put forward an actual program for civil rights and became for Bass, the vehicle by which Black Americans might find an advocate.[31]

Du Bois was officially running as an American Labor candidate, a New York party representing socialists and labor, but his campaign was linked to the Progressive Party, and he argued that a serious third party was needed in the United States. At the Progressive Party convention in October, he argued that "Democracy has not achieved success in any modern state." He told the audience that the US had tried democracy with the two political parties vying for influence with separate and occasionally contradictory programs; but the fact was that there was only one policy and one party. The Democrats and Republicans, he argued, agreed on foreign and domestic policy in almost every respect including "fighting trade unions," and "raising rents and avoiding social responsibilities." A third party was the only thing that could rescue democracy from "oligarchy or plutocracy," and it would allow people to vote for their genuine beliefs. This was why, he argued, there was always such opposition to third parties, because they challenged politicians to represent the views of the majority and not of the ruling classes. For Du Bois, the third party was a necessary elixir to the ailments afflicting US democracy, and fears of that change fueled increased anti-communist reaction.[32]

At a campaign rally Bass continued her criticisms of both Parties urging her audience to see that the differences between their campaign platforms were hardly differences at all. It was a matter of degrees as both were committed to containment and militarism. In her speech she called for unity to build a democratic nation capable of fulfilling its promises. Instead of imposing its will on nations across the world, Bass argued that the US should "solve its own problems" first. She criticized the race for nuclear weapons and concluded her speech arguing that across the world the most important sentiment was peace. The Democratic and Republican candidates believed that elections were about the parties competing over who was more anti-communist, while they ignored dire social issues at home. Peace was what the world desired, but bewilderingly, the United States was pursuing conflict. Bass, Du Bois, and Robeson used their platforms to challenge the parties to commit to ending conflict and dedicate their energies to domestic issues like civil rights.[33]

Bass did not win her election, instead the Democratic candidate, Samuel Yorty, defeated her. Du Bois also did not win, though he received over two hundred thousand votes. Robeson only tallied 2,300 votes; but as Barbara Ransby has argued, the campaign gave her an opportunity to "inject progressive ideas and policies into the conversation" and hopefully influence voters. Bass's colleague, Raphael Konigsberg also ran for office as a Progressive Party candidate for another California congressional seat, which he lost. One of the biggest defeats for progressive voices that year was the defeat of Helen Gahagan Douglas for California Senator. Douglas had been the Fourteenth Congressional District's representative and Bass tried to take on her role when she stepped up to run for Senate. Douglas was defeated by Richard Nixon who famously red-baited her claiming she was "pink right down to her underwear."[34]

The defeat did not dissuade either Bass, Robeson, or Du Bois in continuing to speak out for peace. Bass continued to use her newspaper to criticize the Korean War and the rise of US fascism. In a 1951 editorial she argued that "already we recognize fascism" in the United States as, "American fascists want and need thought control in order to enable them to fasten a police state upon the country." She criticized US spending in the Korean War and its friendly relations with reactionary governments and she warned about liberals who allied themselves with conservative anti-communists. She claimed they "joined forces with the enemy of their own people and the enemy of democracy." It was Black Americans that suffered the most from fighting this US fascism, and they continued to resist and produce brave leaders like W. E. B. Du Bois. She remained optimistic closing the editorial writing, "I am very confident that within my lifetime yet I will see first-class citizenship achieved for all my people, true democracy for all Americans, and peace in all the world!" Bass remained busy throughout this period organizing with the Sojourners, circulating the Ban the Bomb petition, and raising awareness around the *We Charge Genocide* petition and the cases within it. In 1952, Bass would be presented with another opportunity to run for office and once again center the peace movement in her campaign.[35]

CHARLOTTA BASS FOR VICE PRESIDENT

In April 1951, Bass celebrated forty years of working with *The California Eagle*. Friends and organizations sent in congratulations and celebratory remarks that were published in a special anniversary edition. In the same edition, Bass wrote a lengthy editorial about the attacks on her and the newspaper for their growing criticism of US policy. She wrote that those attacking her were "my own people whom I have personally helped over the years." They had "joined forces with the enemy of their people and the enemy of democracy." She was correct on this point as the *Los Angeles Tribune*, a competing Black newspaper founded in 1941, were vociferous anti-communists and critics of both Bass and *The California Eagle*, and employed one of Bass's former journalists, Almena Davis, who regularly criticized her. Bass lamented that her critics had abandoned the fight for democracy and forgotten that it was only in a democracy that their rights could be secured. She asked these "Uncle Toms" as she called them, how they felt being on the side of those who "court-martialed the Negro soldiers, of those who would destroy the colored people's liberation movements all over the world, of those who persecute us daily and keep us and our children from living our lives in dignity and security."[36]

These "American fascists" were not only attacking her, but also her friends and colleagues, she specifically named Du Bois, Paul Robeson, and Claudia Jones. She wrote that even under these attacks, she was heartened by their heroism, as well as the working people of the country and the world. She argued that it was Black people "providing leadership" in the peace movement and liberation struggles and she likened Du Bois, Robeson, and Jones to heroes like Sojourner Truth, Harriet Tubman, and Frederick Douglass. She announced that she was taking a rest and would return to the fight. That same year, Bass sold her newspaper and moved to Harlem. There she worked in closer proximity to other radicals like Beulah Richardson and Louise Thompson Patterson and she became the chairman of the STJ.[37]

John Hudson Jones, writer for the CPUSA's *Daily Worker*, interviewed Bass upon her arrival in New York. She told him "I'm resting a little while after 40 years in the struggle... Let me say this from the start, I'm not fading away, nor am I giving up the battle for Negro rights. In fact I have just begun to fight." She described how the FBI had tried to intimidate her and that she believed the anti-communist attacks were aimed at Black Americans. She told Jones that "our enemies are trying to make Negroes believe that those who fight for peace and freedom are their enemies." Bass was critical of liberal and moderate Black activists like Walter White of the NAACP; their silence in the face of anti-communist harassment was concerning, as was their compliance with red-baiting. She insisted that General MacArthur and his warmongering were a greater threat to the US government and its citizens than the imprisoned or harassed Communist leaders. Bass closed by assuring Jones she would be back at it soon. And she was. Within months of her arrival, the STJ was founded, and she began another political campaign.[38]

In 1952, she agreed to run as vice president on the Progressive Party ticket with Vincent Hallinan. Bass' 1950 campaign was an effort to bring progressive values to Congress, but her work on the 1952 ticket was the most ambitious and optimistic effort. Vincent Hallinan, a lawyer, and the husband of radical activist Vivian Hallinan was chosen as the Progressive Party's Presidential candidate. Hallinan was widely respected in leftist circles for his defense of Harry Bridges, the Australian longshoreman, and radical union activist. For twenty years, the Immigration and Naturalization Services and the Department of Labor tried to deport Bridges. In his efforts to prevent the deportation, Hallinan would be accused of contempt of court, found guilty, and sentenced to prison. He was serving that time when Bass agreed to be his running mate. This left the early part of the campaign to Bass and Vivian Hallinan.[39]

Bass accepted the nomination to the ticket in July 1952 at the Progressive Party convention. Her speech acknowledged that as the only Black woman ever put on a national party ticket, she was a pioneer: "It is a great honor to be chosen as a pioneer—and a great responsibility. But I am strengthened by thousands on thousands of pioneers who stand by my side and look over my shoulder." She highlighted pioneers who " have led the fight for freedom—those who led the fight for women's rights—those who have been in the front line fighting for peace and justice and equality everywhere." She noted that she was on that stage because Black Americans faced regular harassment and discrimination, while the United States sent their sons to fight and die in another war. She argued that Black Americans sacrificed for their country in the two world wars, only to come home to lynching and harassment.

She invoked her nephew's sacrifice to fight fascism, and the case of Robert Brooks, a veteran who was lynched upon his return. Though the US fought to defeat Hitlerism, Bass argued that the seeds of Hitlerism took root in the US and emerged in the form of racist Cold War policy.[40]

Bass included in her acceptance speech a long list of crimes perpetrated by the United States government in the name of democracy: "Yes, it is my government that supports the segregation by violence practiced in ... South Africa, sends guns to maintain a bloody French rule in Indo-China, gives money to help the Dutch repress Indonesia, props up [Winston] Churchill's rule in the Middle East and over the colored peoples of Africa and Malaya." Bass rejected the US's moral authority in claiming to spread democracy by containing the spread of communism and instead accused the nation of terrorism at home and abroad. She argued that US colonial ambitions were coupled with the silencing of Black America using "the rope, the gun, the lynch mob, or the lynch judge" and that the US police state and lynch law were effective methods of containment used against people of color.[41]

She urged Black Americans to work with the labor movement because it was the only movement that could "break down racial differences" and open doors. She linked her activism to end segregation and to create opportunities for Black workers to her interest in and work with labor activists. Her optimism could be seen in cross-racial alliances along class-based lines, like many of her colleagues in the radical peace movement. She argued that true equality would require the radicalization of working Americans against the war state; it was poor Americans whose sons and daughters were dying in war and industries, but it was also poor white Americans who sustained lynch law via indifference to or participation in violence against the Black community, and efforts to secure economic advantages for themselves. Bass warned that these divisions empowered capitalists to continue a forward march across the bodies and territory of people of color globally.[42]

She emphasized that the future for change was in the Progressive Party. She wrote that "In 1948, in the Progressive party, I found that one political world that could provide a home big enough for Negro and white, for native and foreign-born, to live and work together for the same ends—as equals." Importantly, she praised the PP's inclusion of her and other Black Americans in helping to craft the party's principles: "Here no one handed me a ready-made program out of the back door. Here I could sit at the head of the table as a founding member, write my own program, a program for myself and my people, that came from us." She had hope in the 1948 program that created its principles "stone by stone" to usher in an equitable future—but when Wallace was defeated, she realized that her rest was not to come. She told the audience that she could not retire "when I saw that slavery had been abolished but not destroyed; that democracy had been 'saved' in World War I, but not for my people; that fascism had been wiped out in World War II only to take root in my own country." She claimed that she could not rest while Rosa Lee Ingram and her two sons faced execution, or after Harriette Moore and her husband were killed in a house bombing. She made the connection between US racism and imperialism telling the audience: "We fight that all people shall live. We fight to send our money to end colonialism for the colored peoples of the world, not to perpetuate it."[43]

Bass concluded her speech by noting that Black America faced poverty while the US sent billions to re-arm Europe against Asian and African people. That money she argued, could lift millions of Black Americans out of poverty, and out of sickness. "We fight," she told her audience, to end colonialism, and to fight evil. She said that "I am stirred by the responsibility you have placed upon me. I am proud that I am the choice of leaders of my own people, and leader of all those who understand how deeply the fight for peace is one and indivisible with the fight for Negro equality." War spending would be a point that Bass would invoke throughout the campaign trail, noting that war perpetuated inequality against those who fought, and those left behind, and now the war state was US policy and exported inequality and injustice abroad.[44]

Bass centered her peace commitment on the Black freedom struggle and the struggle for women's equality. Bass was STJ president during the campaign, and its interests and demands were integrated into the PP's program. While both pushed for a permanent FEPC, Black political representation, and a focus on social welfare, the STJ did specify that Black women workers needed particular attention and it focused on the need to unionize domestic workers, an occupation with a large representation of Black women. STJ members rallied behind Bass's candidacy and sought a "nonpartisan" unity of Black women behind her "historic" campaign.[45]

The PP was far more progressive on civil rights than the Democratic candidate Adlai Stevenson or the Republican candidate Dwight Eisenhower and issued several statements that linked its campaign to the Black freedom struggle. Bass issued statements that reasoned it was impossible to achieve freedom without dismantling the war machine, cutting off profit centers for capitalists, and securing the bodies of poor and Black Americans from dying in wasteful imperialist wars against other colonized people. In an April 1952 statement, Bass repeated a report from a national NAACP meeting in which its leaders argued that neither of the Democratic or Republican candidates "demonstrated any genuine concern for civil rights." Neither party had committed to

Black candidates for higher office while the PP had not only advanced Bass onto the ticket but regularly ran Black candidates in its local elections. In a pamphlet on the issue, the PP weighed Stevenson and Eisenhower's commitments. Eisenhower opposed the FEPC as did his vice presidential candidate Richard Nixon. Nixon was also credited as a major engineer of the anti-communist state as a supporter and sponsor of bills like the McCarran Act. Adlai Stevenson was "lukewarm" on the FEPC and his running mate, Senator John Sparkman from Alabama was opposed and shared a similar voting record as Nixon on anti-communist legislation. Both tickets "are okayed by the Dixiecrats"; in other words, there was no mainstream support for civil rights legislation and even the liberal NAACP recognized that.[46]

When Eisenhower was formally nominated by his party in July, Bass sent him a telegram urging him to make a statement on civil rights. She wrote that the PP condemned all "bigots who inject class, racial, and religious prejudice into public and political matters." She urged Eisenhower to follow suit and proclaim that "Bigotry is un-American and a danger to the republic." Bass also suggested that he condemn the "Number One bigot," Joseph McCarthy. That same month the PP released a formal statement advocating Black representation at all levels of public office and claimed that this was the "precondition . . . to make our democratic deeds match our democratic words." To increase representation the party proposed a voter registration campaign for all eligible Black voters throughout the country; a platform in all political parties to work with unions, clergy, and other social organizations to identify and choose appropriate candidates; and a call for "Negro representation in every aspect of American life," including courts, municipalities, and higher office.[47]

Peace grounded in a commitment to advancing social justice issues was the campaign's central principal. A PP pamphlet titled "Peace will be on the Ballot in '52" issued an eight-point platform against war and militarism. It started with the demand to immediately end the Korean War, it continued with demands for an end to the arms race, conversion of the US economy to a peace economy, and an end to wartime wage freezes, and the increased tax burden. The final three points linked the peace platform to its social justice demands and included opening world trade to create more jobs, full citizenship, and equality for Black Americans, and the restoration of the Bill of Rights for all oppressed.[48]

At a campaign event in New Jersey, Bass gave a speech advocating reallocating war funds to end poverty, secure global peace, and end discrimination against Black people. She and the PP were concerned that the increased defense spending, US incursion into foreign territory, and the imagined link between social welfare programs and Communist conspiracies meant the gradual dissolution of the New Deal state. This was part of a disturbing trend that associated social justice movements with communism and undermined calls for desperately needed social change. As progressives demanded an end to Cold War policies, liberals and conservatives argued that this weakened the US militarily and created opportunities for the Soviet Union to invade. Cold Warriors concluded that the voices calling for an end to poverty, equal opportunity for men and women, and drastic cuts in military spending were in league with the Soviets to make the US vulnerable to a Communist takeover. This assumed association between communism and the Black freedom struggle empowered intelligence agencies to continue their focus on and harassment of Black activists. The war state justified and to the American public, even necessitated, extralegal harassment.[49]

In April 1952, Bass joined W. E. B. Du Bois and Paul Robeson in a Delegates National Assembly for Peace meeting in Washington, DC. The group traveled to the capital to speak with Senators and Congressmen about the war and to issue their demands. The group's demands included an immediate end to the war, an extension of the Bill of Rights, rejection of an increased war budget and arms race, and a reallocation of funds for housing, education, hospitals, and other social infrastructure. It included a demand to halt the rearming of Germany and the US's new policy in Japan that propped up its conservative government to serve as its allies in the Pacific against communism. It also demanded the recognition of independence and self-determination of all formerly colonized and currently colonized peoples. The call to Washington cited a Gallup poll that concluded that 70 percent of Americans wanted the US to negotiate with the Soviet Union and to end hostilities in Korea. It also noted that the US intervention on behalf of the British and French in securing their empires guaranteed "new Koreas." The group rejected a proposed Universal Military Training bill which would expand and strengthen the draft and concluded that increased militarism led to policy makers ignoring attacks on Black Americans and others.[50]

As part of Bass's VP campaign, the PP circulated postcards to be sent to the White House calling for an immediate end to the war. The text read:

Dear Mr. President,

Why must more blood be shed while the negotiators in Korea settle the last remaining differences between them?

Can't we stop the shooting and killing now, continue and finish the negotiations, and end the war in Korea without any more deaths?

Millions are asking to end the war, add my name.

The PP billed their ticket as the Peace ticket and urged people to "Vote for the Peace Candidates." On the second anniversary of US intervention in the war Vivian Hallinan and Bass issued a statement condemning recent bombings in North Korea and claiming that the two political parties were now just war parties. The statement asked people to send letters of protest to Truman and to join the PP in its campaign for peace.[51]

The PP also responded to the Koje Island incident and the POW repatriation issue. C. B. Baldwin, PP Secretary, urged state chapters to launch campaigns to demand an immediate ceasefire and urged the Truman administration to answer why it was insisting on voluntary repatriation in violation of international agreements. Baldwin cited the Red Cross report that stated US officials were re-interrogating those who chose to repatriate to China or North Korea in a campaign of intimidation. Baldwin claimed that the report had been kept from the US public to perpetuate the lie that the US was seeking an end to the war. He believed the reason that it was "being deliberately prolonged," was to secure an increased arms budget and warned that even if the war were ended immediately, there were other Koreas in the works as both political parties were maneuvering to intervene in other colonial wars. The party argued that a vote for the PP was a vote to end the Korean War and the chance of future wars of intervention.[52]

The Communist Party, embattled by several trials against its leadership, took an interest in Bass's campaign. A *Daily Worker* article described Bass's candidacy as militant because she was forthright in her objections to Jim Crow and every "militaristic utterance" by her opponents. She was, the article explained, a source of "deep pride" to progressive Black Americans and women. In a profile on Bass, the party highlighted her past involvement with the Republican party and her eventual rejection of its policies. She was drawn to the PP, she told the Communist journalist Charlotte William, because she thought it was truer to the spirit of the Constitution and did not work to "soothe factions" rather than address voters' concerns. Her campaign goals were to advance democracy with real programmatic demands like a permanent FEPC, antilynching legislation, an expansion of Social Security payments to the elderly, outlawing the KKK, and peace.[53]

Beulah Richardson celebrated Bass's nomination in *Freedom*. She wrote that the "promise of unity and peace is again in our land" as reflected in Bass's candidacy. Richardson described Bass's politicization as a young woman, when she had become aware that it was the "un-Godly and tyrannical alliance between the rich men of the North and the former slaveholders of the South that severed the unity" between Black and white workers. She claimed that this unity had been present after the Civil War in state legislatures, but the "greedy depravity of a few immoral and murderous men" betrayed that alliance. This realization, Richardson claimed, was what led Bass to take up work as an editor and what compelled her to be an activist. Richardson recounted Bass's work in Los Angeles including helping to secure Black employees at LA city hospitals, protecting Black homeowners in majority-white neighborhoods, and defying the KKK. She wrote about Bass's participation in the sojourn to DC and her demands to the Defense Department to "Bring our sons Home!" She also described Bass's work on the Scottsboro Boys case and her trip to Florida to pressure Florida's governor to investigate the murder of the Moores. Richardson wrote that "here indeed is a woman among women!" She celebrated that a "Negro and a woman" was on the ballot for a major party and she urged readers to celebrate and support her campaign.[54]

Eslanda Robeson gave a radio address in Providence, Rhode Island in support of the Hallinan and Bass ticket. In the address, she argued that the unemployment among textile workers in Rhode Island and their neighbors in Connecticut was because the US had shifted its focus and priorities to the Korean War. She took up the PP message that Adlai Stevenson and Dwight Eisenhower had no plan to end the war, were not committed to improving American lives, and were compromising the working people in the US. Both candidates had been quoted as saying they could see no clear end to the war, but Hallinan and Bass committed to its immediate end. The two parties were "teaming up together" to ensure there were enough guns, but no butter on American tables. Robeson argued that the PP's concern was that if the war did not end immediately it would spread and cause a third world war.[55]

She was particularly proud of her "very good friend," Bass who she described as "one of the most distinguished Negro women" in the US. Bass had suffered, just like the Robeson's, from the "unholy idea of white supremacy." Robeson argued that the PP was the first time since "Abraham Lincoln emancipated the slaves" that Black Americans could find a political home. Black Americans, like herself, had been essential in the PP's founding, in creating its civil rights platform, in its organization, elections, and campaigns. Black Americans were "proud and happy" to see a Black woman running for one of the highest offices in the nation. A vote for the PP, Robeson insisted, was a vote for "peace and equal rights."[56]

As with the 1948 campaign, the 1952 PP bid was dismissed as Communist-inspired. Having a Black woman on the ballot increased attacks. Betty Feldman, writing for the party's "Woman Today" page took issue with the representation of Bass in a *New York Times* cartoon. The cartoon by Doris Matthews titled "Candidette" poked fun at women in political leadership claiming that there might be a new "Department of Interior design," and that fireside chats would be to share recipes. Feldman wrote that it was easy to dismiss such a portrayal as "uncouth and male supremacist. But such ridicule speaks worlds about the class which fosters it as part of its ideological offensive against women." As important, Feldman argued, was that the cartoon author was a woman revealing that "These ideas are not limited to men; in other words, they are accepted currency." Feldman reasoned that the cartoon and the beliefs behind it "In a country which brags to the UN that its women citizens have greater opportunities, are more liberated, than those of other lands" showed the moral bankruptcy behind US democracy. It also showed that power in the US remained in the hands of "banks, and basic industries . . . it is they who make the decisions regarding political candidacies." Feldman wrote that Bass and Vivian Hallinan were part of a "great tradition" of "fighters for peace and decency" along with Harriet Tubman, Sojourner Truth, and Elizabeth Cady Stanton. These women were part of a tradition which revealed "the lie to the tawdry jokes cracked at women's expense." The lie was that women were incapable of leadership, when in fact it was always women at the forefront.[57]

The PP, Feldman continued, had included an expansive program for women in its 1948 campaign which it included in 1952, a program that the Republican and Democratic parties ignored. It called for paid maternity leave, health care and childcare, ending child labor, and equal pay. This platform happened because of women's representation in the PP's highest ranks. Feldman believed that increasing women in political office could potentially lead to ending the increased military spending and more focus on domestic issues. But she argued against falling into the "trap" of essentialism, or as she called it "feminism." Instead, she believed that women in politics would be a challenge to "male supremacist" thinking and "ruling class understanding" of militarism, exploitation, exclusion from meaningful (and well-paid) work, and racism. In other words, Feldman believed that including the oppressed in governance would be a challenge to the status quo, not because women were the same, but because of their shared experience of oppression. She argued that throughout the campaign season, the political parties would offer women the "usual empty gestures," but it was the PP that offered a legitimate program for peace and justice.[58]

Feldman also warned that male supremacism was a capitalist tool, because "the capitalist is no less conscious of women's progressive potential than are the progressives." This is why there was an "unwearying stream of derision directed at women, the insistence that they are ridiculous if they step seriously into the political arena." She warned readers that this was particularly true of Black women and capitalists were wary of a Black woman like Bass taking up a leadership role. Feldman urged women to see the lies behind the attempts to "get the women's votes," as neither political party was committed to women's equality.[59]

At an American Labor Party luncheon, Bass articulated the same concerns and addressed the worry of some voters that it was too soon for a woman to seek high office. She reasoned that when other women claimed the country was not ready for a woman vice president, they were employing the "language of the oppressor" even though they were "echoed by the oppressed." She argued that this language was regularly deployed to put off the aspirations of those most exploited and most disenfranchised. Meanwhile, the oppressed were left to suffer violence and abuse at the hands of the oppressors that counseled it was not yet time. These words, she warned, "closed the doors to a better life" and convinced even the oppressed that those in power were not ready to eliminate racism, sexism, poverty, and violence. Instead, the powers that be counsel that to get ready for those fights, they "waste our money and labors" on "guns and battleships and atom bombs." Citizens are told there was no way to stop the "raging Missouri River" flood waters, but we are ready to "flood the world with guns." Bass instead argued that the time was ripe for women to organize against oppression and for peace because it was what women had always been doing.[60]

Much of Bass' campaign focused her critiques on the shortcomings of the two political parties on women's rights and civil rights. She believed that it was their commitment to anti-communism that prevented the Parties from offering any substantive political promise. Having had experience in both parties, Bass became convinced that neither of them could any longer be the voice for peace while subscribing to anti-communism. At a campaign meeting in Brooklyn, she told her audience that while the American people wanted peace, the "old parties" were preparing for war, and calling it peace. Though the American people wanted freedom, the old parties sought only to keep them in "social, economic, and political" slavery. While Americans sought prosperity, the old parties were advocating funneling money to war, to tanks and planes to suppress the Indochinese and other countries in Asia and Africa. The Democratic and Republican Parties were two sides of the same coin, subscribing to war and condemning Americans, particularly Black Americans, to poverty, violence, and to be soldiers in its imperialist ventures.[61]

In the weeks before election day, Bass summarized her problems with the two parties. They were not distinctive in any major respect; Eisenhower was a Texas-born military man who remained committed to segregation. Adlai

Stevenson was a vocal supporter of states' rights, which allowed Jim Crow to remain in place. Both candidates supported the Korean War and ignored the thousands of American casualties, and hundreds of thousands of Korean injured and dead. Both candidates were motivated to secure capitalist wartime profits. She argued that they claimed to take the "middle of the road" approach, but what that meant was that they took over the middle to shove everyone else off the side.[62]

Both candidates defended states' rights and deplored big government. But big government was code, according to Bass, for a government that gave aid to people, not corporations and war. Even in 1952, Bass noted the shifting tides in party demographics. Democrats were slowly losing their traditional southern segregationist support as the Republican party began to envelop segregationists in its fold. She warned that Dixiecrats remained a force in the Democratic party and both parties were plagued by anti-communists that drowned out talk of social justice and dismissed it as Communist propaganda. Both of the candidates rejected civil rights. Eisenhower's campaign in the south was "based in rebel yells and confederate flags. He feels perfectly at home." Democrat Stephenson was no better. He "praised the Confederate Constitution, which perpetuated slavery and gave constitutional sanction to the slave trade." Each campaign was reduced to "low mud" slinging accusations while trying to come off as the most anti-communist. She said that "both candidates boasted they occupied the 'middle of the road'—and who but a road hog occupies the middle of the road in order to shove the rest of us off to the sides."[63]

The American people were more concerned about the Korean War and the economy, but the candidates focused on proving their anti-communist credentials rather than policy issues. She told audiences that "The American people are sick and tired of the war in Korea. They want peace, an end to the killings." Bass saw the party's commitment to the Korean War as a barometer for their social programs. But the problem was that "those who want an end to the war in Korea—a war that is now picking up in tempo and in killings—cannot choose between Eisenhower and Stevenson." Both are imprisoned in the "cold war formula." Eisenhower, the great and famous general, "proposes the heartless, racist solution of pitting 'Asians against Asians.'" She claimed that he would not end the war but create a much larger war "to turn the colored peoples of Asia into hired mercenaries, ready to lay down their lives for the glory of the house of (J.P.) Morgan and the profit of Standard Oil." She called it a perfect "Dixiecrat" solution, to allow people of color to kill each other, while US capitalists reaped profits. Meanwhile, US troops were engaged in making Korea a "complete ruin."[64]

Stephenson hardly had any solution or sense of the war at all. Bass claimed that all he provided was "limericks and warmed over jokes" and he said he had no "miracles to offer." On the campaign trail, Stephenson claimed that the war had been over when the US troops pushed the belligerents north of the 38th parallel, Bass reminded her audiences that "that victory took place two years ago." Why then, she asked, did the "fighting and dying go on?" She reminded voters that the parties were unified in the commitment to the voluntary repatriation which held off a ceasefire and prevented the end of the war.[65]

Bass concluded that the parties were indistinguishable in their warmongering. Neither cared that manpower and "woman power" were being expended overseas, the blood of American youth and the "spirit and optimism" of the nation were being destroyed, while both parties pushed forward in their "perverted" holy war against communism. The enemy was not "poverty, disease, ignorance" nor was it high prices and higher taxes, it was the so-called enemy within and overseas. She argued that rather than debate actual issues, the parties debated which Communists, labor leaders, or immigrants to put on trial and jail. Republicans might be licking the boots of McCarthy, but she felt the Democrats were tripping all over themselves to prove they abandoned Alger Hiss first. Bass highlighted the absurdity of the anti-communist trials and their link to the containment policy abroad as a steep price to pay to ignore the real issues that Americans were concerned about—safety, security, and peace.[66] She recommended that rather than a war on communism, the US needed a "war on poverty," and neither party nor their candidates were prepared to wage that war. She appealed directly to women on this point urging American women to reject both parties, since both were prepared to take their children and send them to war.[67]

In a speech given at Madison Square Garden eight days before the election and hosted by the American Labor Party, Bass tried to soften the blow of a predicted loss. Bass told the audience that even in losing, they would win. She urged supporters to see their vote as a political statement, a statement that neither party could count on the Black vote, that neither party could count on women or laborers. What they demanded was more, more emphasis on peace, more emphasis on social policy, and an end to discrimination and poverty. More important, Bass believed that a vote for the Progressive Party was a vote for continued struggle, a vote to keep the civil rights movement at the forefront of politicians' concerns as they moved forward. She wanted both political parties aware that people were no longer willing to let the old parties dictate policies that kept the US at war, kept Americans impoverished, and ignored racist and sexist practices.[68]

The 1952 PP results were even more dismal than in 1948; Hallinan and Bass received less than one percent of the vote. At a meeting weeks after the election, the candidates noted that they were committed to continuing their work with the PP and to ending the Korean War. Vivian Hallinan wanted to organize a march on Washington to protest the war and Bass was appointed to a committee to formulate a statement to present to the UN the following month urging the end of the war. Bass made a statement arguing that the party had made important strides with Black voters and needed to continue to focus on its civil rights platform and work against racism; she encouraged organizing for the freedom of Rosa Lee Ingram and her sons.[69] She reflected in her autobiography that the victory of the campaign was that progressives realized the two political parties did not focus on the needs of the people and that real and important alternatives to the major parties were needed. She believed that the campaign raised the awareness of voters that they did not have to settle for the Democratic or Republican Parties, and despite the Progressive Party's failure, its influence lingered on.[70]

The PP National Committee issued a statement calling on Eisenhower to end the war. They feared that with his election the "big anti-Roosevelt corporations" were now in a position of power and these corporations were invested in the expansion of US militarism. The group adopted a seven-point program for its state chapters to take up. The first point was to pressure Eisenhower to immediately end the war. The remaining points instructed the PP membership to visit their congressional representatives to urge them to end the arms race, end the filibuster that had so effectively been deployed against civil rights demands, repeal anti-communist legislation, and an expansion of labor union rights and economic demands.[71]

The PP expressed concern that with the end of Democratic leadership in Washington a reactionary era would be ushered in that would mean the end of the Democratic party's labor coalition that worked with Black Americans and farmers. Given that even that coalition was often unable to usher in the reforms progressives sought, they feared that the Republican party would dismantle the remaining hope they had. In another statement, the National Committee noted that their own poor returns meant that US voters had sided with reactionaries who would usher in a period of Wall Street ascendancy and the continuation of and increase in war and militarism. The Democratic party, in its failure to end the Korean War, had "dug its own grave"; it had no program to remove troops from Korea, and "offered no positive domestic program." The Democrats instead tried to justify the war and effectively allowed for the ascendancy of a Republican coalition of reactionaries and "dominant financial and industrial groups." The job of progressives was now to prevent this coalition from "turning this country into a private preserve" of capitalists.[72]

The party's humiliating defeat proved to the National Committee that the electorate had chosen reaction against progressive reform, it had chosen war over peace, and it rejected civil rights. Radicals, however, argued that US elections were hardly democratic given that large numbers of Black Americans were prevented from voting with legal means but also with violence and intimidation at the polls. Additionally, the political atmosphere had been worsening and criticism of the Korean War and containment policy put the PP at odds with liberal activists. The peace movement and the radicals involved found themselves isolated and the targets of intelligence agencies devoted to making organization difficult. Bass never expected to win and from the beginning, she saw her campaign as a protest against the very climate that would doom the Progressive Party.

CHAPTER FIVE

The High Price of Peace

On May 9, 1952, Shirley Graham and W. E. B. Du Bois arrived at Ontario's Malton airport to attend and speak at a Canadian Peace Congress held in Toronto. The Congress was organized in part by the American Peace Crusade, an organization created after the Peace Information Center was forced to disband. Weeks before they left, W. E. B. Du Bois warned the organizers that the US State Department would likely prevent their entrance into the country. The couple had recently had their passports denied for a trip to Brazil, so he expected opposition; but Canada and the United States had always had "porous" borders with passports regularly required only in the twenty-first century. A driver's license or birth certificate would often suffice for entry between the countries. There was reason to be optimistic, but careful.[1]

Within just over an hour after their arrival, the couple was detained, deportation orders were issued, and they were put on a flight back to New York. The Du Boises had arrived at 12:30 p.m. and were back in New York by 3:30 p.m. A Quebec newspaper claimed that there were no facilities at the airport to process the New Yorkers. Given that Malton airport was an international airport, that does not seem likely. More likely is what one of the event organizers learned from friends of his close to the Canadian government; the US State Department contacted officials to prevent the Du Bois' entrance into Canada.[2]

W. E. B. Du Bois and Shirley Graham Du Bois were deported from a friendly neighboring country because they were both vocal and active voices against US Cold War policy and advocates of peaceful coexistence between the US and the Soviet Union. Their deportation is a dramatic example of the Cold War state's criminalization of radical Black activism. Criticism of Cold War foreign and domestic policy and advocacy of peace was criminalized in the middle of the twentieth century. Intelligence agencies, legislators, and patriotic, religious, and educational institutions put forward enormous energy to silence Cold War peace activists effectively outlawing peace advocacy.

Scholars have argued that the notion of the first and second red scares is misleading. Anti-communism and antiradicalism are foundations of the US's body politic and formative to defining the rights of citizenship, especially during times of national crisis. Charisse Burden-Stelly describes this as anti-communism's "durable mode of governance" that operates along with anti-Blackness to circumscribe progressives and target Black Americans, specifically radicals, with the carceral state's expansive punitive measures. What is notable about these red scares is the scale and viciousness, but they stand together with efforts on the local, state, and national levels to criminalize challenges to the status quo. This escalated during the Cold War as state officials forced consensus and punished those who criticized state policy.[3]

These civil rights violations were justified as national security imperatives. The Korean War enabled US anti-communism and the legalized harassment of radicals as necessary for domestic and foreign defense. Though it has pejoratively become known as McCarthyism, Phillip Jenkins believes it might more appropriately be called the "Korean War Red Scare" because it "fundamentally changed" the ability of activists to voice their opposition to the war or their commitments to other social justice causes. Hajimu Masuda describes it as "social warfare" and he defines it as a time, not confined to the United States, when people wanted to attack Communists, though the only understanding of a Communist was someone whose beliefs or actions were "unharmonious" to the social order.[4]

The Cold War created an interminable period for the suppression of progressive activism. Mary Dudziak shows that wartime in the US has become synonymous with restrictions on civil liberties. The problem in the US is after World War II, war was no longer "an exception," it became an "enduring condition." During the Cold War and beyond, "wartime has become normal time in America" and the "only time we have" making civil liberties even more precarious. The justification for the war, widespread anti-communism, also justified the determined legal harassment of those opposed to it.[5]

Every woman in this study had been monitored and harassed, faced punitive measures, and unbeknownst to them, they worked alongside informants. Legal authorities leaned on the questionable evidence of informers and professional witnesses and used extralegal methods to restrict travel, imprison, and sometimes deport radicals. This chapter explores the organized and sustained assault on the Black freedom and peace movements by the FBI and other agencies, and their efforts to make communism illegal and temper the gains made by the civil rights and peace movement. I argue that the Cold War created dual and paradoxical imperatives for the United

States. It required the US to prove it was a democratic nation yet required the silencing of those that challenged that view. First World War II, then the Korean War provided cover for this harassment and demonstrated that anti-communism has been a detriment to civil liberties and the free exercise of constitutional rights. It was used to silence criticism of Cold War policy, undermine the Black freedom struggle and the peace movement, and enable the rise and dominance of the national security state.

RED-BAITING AND WAR

Christine Hong reasons that the defeat of the Japanese in 1945 led to the introduction of an "anti-Communist necropolitical order" that deployed racist policy and presented it as colorblind effectively introducing "unfreedom" as freedom, "democratization as democracy," and militarism came to define all US relationships. In other words, while the US could claim it was democratic fighting its wars with an ostensibly integrated military and supporting allegedly independent regimes throughout Asia, it had in fact "expanded the concept of the military target" and made "indiscriminate death" policy. It also allied itself with undemocratic regimes to appear as if it was part of the liberatory projects in formerly colonized states. Cold War US militarism became a "modality of racial capitalism" and it "institutionalized colorblind policy." The reality was that the US became a "military imperial" devoted to total war. That total war "furnished the rationale for the targeting of domestic populations as potential enemies of the state." On a global level, the appearance of the "racial integration of humanity into the US war machine" became essential to "militarism's democratizing promise." The US masked its increased militarism behind promises of democracy and deployed that militarism against its citizens to suppress dissent.[6]

Gerald Horne argues that in the post-World War II years, opportunities for Black Americans were expanded; this was in part to improve the US image abroad. One important example is Executive Order 9981, which ostensibly integrated the military. It became an example of racial progress, began to alienate Southern Democrats from the Truman Administration, and eventually the Democratic party, and it promised Black American men integration into what was fast becoming the world's largest military. The federal government, however, failed to enforce integration at Southern bases or in combat units. Black servicemen continued to face racist treatment by officers, in the administration of supplies, and in military punishment and courts. This alleged democratization occurred simultaneously with government agencies shutting down the civil rights movement's "traditional allies" in the American Communist Party. The repression directed at the party did not lessen as the party's influence and power declined. Even moderate voices faced harassment and silence because the US government wanted to contain civil rights gains. For Horne, this meant that the movement could "only go so far."[7]

Erick McDuffie describes this as "Horne's thesis" which emphasizes white supremacy and anti-communism as essential in shaping post-WWII life. The US had to address Jim Crow segregation so that it could appeal to the "hearts and minds" of the people in decolonizing states across Africa and Asia. But the state wanted to simultaneously shut down radical demands for economic and racial equity at home. It conspired to limit civil rights gains by suppressing radical Black activists. In collusion with businesses, the government permitted some civil rights demands but this created an "ideological vacuum" in the civil rights movement which was filled with "narrow nationalism." This meant that anti-communist liberals ascended to the leadership of the movement, which would then shape "freedom movements across the African diaspora."[8] The Cold War led liberal activists to distance themselves from radical Black activists and turn their focus on integration. For Dayo Gore, anti-communism meant that Black activists had to shift focus to fighting communism rather than focusing on movement demands. They also had to toe a careful line to prevent accusations of communism leveled against them. Radical activists found themselves marginalized, harassed, and under constant surveillance. This shut down movement coalitions and prevented substantive progress.[9]

Red-baiting has been deployed against civil rights demands long before the Cold War. What Robbie Lieberman calls "defenders of the racial status quo" frequently used both anti-communism and violence to undermine the Black freedom struggle. Red scares are an "attack on civil liberties" in the name of patriotism. They are used to undermine social justice organizations and individuals within them; therefore, anti-communism is anti-democratic and regularly deployed against social justice demands. Lieberman dates this to the post-World War I period, but Nick Fischer has argued that anti-communism has been used against dissenting populations often described as "unruly," including labor advocates and people of color since the end of the Civil War.[10]

Anti-communism also has a gendered element. Anti-feminists used it against women's rights activists starting in the wake of the Bolshevik revolution. Women demanding equality were depicted as Communist agitators seeking to undo the natural order and usher in gender chaos under

Bolshevism. Anti-communism hinged on a "patriotic white masculinity" that leaned on heteronormative familial expectations. Anything that deviated from expected gender and sexuality was not just deviant but traitorous. This "heightened concern" with masculinity fueled homophobia. Not coincidentally, anti-communism emerged with renewed force in the Cold War just as disenfranchised people made modest gains but sought expanded rights. Red-baiting and framing calls for justice as communism has served (and continues to serve) powerful government and business interests to prevent social justice and justify war, imperialism, and wealth concentration.[11]

Those most in need of progressive change were the same populations that were targeted. This is the contradiction at the heart of US Cold War policy; those who advocated for the oppressed found themselves in the position of having to defend themselves. Anti-communism became a "Cold War technology" that was used to "discredit, repress, and criminalize" peace activism and the Black freedom struggle. These activists were internationalist, and linked peace, "disarmament and non-proliferation" with "antiracism, anti-colonialism, anti-imperialism, and socialism." Officials interpreted their organizing as part of a treasonous plot against the state.[12]

Burden-Stelly argues that anti-Blackness and antiradicalism were the "architecture" of racial capitalism in the modern era. She identifies the "trifecta of foreignness, Blackness, and radicalism," as "mutually constituting forms of subversion and sedition" that the state sought to punish. The "Black Scare" dominated and convinced white America that what Black Americans wanted was to dominate "superior" whites. Black skin effectively signaled "disloyalty" no matter political affiliation. This is evidenced by accusations of communism against anti-communist Black activists like Marcus Garvey. Coupled with anti-communism that convinced Americans that Bolsheviks wanted to upend the federal government and usher in dictatorship, anti-Blackness became akin to antiradicalism. Burden-Stelly shows that the US government in coalition with capitalist interests constructed the Black freedom struggle as a seditious attempt to undermine the US government.[13]

Anti-Blackness also applied to "ideas and internationalist politics" specifically "Radical Black internationalism." This along with anti-communist legislation endangered the citizenship of all Black radicals "irrespective of citizenship status." Because Black radicals challenged not just racist institutions but the legitimacy of a liberal democracy at war that marginalized and oppressed its citizens, the state, and its agents (quite literally FBI agents but also elected officials, law enforcement, and all state actors) were justified in their harassment. Peace radicalism posed such a threat that it was "systematically targeted" and Black radicals faced "exclusion, defamation, deportation, and incarceration." All radicals faced harassment, surveillance, and the removal of constitutional rights but, as Gerald Horne has argued, "Black Reds were virtually flagellated."[14]

As the women in this book argued, war and the US's increased commitment to militarization drove corporations to seek constant profit and thus constant war and conflict; this, in turn, required the "endless construction of threats" identified as nations and people of color. Liberation movements abroad were viewed as a challenge to US and thus capitalist control, and domestic radicals who allied themselves with liberation movements were equally as dangerous. The government in league with business and conservatives could claim to be defending "progress, prosperity, freedom, and security" while simultaneously denying rights to its citizens and waging war against people of color abroad. As Burden-Stelly shows, seemingly innocuous concepts like "peace and freedom" were framed as "threats to national security" and used to legitimize "racialized carcerality and expulsion."[15]

These attacks were not confined just to radicals as even liberal peace activists found themselves targeted, reifying that anti-communism criminalized even the most temperate calls for peace. Joyce Blackwell has shown that even the moderates in the Women's International League for Peace and Freedom were targeted by official bodies as disloyal and the Cold War proved "extremely trying" for these activists. The organization already had a low number of Black members, and its membership, both Black and white suffered for fear of being labeled un-American. But it was particularly acute for Black members who were interested in working toward racial justice. Several of its members were called before the HUAC and some of its local affiliates were torn asunder because of accusations of communism.[16]

Cold War anti-communism was a mechanism of US empire building and it was an "instance of empire 'at home.'" The Black freedom struggle and I would argue Cold War peace activists, were anti-militarism, anti-imperialist, and anti-colonialist which the US government interpreted as "an especially subversive form of solidarity." John Munro defines US imperialism as a "structure of power" that extends beyond its borders, dominates others, and "accumulates unevenly distributed benefits along intersecting axes of inequality." There are "imperial dimensions" of US history and individuals like Claudia Jones recognized the operations of imperialism within the anti-communist infrastructure. Importantly, this was part of a long history within the United States, one that has gone understudied in the post-WWII era when the US empire expanded, solidified its power, and militarized itself and its allies to secure global hegemony.[17] While there were piecemeal civil rights gains, including the 1948 order to integrate the military, politicians further expanded the US's already expansive surveillance and punitive state.

The Korean War enabled the passage of even more repressive anti-communist legislation. In September 1950, the Internal Security Act (McCarran Act) created the Subversive Activities Control Board (SACB), it required organizations or individuals to register as an agent of a foreign power. The SACB was empowered to investigate groups to determine whether they were subjects of a "totalitarian power"; it was this act that led to the dissolution of the Peace Information Center (PIC). The Act was also used to deny passports to radicals including the Du Boises and the Robesons. At the time passports had to be renewed every two years empowering the State Department to deny radicals travel documents and contain them within US borders where it was easier to surveil them.[18]

In 1952, Congress passed the McCarran-Walter Act, an act that has been celebrated for eliminating immigration restrictions from some Asian countries as well as naturalization requirements based on race. However, the law used the 1920 census rather than the more recent 1950 census to create national quotas (rather than race-based quotas). This might have provided opportunities for some, but others found further restrictions; Caribbean immigrants were limited to just 100 per year while the number for Northern Europe increased. It also strengthened existing deportation laws and allowed for the removal of immigrants who were Communists. Though many of these laws would later be overturned or see some provisions stripped, the immigration restrictions on radicals remained largely in place until 1990. Still today individuals who are in the process of naturalization must answer whether they are Communist.[19]

Anti-communists used propaganda to convince the public to invest in this antiradical suppression, though it was a clear violation of civil liberties and constitutionally protected rights. The Korean War and the US's containment policy further convinced the public that suppression was necessary; but it was based on contradictions. Anti-communists expressed "horror and outrage" at conditions in the USSR to increase fears around communism, though it was not unlike parts of the US. For Fischer there was a clear cognitive dissonance as anti-communists deplored poverty in the Soviet Union while ignoring it at home; excoriated the Soviets for suppressing information and free speech while actively litigating against and harassing American radicals; attacked the USSR's silencing of labor unions while doing the exact same thing. He argues that anti-communists deployed "semantic contrivances" to ignore their own actions and to justify them to the public. The federal government masked its harassment of its own citizens as a democratic process; one it was claiming was its most important export during the Cold War. HUAC made this clear when in 1949 it claimed that a Communist could not be a good US citizen.[20]

What follows is a brief exploration of the legalized harassment the women in this book faced. What they endured varied depending on their own organizational affiliation and leadership, their career visibility, and their spouse's harassment. What they have in common is that FBI surveillance and legalized harassment began and intensified during wartime. The FBI saw its power expanded during the Great Depression and further during World War II. Its previous surveillance, especially of radicals, had been curtailed in 1929. But by 1940, Franklin Roosevelt feared internal forces could disrupt US war preparations, he was specifically concerned about "Nazi and Soviet . . . threats to national security." He approved extralegal wiretapping "of persons suspected of subversive activities against the government of the United States, including suspected spies." In 1942, the FBI launched RACON targeting the Black freedom struggle. Hoover and his agents believed the NAACP had Communist connections; RACON sought out "foreign inspired agitation" among Black Americans. The expansion of bureau authority led to wide-scale surveillance of Black radicals. In 1941, the agency opened its file on Louise Thompson Patterson and Paul and Eslanda Robeson. The following year the bureau began its surveillance of Claudia Jones and in 1944 Charlotta Bass. Shirley Graham DuBois, Lorraine Hansberry and Beulah Richardson's files were opened during the Korean War because of their peace activism. Concerns about national security justified surveillance, racism fueled harassment of Black radicals.[21]

CLAUDIA JONES

As an immigrant and a Black woman, Claudia Jones was an obvious and vulnerable target and the state viciously narrowed in on her. Her first arrest came in January 1948. FBI agents raided her apartment in the evening, forced her to get dressed, and took her into custody, all while her sisters Yvonne and Sylvia looked on. Jones did not easily submit to authorities. They reported that she questioned why she was being arrested and the agents noted that she "ridiculed" her arrest. She was left at a detention facility on Ellis Island. The next day she was out on $1,000 bail.[22]

The bureau had begun its monitoring of Jones six years earlier during World War II. As a Young Communist League leader, she captured the bureau's attention. But the agency took years to finally piece together her origins. The bureau was confused because Jones was her pen name, her surname was Cumberbatch, and in 1940 she married Abraham Scholnick (they divorced in 1947). Her name appeared in city directories as Scholnick, but in Communist publications as Jones; therefore, the bureau was investigating Claudia Jones. Importantly, women's maiden names were listed as aliases, heightening suspicion of their activities.

The bureau found little biographical information under the name Claudia Jones. Until 1946, agents believed an informant's incorrect claim that she was born in Lawrenceville, Virginia. The bureau's investigation is a testament to the dogged attempts to find information. Agents questioned elementary school teachers in Lawrenceville, talked to principals and local businessmen, and searched local records. Because she lived in New York City at the time, they did the same there. Meanwhile an agent was following her every move noting the meetings she attended, where she lived and worked, who she interacted with, and everything she published in the CPUSA press.[23]

The FBI realized she was not a citizen by examining her sister Yvonne's and her husband's records. In the spring of 1947, the bureau found the ship manifest that carried Yvonne and Claudia along with their other sisters and Aunt from their birthplace in Trinidad to New York City. After confirming they were sisters and failing to find documentation that Jones was a citizen, the bureau was poised to act. Jones tried to become a citizen on two separate occasions but was denied because she was a Communist. The US government effectively used a political litmus test to deny her citizenship. Once it confirmed she was not a citizen, the bureau decided to seek deportation using the 1918 immigration law.[24]

What followed was eight years of further arrests, surveillance, harassment, detention, and eventual deportation in 1955. None of the harassment dissuaded Jones from her political work, and as Cold War military proliferation and conflict increased, her resistance increased. The CPUSA and its adjacent organizations mobilized in Jones's defense. She was bailed out by the American Committee for the Protection of the Foreign Born (ACPFB), an organization that helped defend immigrants from state harassment. The National Committee to Defend Negro Leadership would also emerge as a voice for Black Communist leaders arrested, under the threat of prison and deportation, or those stripped of their right to travel.[25]

After her first arrest, the Immigration and Naturalization Service (INS) issued a deportation order. Over the next year and a half, Jones and her attorneys attended hearings to challenge the order. The primary issue was that the existing legislation required the courts to prove Jones advocated the overthrow of the US government. The CPUSA and Jones both insisted that the organization never advocated revolutionary violence; this left the government to try and prove that Jones knew a conspiracy existed. To do this the bureau used Jones's own words against her. The agency compiled her written work, speeches she made, and radio shows she was on. Her membership and leadership in the party was enough for authorities who believed she knew a conspiracy existed. The most potent weapon in the bureau's arsenal was the professional witness. Professional witnesses were former Communists willing to testify that a conspiracy did exist, even if they could not pinpoint the individual role of people in the alleged conspiracy. These witnesses were often able to gain a level of celebrity among anti-communists, and for some, among the public. It proved to be a lucrative career move that could lead to book deals and paid speaking appearances. But the witnesses produced hearsay testimonies that proved problematic as they often contradicted each other and just as often themselves or offered up unproven and sensational claims.[26]

In the meantime, the Internal Security Act was passed which further empowered the INS's deportation powers. Jones was remanded to custody again in October 1950 on Ellis Island, where she was held with other immigrant Communists in what they dubbed the "McCarran Wing." She wrote a letter that was published in the *Daily Worker* about the conditions and accused the "atom makers of war and fascism" of trying to silence them. She believed that it was her anti-racism and peace advocacy that led to her imprisonment and harassment, and she reminded readers that the war state would not tolerate dissent. Jones also described the poor conditions of the facilities which affected her health. She had suffered from tuberculosis as a youth and while detained she suffered from a recurrence of a recent bout with bronchitis. After three weeks the ACPFB secured bail.[27]

During the period between Jones's first arrest in 1948 and her deportation in 1955 she wrote some of her most significant theoretical work for the party. These included her writings on the peace movement and these writings and her speeches on peace were highlighted by the FBI in her file. Jones was regularly featured on the radio, but the bureau included only one radio show transcript in its file. The transcript was over a debate about mandatory military conscription, which Jones opposed. It was her speech on International Women's Day in 1950 (which was turned into an article), however, that led to her third arrest. That article and her others on peace were included in the state's indictment which claimed that she "issued a directive" sometime in March 1950. As Lydia Lindsey argues, what issuing a directive meant was unclear, but in the speech Jones urged women to organize for peace, something the government considered treasonous.[28]

The full text of her articles "For the Unity of Women in the Cause of Peace" and the International Women's Day article were included in her FBI file along with others in which she was critical of the Korean War. These and other written and spoken statements were gathered as evidence to be used against her in court. The bureau was poised to oust Jones and a deportation order was issued for November 1952; but that order would be canceled. The bureau instead decided to press for criminal charges against her and on June 20, 1951, she and sixteen other party leaders were arrested for violating the Smith Act.[29]

In 1948, after Jones's first arrest twelve CPUSA leaders were arrested and charged under the Smith Act. Their trial lasted ten months. Eleven of the men were convicted and sentenced to prison terms of five years and a $10,000 fine. On June 4, 1951, the Supreme Court upheld the decision; two weeks later Jones and her comrades were arrested. Ellen Schrecker argues that the 1948 Smith Act convictions and the 1951 affirmation removed any "restraints" the government had in harassing Communists; the Supreme Court decision upholding the convictions, *Dennis v. US*, further empowered the state. Communists, and arguably their allies, "had few rights that any official body had to respect."[30]

Only thirteen of Jones's fellow defendants were put on trial, which began March 1952; the other four were either acquitted or too ill. The trial featured professional witnesses and the written and spoken work of the defendants, which Jones noted was not read into evidence because the courts feared sympathy with the Communist position. To no one's surprise each of the defendants was found guilty and on February 3, 1953, sentenced to between 1 to 3 years and fines. Jones received a lighter sentence of one year and a $2,000 fine because of her health. She was hospitalized twice during the trial requiring postponement and her attorney Mary Kaufmann worked to get a reprieve from serving jail time because of her worrisome health.[31]

The defendants each made a statement at the sentencing hearing. Jones's statement attacked the proceedings as an unconstitutional violation of the Communist's first amendment rights and as a sounding board for the false accusations of witnesses. One of which, Harvey Matusow, would later admit to lying in Communist trials. Another of the witnesses, Paul Crouch, regularly contradicted himself on the stand. Because Crouch continually got caught in his lies Attorney General Herbert Brownell ordered an investigation into the informer system; some journalists began to catalogue his lies in what they called the "Crouch Index." In Jones's statement before the court, she focused on her peace advocacy and work for Black Americans as the heart of her prosecution. She stated that she was "being found guilty of struggling against military supremacy, specifically to 'end the bestial Korean War, to stop 'operation killer,' to bring our boys home, to reject the militarist threat to embroil us in war with China." She also noted that as a Black American she was silenced by a racist court. Jones and her fellow defendants rejected the government's position and still held out hope that justice would prevail.[32]

The defendants lost their appeals in January 1955 and were remanded to custody; Jones was sent to the segregated women's federal penitentiary in Alderson West Virginia along with Elizabeth Gurley Flynn and Betty Gannett. Her health continued to decline while incarcerated, and she was hospitalized several times. In May, she was denied parole (because she would not admit guilt) but was released for good behavior in October. All the while Jones was imprisoned, the FBI maneuvered to have her deported. They hoped to have her deported immediately upon release, but because of her poor health her attorneys managed to hold off authorities until December. Exhausted and battered from the legal efforts and her illness, Jones agreed in November to be sent to England.[33]

Jones was forced out of the country on December 9, 1955. She would live only nine more years, dying on Christmas Eve 1964, two months short of her fiftieth birthday. Many speculate that it was the government harassment, imprisonment, and then deportation that led to her poor health and premature death. Jones remained a fighter until the end of her life becoming an important part of London's West Indian community; she is remembered there more widely as the founder of the *West Indian Gazette and Afro-Asian-Caribbean News* and Carnival. Today Jones is being remembered by young activists more sympathetic and open to her socialist vision.[34]

Jones was one of the most outspoken party members against US militarism, the Cold War, and the Korean War. FBI surveillance of her began during one war and escalated during another and while it continued after the Korean War ended, Jones's anti-Cold War rhetoric did not end. She continued to speak out against US policy and the conflicts it created. Jones reasoned that the US crusade to spread democracy and contain dictatorship only spread authoritarianism as the US increasingly supported right-wing dictators and engaged in military campaigns in formerly colonized states. It was all, she believed, motivated by Wall Street imperialists who deployed the US military as their own tool to secure wealth. War and imperialism would continue under capitalist regimes; therefore, the US was committing itself to endless war.

SOJOURNERS FOR TRUTH AND JUSTICE
AND CHARLOTTA BASS

In attempting to excavate the government's harassment of Communists and fellow travelers' researchers are paradoxically reliant on the government's own concession to release documentation. The Freedom of Information Act (FOIA), passed under the Lyndon Johnson administration in 1966, and amended several times after that, is meant to create transparency in government, though not all documents are covered, and the bureau has used its own discretion to release its files. FOIA was passed as a reaction to the government secrecy that reigned during the early Cold War, and to avoid conspiracy theories. But to understand the government's secrecy, the government must be willing to reveal its secrets, and that has proven difficult which has only fed conspiratorial thinking. Limitations on document releases is particularly true of the Charlotta Bass file. The FBI processed Bass's file and made it available in the 1990s but has recently only released fifty-one pages to researchers.[35]

Today the full file, which includes over 200 pages has circulated thanks to activists. Bass's file began in 1944. As a high-profile activist and editor of a popular Black newspaper, the bureau had her in its sights. Its surveillance continued even after her death in 1969 as it monitored the executors of her estate. The bureau was particularly interested in her newspaper, how it was used, and its function as an alleged organ of the Communist Party. It also followed her movement overseas to the Prague conference, her trip to the USSR, and her favorable statements about the Eastern bloc.

The bureau claimed that though there was no evidence of her membership in the CPUSA, she followed the party line. To the bureau and its agents, the "Communist line" included advocating the destruction of Jim Crow, anti-lynching, abolition of poll taxes, and during WWII, opening a second front. It noted her opposition to the Winston Churchill Iron Curtain speech, her previous opposition to communism, but more important to the bureau, her association with party members and other radical organizations. Her trip to Prague was closely monitored and her report on her 10-day visit to the Soviet Union was of particular interest. When the FBI found that she traveled on a passport with limited travel permission (she was only permitted to travel to France, Haiti, UK, West Africa, and Switzerland), the agency informed both the Department of State and the CIA. Based on that information, the Department of State sent a local California agent named Frank Patten to interview Bass and to "request the return of her passport." He was told she was not available, and he sent a letter to her demanding the return of her passport; in response, Bass secured the services of attorneys to deal with the matter. According to the FBI there was no indication that the Department of State was able to collect her passport.[36]

The bureau also followed her association with the Progressive Party and both her 1950 run for Congress and 1952 campaign for vice president. Agents made certain to record her opposition to both HUAC and the Korean War and catalogued the articles that appeared in *The California Eagle* on the war and her accusation that the US military was a Jim Crow army. The bureau claimed that her newspaper had effectively been bought by the CPUSA believing it bailed Bass out of financial troubles making it a Communist organ. This information came from a former and unnamed Communist party member that had been expelled.[37]

Bass features prominently in the Sojourners for Truth and Justice FBI file. The STJ file is a disturbing peek inside the minds of an agency willing to go to any lengths to prevent Black radical organizing. The bureau was tipped off by an informant about the group's creation and it immediately began surveillance. The agency was specifically interested in the "Call for Negro Women" to descend on Washington in the fall of 1951. It mentioned that the women wanted to meet with the President, State Department, Justice Department, and Congress to discuss "grievances regarding civil rights" and the billions spent on war spending. The women were also, according to the agents "embracing the cause" of William Patterson and W. E. B. Du Bois who were both "indicted Communists." Both men had been arrested and were on trial, Du Bois for his involvement with the PIC and Patterson for his leadership in the Civil Rights Congress.[38]

The bureau was very anxious about the march and followed the prominent women in the STJ leadership—Eslanda Robeson, Shirley Graham Du Bois, Louise Thompson Patterson, Beulah Richardson, and Charlotta Bass—all of whom were already under surveillance. At the march, the bureau's informants reported on the speeches, the conversations, and the new organization's plans. It also watched the reporting on the march in the Communist press. The women accused the bureau of taking pictures of them as they were marching; bureau agents followed up and confirmed that the Secret Service and the United States Army Counterintelligence Corps took the pictures. The "Call to Negro Women" (also included in the file) was only issued in early September. The march took place the last weekend in September into October; within weeks there were three intelligence agencies monitoring the group. Later the Office of Naval Intelligence would surveil the women. The official response to the STJ prove that peace and civil rights were interpreted as dangerous to the anti-communist state.[39]

The bureau informants were central to the monitoring of the STJ. One informant in particular, Julia Clarice Brown, revealed herself in 1966 when she wrote a tell all about her time working for the bureau. Her book, *I Testify: My Years as an Undercover FBI Agent*, made Brown a right-wing hero. She had originally joined the CPUSA and CRC out of concern for segregation laws and lynching. She later decided that the CRC propaganda was "misleading and un-American" and she did not like that the CRC was defending CPUSA leaders in the Smith Act trials. She also feared that the CRC's actions were leading to a "violent overthrow" of the US government. In 1948 she quit the party and approached the FBI to share information, but the agency was not impressed or surprised by her information and Brown returned to her life. In the summer of 1951, the agency approached Brown and asked her to join the CPUSA again and act as its informant. The bureau convinced her that she would be doing a "great service" to her country. She agreed.[40]

Brown described in the book her descent into the "Marxian morass," and she parroted government anti-communist propaganda. She wrote that communism was a "multi-faceted evil" because it wanted to violently overthrow the government, it was treacherous and sought dictatorship, and it was antireligious, and immoral. She was asked to be a delegate at the Sojourners March in Washington, where she claimed the executive committee, including Graham Du Bois, Thompson Patterson, and Richardson, dominated the meeting. After the march, Brown joined the Cleveland branch of the group. She claimed that local branches were created by Communist white women with "axes to grind" though it was meant to be a Black woman's organization.[41]

Brown was asked to travel to Florida to attend the funeral and protest the murders of Harry and Hariette Moore. She wrote that their killing was "the sort of tragedy that delights Communists" and that local party branches immediately organized to propagandize it "lest the Kremlin think they were dragging their feet." She was prominent in the organizing because the party wanted to have a Black woman at the center of its propaganda. She was part of the delegation that met with Governor Warren to encourage an investigation into the murders. Brown claimed that the group was led by Communists who were "willing to do and say anything to make a propaganda mountain out of a discrimination molehill." Brown was involved in several organizations at the FBI's behest and she saw all of them and the individuals involved, including Beulah Richardson, as Communist puppets.[42]

Brown also had strong feelings about the peace movement. She described the Korean "police action" as the US's first defeat which led to a loss of prestige in the Communist world. She believed that peace could only be secured using force against Communists. It was "never achieved through weakness and a lack of determination" and she warned that "doves of peace" are actually just agents working under the Communist aegis. She believed that the Stockholm peace petition was "masterminded by those who would deprive us of those cherished rights."[43] She articulated what anti-communist liberals and conservatives believed: that the US could only secure peace through force, that militarism was justified, and that the US was empowered to intervene in other countries. Brown told the FBI that when Communists began losing control in the STJ they dissolved the organization.[44]

Another informant claimed that Bass was a secret member of the CPUSA and that she was the "mistress of ceremonies" at a CRC event. This was meant to link the STJ to the party. Bass was accused of following the CPUSA line and under her leadership the STJ was under "complete Communist control." She was listed, along with Louise Thompson Patterson, as one of the organizers of the proposed Georgia march that was alleged to be a test for launching a revolution. The STJ endorsed Bass's 1952 vice presidential campaign and she gave a speech at one of its meetings about her candidacy. The bureau noted some lines from her speech indicating that she urged Black women to "fight for their freedom." The STJ also celebrated Bass as the first Black woman to appear on a major party ticket in a presidential election.[45]

The bureau observed that by 1952 the organization was at a "low ebb." It nevertheless continued monitoring it and its members and warned that if it became active again it would "pursue action." Until 1956, it kept an eye out for any sign that the STJ would reemerge.[46] Bass retired from political work and editing in 1966. After her failed 1952 campaign, she moved back to California. Even with retirement she remained active in radical organizations, but mostly as an attendee of events. She also served on the board of the CPUSA's *People's World* and as an honorary member of political organizations. Even when Bass was hospitalized, the bureau had agents make pretext calls to hospitals to inquire about her status. Both the bureau and the Secret Service kept tabs on the elderly and infirm Bass. Agents concluded that her health and age meant she was not appropriate as a potential informant, but it did not mean constant surveillance would end even when she was "crippled by arthritis" and "partially bedridden." She died from a cerebral hemorrhage on April 12, 1969. An informant told the agency that Bass intended to leave her estate to the Communist Party, so her file continued for two decades after her death. In it, the bureau monitored her attorney Ben Margolis, who was affiliated with the National Lawyers Guild, an organization of radical attorneys. Margolis had a reputation for representing Communists, which justified the surveillance. Death, it seemed, was not enough to end monitoring.[47]

SHIRLEY GRAHAM DU BOIS

In 1950, Louis Budenz claimed that Shirley Graham Du Bois was one of 400 concealed Communists. A concealed Communist was defined as someone who would "deny membership" in the party and would not present themselves as a Communist. Budenz, who admitted to not knowing Graham Du Bois himself, claimed he was told by another Communist that she was an active and enthusiastic party member. This secondhand account was enough for the bureau to begin its surveillance, which would last twenty-seven years and result in a larger file than her famous husband. Budenz's accusation might have prompted opening the file, but it was Graham Du Bois's involvement in the peace movement that the bureau would follow and note with great interest.[48]

Budenz was at one time the editor of the CPUSA's *Daily Worker*. He claimed that this role gave him access to the party's secret apparatus. He made probably the most dramatic exit from the party when he publicly knelt before anti-Communist Monsignor Fulton Sheen and returned to the Catholic church. All of this was done without the party knowing anything until it was reported in the press. Budenz became, according to Robert Lichtman, a prolific informer, and a professional witness. He accused several individuals, especially Black radicals like the Du Boises, Bass, and the Robesons, of being secret members. Budenz was a "prototypical excommunist" informer, providing information to the bureau based on shaky evidence and his own alleged knowledge of the party apparatus. His evidence was often that their names appeared on Communist adjacent organizational letterhead. Budenz would later claim that he abhorred racism and proudly recounted his father's friendship with a "mulatto porter," but he eagerly informed on Black radicals, suggesting his complicity in attacking and undermining the most important voices in Black radicalism. He assisted in effectively drowning out their voices while making money as an informer (in one year he reported $70,000 income as an anti-communist witness and speaker). One thing that few officials considered was that these witnesses, some of whom had been out of the party for years, were no longer privy to party actions. This did not hamper reliance on their testimony.[49]

Whether Shirley Graham Du Bois was a Communist or not, she was a well-known radical activist who worked with known Communists, and mere association was enough for the bureau. Her assistance in organizing the Scientific and Cultural Conference for Peace in New York City was noted by the bureau and HUAC. Even before the conference began, the State Department called the conference a "likely sounding board" for communism.[50] Graham Du Bois wrote that many of the attendees would later have their careers destroyed because of their concern for peace and the federal government's harassment. HUAC released a report on the conference listing it as a Communist front and including the names of individuals in attendance along with their political affiliations. The report reveals that not only was peace activism criminalized, but that the activists involved were so thoroughly investigated that HUAC could list petitions they had signed, events they attended, and political activity they participated in. It listed several people who had been involved in the 1948 Progressive Party campaign, including Graham Du Bois.[51]

The Cold War surveillance apparatus was far-reaching, aggressive, and eagerly focused on Black radicals. The FBI followed Graham Du Bois's movement across the globe to the Paris Peace Conference and the Cuba Peace Conference, to the White House for a vigil, to Chicago for a convention, to states across the country where she advocated for the end of war. It was a Herculean effort that included the work of agents abroad and at home, and informants across the country. Like Jones's file, it included articles she had written, speeches she made, and people she interacted with. The bureau was especially interested in her tour of the United States to raise money for her husband's defense in the PIC case. Agents noted where they traveled, what they said and who they said it to. This culminated in their 1952 deportation from Canada and the revocation of her passport. Between 1949 and 1958, Graham Du Bois's passport was denied several times. In the 1958 *Kent v. Dulles* decision (involving Graham Du Bois friend artist Rockwell Kent), the Supreme Court ruled that the Secretary of State did not have the authority to deny passports to citizens.[52]

When the Du Bois' passports were returned, she and her husband left the United States and became sojourners first in Ghana where W. E. B. Du Bois died in 1963. While there they had their US passports canceled and became Ghanian citizens. The Du Bois' case highlights the precarity of Black citizenship. Once the State Department could no longer control their movements, it effectively restricted re-entry into the country. Graham Du Bois would spend several years out of the US and was denied a visa to return in 1970, but she finally made her way back, all the while the FBI kept a watch on her movements until 1975. She died in China in 1977.[53]

ESLANDA ROBESON

Paul Robeson's passport was famously seized creating enormous career and financial problems; Eslanda's was also taken. The Robesons were left without passports for eight years, and when they were finally returned, they immediately left the country where they would join their friend Claudia Jones in London. Paul Robeson has received more attention and notice for his activism, but intelligence agencies took notice of his radical wife too. In 1953, she was subpoenaed to testify before a Congressional committee.[54]

She was subpoenaed to testify before the Senate Permanent Subcommittee on Investigations with the infamous Joseph McCarthy presiding. McCarthy is the name and face of US anti-communism, but the truth is few of the people under investigation had the opportunity to face off with the man himself. His reputation is perhaps from his bombast, his outspoken criticism of his own critics, and the power his own political party afforded him. Barbara Ransby speculates that Eslanda was called because her books appeared in embassy and US government libraries around the world; but the government's interest in her husband was also a motivating factor. Additionally, Eslanda had become a force of her own in peace campaigns and in the Progressive Party.[55]

Congressional testimonies are perhaps the most remembered part of the so-called "McCarthy era." Some hearings were televised or broadcast on the radio, thus bringing anti-communism into the US living room. While these hearings have come to symbolize anti-communism, they are only one small aspect of the hysteria that gripped the country. Alongside FBI surveillance, criminal prosecution, arrest, detention, incarceration, travel restrictions, and deportation, the humiliating prospect of being dragged before a large audience with the potential to lose jobs, friends, and housing was daunting. Robeson, however, was not cowed and went before the committee with every intent to challenge its legitimacy.

As Ransby has written, she was a "hostile witness" who questioned the legality of such hearings and accused them of "racism and repression." Robeson was described by the bureau as "unfriendly, evasive, and uncooperative." She was intentionally uncooperative and she had created a "highly politicized public persona." The hearing began with simple enough questions: what was her name, is Paul Robeson her husband, was she the author of certain books; but then the infamous inquisitor Roy Cohn asked whether she was a member of the Communist Party. Rather than invoke the Fifth Amendment, or even the First Amendment, as some individuals tried to, Robeson invoked the Fifteenth Amendment. When Cohn asked why the Fifteenth Amendment, which prohibits denying the right to vote based on race, she answered that as a Black woman she was taught to seek protection under the Fifteenth Amendment. Cohn tried to press the point, but Robeson insisted that as a "second-class" citizen, she was not seen as an equal to her fellow white citizens and thus sought the protection of the Fifteenth Amendment. Robeson was challenging not just the committee's ability to question her but also forcing the committee to recognize that she was not considered a citizen and that the US had failed to protect Black Americans. This was a direct challenge to the democratic mythology the US promoted. This moment highlighted the coupling of anti-communist harassment with racist inequality; Robeson was denied her rights as a citizen because she was both a radical and a Black American.[56]

The committee continued its questioning asking if she was refusing to answer or use the Fifth Amendment because it would incriminate her. Invoking the Fifth Amendment was interpreted as an admission of guilt, and it was a tactic the committee used to confirm guilt. Robeson's claim to the Fifteenth Amendment confused and befuddled her inquisitors. Other questions followed including whether she was the sole author of the book *This African Journey*; Robeson told the committee that she was offended by the question because it implied she could not write a book. Cohn continued by asking if she ever taught the Communist line, whether she advocated the overthrow of the government, whether she had ever heard anyone else advocate it, whether she had engaged in sabotage or espionage, and so on it went. Robeson did not want to make the committee's job easy, and McCarthy told her at the end of the hearing that if she was not a woman she would have been found in contempt. McCarthy's posturing did not dissuade the Black press who "applauded [her] cool, intelligent, and confident" demeanor.[57] Robeson, like her radical friends, faced FBI surveillance and harassment, the revocation of her travel privileges, and the contempt of her political leaders. She was also dragged before the public's attention before the infamous anti-communist villain Joseph McCarthy. Despite the personal and political costs, she remained an activist devoted to peace and anti-racism until her death in 1969.

LOUISE THOMPSON PATTERSON

Louise Thompson Patterson's FBI file is extensive, spanning thirty-three years (1941–1974), and covers almost a thousand pages. The bureau began its investigation on Thompson Patterson in 1941 and over the next three decades kept close surveillance on her personal and political activity. Thompson Patterson's prominence and activity in the CPUSA made her a special target as the bureau worked to curtail the influence of Black radicalism. Despite the harassment, Thompson Patterson remained a formidable activist throughout the Cold War and during the Civil Rights movement; she also maintained her allegiance to communism and the party and unapologetically pushed for radical change until she died at ninety-eight years old on the eve of the millennium.

Thompson Patterson's file follows her Communist career working on the Scottsboro defense and for the International Workers Order, but in the post-WWII years the bureau's anxieties about Communists increased its interest in her. In 1946, an order was given to find out what her affiliation with the party was and knowledge of the party's assumed revolutionary goals. Agents did not appear to follow up on that order. By 1948 an admonishing letter from J. Edgar Hoover appeared that scolded the agents for ignoring Thompson Patterson even though she was not a "top functionary." This might have been because agents, succumbing to gender stereotypes about women's work, viewed her as an auxiliary of her husband. Hoover is not known for his gender egalitarianism, but even if his own agents did not agree, he believed that women could be just as much a threat as their male partners. Citing the "tense international situation" Hoover ordered a review of Thompson Patterson and her Security Index updated. She was in good company on the Security Index, and was joined by her friends Claudia Jones, Shirley Graham Du Bois, Charlotta Bass, Lorraine Hansberry, and Beulah Richardson.[58]

The Security Index came from Hoover's 1939 Custodial Detention program which was supposed to "identify persons of German, Italian, and Communist sympathies," and those who it assumed had loyalties elsewhere. The program encapsulated the xenophobic and antiradical fears that left even citizen status precarious. The program was directed at "aliens and citizens" whose freedom during war, or during a national security crisis was considered dangerous. Custodial detention was obviously unconstitutional, and Hoover understood that; therefore, he anticipated legal challenges by discussing it with the attorney general nine months after he ordered his agents to begin compiling it. He also resisted any supervisory role for other departments but conceded to those citizens on the list being prosecuted under legislation before detention; aliens were not given the same consideration. It was a program that revealed the vulnerability of both immigrants and radicals to the whims of the state and the malleability of citizenship in the face of anti-communism. Hoover changed the name from Custodial to the somewhat more benign Security Index and urged his agents to keep the files updated. Even in her later years, the bureau maintained Charlotta Bass's index file. In June 1968, the Los Angeles FBI office recommended that Bass be removed from the Security Index where her status was DETCOMM. This meant that she was identified for detention as a Communist. Instead, she was recommended for the "reserve index" which would maintain surveillance. Not until August 1968, at age 91, was Bass removed from the Security Index. Claudia Jones was only removed after the bureau confirmed that she boarded the ship for her deportation.[59]

The bureau's report on Thompson Patterson listed all of her affiliations that were considered Communist by the attorney general to justify its surveillance and her inclusion on the Security Index. The organizations she was affiliated with included the Council on African Affairs, the CRC, the CAW, and the IWO. Her file included articles she was featured in or wrote, and CPUSA meetings she attended. It also listed people she had spoken to and informant information; most of the informants confirmed her association with the CPUSA, her attendance at its events, and her participation with adjacent organizations. The bureau dutifully updated her Security Index to reflect the new information.[60]

By 1950, Thompson Patterson's file included her criticism of the war and the atomic bomb. At a CAA event, she was recorded as denouncing "American aggression in Korea," and she claimed the US government would never use the atomic bomb against a white nation. Months later the bureau noted that she was quoted in the *People's Daily World* arguing that the US's colonial aggression in Africa was shackling the continent to Wall Street warmongering. That same year her husband William Patterson was indicted for contempt of court for refusing to turn over the CRC's records to authorities.[61]

William Patterson tirelessly led the CRC through its many campaigns to rescue Black Americans and Communists from the injustices of the legal system. In August 1950, he was summoned before a Congressional Committee to testify about the CRC; what it wanted was for him to give up the names of members and its funders. Socialist congressman Vito Marcantonio warned Patterson that if he refused to give up names he would be held in contempt. To prove a Communist conspiracy, especially among those that were in the public-facing organizations, required officials to make imaginative leaps. Refusing to testify or to surrender information was one way to trap someone, and Patterson had been set up to fail. Patterson's testimony led to a confrontation between him and a southern congressman who called him a "Black son of a bitch" and who would insist on contempt charges.[62]

In 1951, William Patterson escaped a contempt conviction. In the meantime Thompson Patterson had to testify before a New York State committee about her work with the IWO. The IWO was a mutual aid insurance organization, but it was designated subversive and a "national security threat." Her biographer Keith Gilyard argues that as anti-communist trials went, this one was "low stakes." Governor Thomas Dewey and the New York

State Insurance Department wanted to eliminate the IWO; their opportunity would arrive if they could prove its affiliation with the CPUSA. To do so meant to prove its leaders, like Thompson Patterson, were Communist. Another anti-communist tool was perjury. Thompson Patterson had to testify before a state committee and deny her communism if she wanted to avoid jail; but admitting to it would doom the IWO. Gilyard argues that the prosecution only needed her to plead the Fifth, proof enough that she was a Communist. Thompson Patterson did not answer whether she was a Communist, but as Gilyard notes, it did not matter, the IWO was doomed. Though she would not face any jail time, the IWO was forced to dissolve. Meanwhile William Patterson was facing a retrial.[63]

Such was the life of an American Communist in the 1950s: testimony, trial, arrest, prosecution, perhaps imprisonment and deportation while watching their comrades endure similar treatment. The Korean War provided the government cover to continue this extralegal and unconstitutional harassment. Black American citizenship was (is) precarious; Black American radical citizenship was (is) believed to be potentially traitorous and the state was primed to strip citizenship rights for anything it deemed an offense.

Thompson Patterson's FBI file tracked her political activity, including her work supporting her husband against his contempt charges. It also focused on her role in creating and working for the STJ. The planning meeting for the march to Washington was held at her apartment, and the bureau noted that the organization was meant to separate Black women from white women radicals, an interesting contradiction given that Julia Brown said that the local branches were dominated by Communist white women. Contradictions like these never hampered the bureau's assumptions about the women and their organizations. The bureau also noted that it was Thompson Patterson who organized the group's activities once in Washington. Her file often conflated her support for her husband with organizational support, but it was implied that her support of William Patterson meant the STJ's support. The organization did raise awareness around both Patterson's and Du Bois's indictments and trials; what made it criminal and worthy of the bureau's notice was the bureau's anti-Black anti-communism.[64]

The bureau found little difference between the STJ's and the CRC's work against the Korean War and US militarization and the groups' advocacy for Black Americans. But neither did the Pattersons; both understood that US militarism was a domestic and foreign policy issue. The United States commitment to war against people of color abroad translated into war against people of color at home; militarization meant shifting resources away from the impoverished and disenfranchised at home toward impoverishing and disenfranchising people abroad. There was no difference between making war and Black oppression; it was the state's means to control its citizens. After the STJ's activities declined, Gilyard argues that Thompson Patterson's political work declined and may have become "less exuberant." Part of this had to do with William Patterson's conviction and detention in a federal penitentiary. Meanwhile, the organizations that both Pattersons had led disappeared—by 1955, the STJ and CRC were gone. This did not end the surveillance, which continued for Thompson Patterson well into the 1970s. She did remain a committed activist and Communist and took a prominent role in the campaign to free Angela Davis, which kept her on the FBI radar. But the state harassment had left much of the radical Black left exhausted and demoralized.[65]

BEULAH RICHARDSON AND LORRAINE HANSBERRY

Both Lorraine Hansberry and Beulah Richardson (under the stage name Beah Richards), would be remembered as artists and entertainers. But both women were committed to peace during the Cold War, which meant the FBI would consider them national security threats. Both were monitored, followed, and informed on while they watched their friends being arrested, imprisoned, and deported. Their eventual fame kept the bureau at bay, but the women's continued association with their radical friends and their activism kept their files open. Despite the treatment, they continued their creative output which was inspired by their commitment to the Black freedom struggle. While Beulah Richardson would go on to a long career in theatre, television, and film, Lorraine Hansberry unfortunately died at a young age leaving behind her rich creative legacy inspired by her radical commitments.

The popularity of Richardson's 1951 poem "A Black Woman Speaks . . . of White Womanhood, of White Supremacy, of Peace" and the pamphlet reprint of it caught the attention of the FBI which opened a file on her that same year. Richardson's file, under her stage name Beah Richards, is one of the shorter files compared to some of her peers. This could mean that she was believed to be a low-stakes person (though bureau language would not reflect that assumption). It could also mean that the bureau is not releasing the entire file. Whatever the reason for the short file (317 pages), the bureau certainly took her seriously. Initially, however, the agency could not quite figure out who she was. Early in her file, Richardson was confused for Charlotta Bass. It appears to have taken months for the FBI to realize that she was a completely different person who was almost fifty years younger than Bass.[66]

The confusion might have come from an informant that claimed Richardson had joined the California Communist party in 1946; but Richardson was not living in California at the time. She was attending Dillard University in New Orleans where she graduated in 1948. The bureau, finally realizing that Richardson and Bass were two different people, began earnestly following Richardson, but it continued to operate under the assumption that she had been a California CPUSA member since 1946. As it so often did, the FBI struggled to find biographical information on its subjects. Claudia Jones's pen name caused no end of confusion for agents; bureau informants believed for years that Shirley Graham Du Bois was from Evansville, Indiana, when she was in fact from Indianapolis. The bureau did realize that Richardson was from Vicksburg, Mississippi, but could not locate information on her mother and found no one under her mother's name there.[67]

Richardson's file is an example of how the bureau justified its determined and extralegal surveillance because the person under investigation was associated with organizations designated as security threats. The bureau believed, again using informant information, that she was a member of the CPUSA. It claimed that the informant said she joined in 1946, dropped out, became active again in 1950, and then rejoined in 1951. At another point in the file the FBI listed her date of CPUSA membership as 1947. Because it failed to secure reliable biographical information, the bureau assumed she was a Communist. Its own investigation had contradictory information about her, but it could not confirm her California residency until 1949.[68]

The agency also linked her to the CRC because it used Richardson's poetry in its *We Charge Genocide* campaign. Richardson was a prominent leader in the STJ and one of its cofounders, which was noted. Her file also indicated that she advocated destroying white supremacy, and the bureau listed everything she wrote that was published in left-wing periodicals and every meeting she attended. This was enough to include her on the Security Index along with her friends. Richardson was under surveillance solely because of her association with organizations and individuals close to the CPUSA and her commitment to anti-racism and peace.[69]

By 1957, her Security Index was updated to reflect her stage name Beah Richards. The organizations that Richardson had been associated with had been dissolved, but the bureau still felt that she presented enough of a threat that she should remain on the potential detention list. It continued to monitor her activities, which included a conference she was invited to at the Marxist Jefferson School of Social Science in 1956—the same year the school closed because of anti-communism. She also performed at a fundraiser for the Montgomery Bus boycott, and perhaps more damning, her roommate

Alice Childress was reported to be a CPUSA member. It is hard to locate a crime in her file, aside from her advocacy of civil rights and her association with individuals believed to be Communists; yet, this was crime enough for the FBI. Richardson's file reveals that assumptions about party membership were solely based on informant information, and even inconsistency in dates did not trouble agents. Certainly, many people were open about their membership, like Jones and Thompson Patterson, but suspected membership was considered just as dangerous.[70]

The bureau had been making pretext calls to Richardson as early as 1952 to gather information. By 1957, the agency determined that interviewing her based on her reading poems at events or publishing in left-wing magazines could prove embarrassing, a tacit acknowledgment that the evidence of subversion was insufficient. By 1958, the agency had changed its mind and tried to secure an interview, though it suspected it would not reveal new information. One of the reasons for the change of heart was that she had moved in with the Pattersons, known Communists, and this would make it no longer embarrassing. The bureau's reliance on association in Richardson's case and in other cases reveals the shaky foundation of its mission and the questionable legality of its activity. By 1959, the bureau was listing her association with the Pattersons as evidence that her "subversive thinking" had not changed. The agency decided that there was "little doubt" that she was still linked with the CPUSA and was in full support of its leaders and members. The conclusion was that she had to be considered a person "potentially dangerous to the national security."[71]

Though Richardson was under scrutiny and the bureau made pretext calls to her as late as 1962, she seems to have escaped the kind of harassment her colleagues experienced. The bureau continued to monitor her until 1972 when it determined that she was still "potentially dangerous." Richardson would go on to have a successful stage and film career. She starred in several films and television shows including *Sanford and Son*, *The Cosby Show*, *ER*, and the film adaptation of *Beloved*. She was nominated for an Oscar and won an Emmy. When she died in 2000, her obituaries did not mention her radical politics or that the FBI saw her at one point as "violently dedicated" to communism and a national security threat.[72]

Richardson's and Hansberry's success by the late 1950s and 1960s might have insulated them from more serious retribution. A decade before the federal government could easily vilify the entertainer Paul Robeson and describe his activities as un-American. But a public weary of anti-communist hysteria might have been less receptive by the late 1950s and early 1960s. Gender might have also provided some insulation, though the treatment of Claudia Jones would belie that assumption. The public censure of Joseph McCarthy in 1954 indicated the declining social power of anti-communism, but it did not stop the surveillance and monitoring or legal pressure. As the decade wore on, the FBI frequently noted in Richardson's file, and later in Hansberry's file, that securing an interview with them could be "potentially embarrassing" to the agency. This was especially true for Hansberry after *A Raisin in the Sun* premiered in 1958 and made her a public figure.[73]

Hansberry's file is extensive, spanning the year 1952 to her premature death in 1965 and covers over 1,000 pages. Surveillance began in 1952, when she traveled to Montevideo, Uruguay, for the Inter-Continental Peace Conference in place of Paul Robeson whose passport was revoked. The FBI noted that the conference had been cited by the HUAC as "Communist established." The State Department retaliated by revoking her passport. The bureau was interested in not just her association with the CPUSA but her continued work with organizations, including the CRC and STJ. [74]

The bureau's file on Hansberry is not dissimilar to her colleagues. There are informants claiming that she was associated with the party, and one informant claimed that her mother-in-law was a "fanatical Communist" who raised her kids to be the same. Hansberry's association with or advocacy of organizations; her friendships with people like Jones (briefly her roommate), W. E. B. Du Bois, and Paul Robeson; her work on radical publications like *Freedom* and *New Challenges*; and her work with the STJ and attendance at the STJ march to Washington were all included as indications of subversion. Unlike her friends though, Hansberry was briefly taken off the Security Index. One agent seemed to think that because there was no proof she was a CPUSA member, she should be removed. She was promptly returned not long after; the reason for her return is redacted.[75]

When *A Raisin in the Sun* was released and met with critical and popular approval, the bureau immediately tried to ascertain whether the play was controlled by the party or followed the party line. It was initially released in markets outside Broadway, and the bureau had an agent attend a showing in New Hampshire in February 1959. The agent wrote that there were no comments about communism and that it dealt primarily with "negro aspirations." The agent also noted that audience reaction was not to the "propaganda messages" but for the acting; though occasionally there was a reaction "on a racial basis." By March 1959, the bureau had officially decided that the play was not controlled by the CPUSA; but its success did suddenly make it embarrassing to try and interview Hansberry. This did not end surveillance; the agency monitored her, followed her on dog walks, noted her continued work with activists, and considered her a national security threat. She was only removed from the Security Index when she died at 34-years-old.[76]

To be sure, there were white Communists who were arrested, imprisoned, and deported; but each of them were anti-racist advocates, vocally opposed to imperialism and colonialism. They were some of the most vehement and loyal allies of Black Americans, and they stood side by side with their Black colleagues to demand justice, even after liberal anti-communist organizations and individuals abandoned them. The Communist Party was the most outspoken interracial organization to challenge racism, demand justice, and put forward programmatic solutions to the US's ills. Did the organization advocate revolution? The answer is complex, it certainly advocated revolutionary change, but it did not advocate, nor did it plan for, violence. Even the federal government could not prove that Communists sought a violent overthrow. Instead, the forces of the state had to engage in slipshod, unconstitutional, and illegal harassment, using the fear of war with the Soviet Union and war in Korea as justification, to try and prove there was a fifth column operating within the United States.

What it managed to prove was that people like Claudia Jones, Charlotta Bass, Eslanda Robeson, Shirley Graham Du Bois, Louise Thompson Patterson, Lorraine Hansberry, and Beulah Richardson believed in a better future—without war, poverty, and injustice. What it failed to prove was that any of these women sought, organized for, or engaged in violence against their government. But during wartime, any criticism of the state apparatus could be dismissed as potentially treasonous. As the long history of anti-communism proves, authorities operated under the assumption that Black radicalism is a danger to the state, and war excused the punitive measures that followed.

Conclusion

In 1959, Shirley Graham Du Bois reflected on the ten years since the Paris Peace conference in the magazine *Soviet Woman*. She wrote about the challenges of advocating for peace in a world of legal consequences. She wrote that even ten years later, Americans had no appreciation for the peace movement because they had not seen the devastation of war firsthand. She believed that this made Cold War militarism palatable as the US brought war and destruction to other nations, while unseen and unfelt by the American people who endorsed and paid for war with their tax money. There were voices for peace in the US, but they were shouted down or legislated out of existence. Meanwhile, Americans had, what she described as an "extraordinary lack" of understanding about war. Ever the optimist, Graham Du Bois wrote that there were women in the US who faced off against the greatest odds to advocate for peace and to denounce US policy. Black women, Graham Du Bois noted, were particularly vocal against war. Their economic and social condition was never raised during war, their husbands and sons never saw their status improve after war, and their children went hungry while the war machine was overfed. She understood that anti-communism was sold to the American people to preserve democracy, but it was a smokescreen which allowed the federal government to use taxpayer funds to secure capitalist resources. Her hope remained that the global resistance that once had so much momentum would stand against US militarism and the death and destruction left in its wake.[1]

The women in this book feared the power anti-communism could wield in defining domestic and foreign policy and that it was in service to capitalists who were always willing to send people to slaughter to secure their own profits. Graham Du Bois, Louise Thompson Patterson, Claudia Jones, Charlotta Bass, Eslanda Robeson, Lorraine Hansberry, and Beulah Richardson argued that anti-communism fed racial fascism, circumscribing the rights of Black radicals and their allies. It distanced them from other progressives allying liberals with conservatives which created a united front against progressive change. This liberal conservative alliance ushered in the destruction of the New Deal state, the rise of incarceration and militarism, the ascendancy of corporate control, and the maintenance of racial fascism. What radicals advocated was social justice grounded in peace, and this meant the destruction of the US war machine and the dissolution of capitalist power. Peace meant freedom and freedom required the end of capitalist monopoly and militarism. Theirs was a vision of peace that was anti-capitalist, anti-imperialist, but more importantly for equity, peace, and freedom. The war state could not sustain justice; only the peace state could ensure freedom.

ANTI-WAR AS PRESAGE TO NON-ALIGNMENT

The Cold War peace movement predated the non-aligned movement famously inaugurated at the 1955 Bandung Conference. Elizabeth Armstrong argues that the November 1949 Asian Women's Conference in Beijing, the same conference Charlotta Bass was barred from traveling to, anticipated the non-aligned movement. Anti-Cold War activism and organization, particularly organized by the WIDF, presaged these non-aligned solidarities and helped to create an internationalist, anti-imperialist feminist movement. The WIDF hoped to create a women's global solidarity movement that unified women in colonized and formerly colonized states with women from the imperialist states. The women from imperialist nations were encouraged to resist their country's murderous policies and to support liberation movements. This, Armstrong argues, "mobilized rather than ignored or universalized women's differences." Thus, the Bandung conference was not, what she calls, the "opening salvo" in feminism's internationalist solidarity movement.[2]

At the 1949 conference, Armstrong shows that the women created a "solidarity of commonality for women's shared human rights, and a solidarity of complicity that took imbalances of power between women of the world into account." This feminist solidarity necessarily integrated the differences among the women and transformed it into a source of unity and strength rather than division. For Armstrong, there were many different feminist strains in collusion at the conference, but what she called a leftist feminism was the "ideological root" of the conference which would influence "anti-imperialist regional cooperation" that would eventually emerge from Bandung.[3]

These leftist feminists also coalesced around anti-Korean War activism, particularly in the United States as chronicled in this book. US and United

Nations interference in the Korean Civil War drew the attention of activists that recognized this as the culmination of US anti-communism and its stated commitment to capitalist ascendancy. Policymakers confirmed that the war was the first theatre of conflict to shore up US alliances in Asia against Communist influence. The solidarity forged at the 1949 conference continued into the next decade as activists rallied against the spread of a US empire. By the time of the Bandung Conference in April 1955, which brought together Asian and African representatives to discuss decolonization and the superpower rivalry, US officials were actively trying to silence Black radicals. Claudia Jones was serving time in prison; the Du Boises, Robesons, and Lorraine Hansberry had their passports seized; and all of them were being monitored and were placed on special detention lists. The passport seizures prevented W. E. B. Du Bois and Paul Robeson from attending the Bandung conference.[4] Despite the harassment, the spirit of their anti-colonial activism against the Korean War and their resistance to US incursions, inspired by anti-communism, foreshadowed Bandung.

Fanon Che Wilkins describes Lorraine Hansberry's activism as "Beyond Bandung" and argues that her challenges to "Cold War orthodoxy, liberalism," and the attacks on the Black freedom struggle were reflective of Bandung's radicalism. Wilkins argues that Hansberry's optimism was tempered by fears of elites in postcolonial states, particularly in Africa, in perpetuating exploitative conditions. But it was her journalism for Paul Robeson's paper, *Freedom*, that helped her shape her anti-imperialist commitments, and it was at this paper that she wrote about the need for peace. This journalism inspired the artistic work she is remembered for.[5]

Eslanda Robeson reported on the Bandung conference for the *New World Review*. She saw it as an opportunity to tear down "Western Hegemony" at the United Nations. Of the twenty-nine countries that had representatives at Bandung, seventeen created a bloc within the UN to "initiate and support all measures for peace, disarmament, self-determination, non-interference, human rights, friendly international relations, and economic cooperation." These nations hoped to remain neutral in the superpower contest and stand firm against US imperialism. The goals that Robeson and her comrades sought in their resistance to the Korean War, namely disarmament, peace, and the end of US neo-colonialism, were shared by activists and politicians in other nations.[6]

After Bandung, Black internationalists, including the Robesons, the Du Boises, and Claudia Jones, turned to China as the leader of world communism. This move away from the Soviet Union was inspired in part by the Soviet's willingness to work with the US and Mao's recognition of Black liberation, and the liberation of formerly colonized nations. As Zifeng Liu argues, in the years after Bandung, China actively promoted itself as the "central node in a Third World Internationalist Network." Gao Yunxiang has demonstrated that the travel of Black internationalists, including Du Bois and Robeson, influenced their fascination with China, and after 1949, its place in the socialist world. Gao argues that Graham Du Bois played an important role in interpreting the importance of China to Black internationalism for her husband. After their passports were returned, the Du Boises traveled to China in 1959 against State Department rules that prevented travel there. After Du Bois's death in 1963, Graham Du Bois continued her relationship with China, living there during the Cultural Revolution, which for Gao demonstrates a "new understanding of the ties between Red China and Black America."[7]

Claudia Jones's 1955 deportation to London did not end her legal struggles. She was not issued a British passport until 1962; but as soon as she had one, she traveled to the Soviet Union, Japan, and China where she had a brief audience with Mao Zedong. As Liu demonstrates, the Soviet Union did not abandon third world revolutionaries, but it sought to calm its relations with the US and secure "peaceful coexistence." China under Mao's leadership promoted liberation movements and sought to "build up momentum for world revolutions." In 1963, Mao issued the "Statement Supporting the Afro-American in Their Just Struggle Against Racial Discrimination by U.S. Imperialism," which further endeared Black radicals to China. Jones gravitated toward China as a new leader in world communism and among third world revolutionaries.[8]

It is not clear what role China's interference in the Korean War had in endearing it to Black radicals and anti-colonial struggles globally. This is an area of study worth exploring as our understanding of the Korean War in anti-imperial and anti-colonial struggles continues to expand. Chinese intervention in the war reversed its course and prevented a US and South Korean victory. While this has had long-lasting implications on US-Chinese diplomatic relations, the question remains: What (if any) role did it have in inspiring national liberation movements, the US Black freedom struggle, and China's leadership among third world revolutionaries?

ANTI-COMMUNISM, WAR, AND MILITARISM

Anti-Korean War activism was a moment when the full power of the Cold War state collided with the US's growing militarism and would come to characterize geopolitics until the present. The liberal abandonment of radicals is one of the lasting legacies of the Cold War. Liberals in organizations like the NAACP and ACLU and in labor unions under the AFL-CIO banner ousted Communists and fellow travelers from their ranks and actively operated against them to distance themselves from anything considered or alleged to be red. This prevented unity against anti-radical policies, solidarity against corporate malfeasance and exploitation, and provided the government cover to actively pursue and undermine radicals, (arguably) leading to the rise of the permanent national security state. Anti-communism undermined progressive unity, which fed the growth of US militarism and allowed US leaders to commit to endless war.

This has been enabled by what Suhi Choi calls "lingering McCarthyism" or the "longue duree of McCarthyism" as defined by Charisse Burden-Stelly. Both show the prolonged power of anti-communism within US domestic and foreign policy. Burden-Stelly's understanding of anti-communism as a "durable mode of governance," demonstrates the ongoing limitations to secure progressive change, how anti-radicals link Black radicalism to a treasonous conspiracy, and ongoing war and its concomitant wealth accumulation. The power of McCarthyism also resides in other institutions and individuals that are "invested with state power" to engage in "fascist-like repression," which would include liberal organizations. This "soft power" means that Black radicals face both social and political ostracization and punishment. The Cold War with the Soviet Union may be over, but the power of anti-communism remains.[9]

As Beverly Gage has argued, McCarthyism should be more aptly named Hooverism to describe the power of the FBI director over intelligence gathering and his targeting of leftist activists during his entire tenure at the bureau.[10] Considering the continued effects of anti-communism and the anti-progressive harassment at all law enforcement levels, it might be more accurate to call it omnipresent Hooverism, which has conspired to silence the voices of the women in this book and their allies that stood up to US anti-communism and empire building. The surveillance state fortified in this period has survived long past Hoover's death in 1972 and set a precedent to target Black freedom struggle activists and their allies as a radical threat to national security. It has also obfuscated the history of anti-war activists under the anti-communist veneer.

Silencing critics of Cold War anti-communism meant that there were no objections to the rise of and omnipresence of US militarism and defense spending, which led to what Michael Brenes describes as a new political economy. Pejoratively known as the military-industrial complex, it included "large scale defense appropriations" that function as the "social welfare state" for many Americans. This militarism, in part because of the Korean War, has had enormous consequences on the US economy. The phrase, coined by former General and outgoing president Dwight Eisenhower, describes, according to Ruth Wilson Gilmore the "set of workers, intellectuals, bosses, boosters, places, materials, relationships, ideas, and political-economic capacity to organize" the "social order" and production into the "machinery of death." This machinery is the foundation of both the US economy and its culture. This means that in the US, proposals for social legislation that could remedy racial and economic injustice are dismissed as "too expensive and inflationary [but] a trillion dollars for 'lethal aid' and 'defense' that ensure aggression in international relations, and for bank bailouts that effectively amount to the redistribution of wealth upwards" are readily and eagerly approved.[11]

Also significant is the role US militarism plays in the global climate crisis. Eleana Kim notes that the year 1950 is significant because it "marked the beginning of the Korean War and the attendant expansion of US bases but is also the year that geological scientists point to as the beginning of the Great Acceleration." The Great Acceleration describes the "point at which industrial production and mass consumption began their exponential rise." US military production is an essential part of that as it used the alleged threat of a Communist conspiracy to justify its military presence globally and the need for constant weapons proliferation, and thus resource extraction. In 2019, the US military was the "largest single institutional consumer of hydrocarbon," which "is unlikely to change as the USA continues to pursue open-ended operations around the globe." A group of climate organizations produced a report in 2023 that showed NATO spending could be used to combat the climate catastrophe for years; instead, that spending is only increasing the crisis.[12]

The war also fundamentally changed US governance. Mary Dudziak has argued that the Korean War's impact has been integrated into the Cold War obscuring its legacy, and this conceals that the war changed the "structure of government." The Cold War "drained . . . the nation's resources" making it the "most important threat" to anything that remained of the New Deal state. It was this moment "when the question of whether the nation was on a permanent war footing was answered in the affirmative." Dudziak has also demonstrated that Truman's police action has had far-reaching legal consequences for presidential power, allowing the executive branch to commit US troops to conflict (not officially considered war) without congressional permission. The post-Vietnam War Powers Act did not wholly restrain presidential power, but it did limit the size of the conflicts. Marilyn Young has shown that this means that president's do not need to seek public approval to wage endless war. The permanent national security state thrives with an indifferent constituency, using its tax dollars and bodies to fight in endless and unsuccessful wars. This was enabled by anti-communism, and it has facilitated the maintenance of racial fascism, which has contributed to the recent rise of authoritarian efforts to further delimit constitutional rights.[13]

Erik McDuffie argues that the far-right movements of today "share common characteristics" of fascism. This includes "a promotion of hyper-nationalism; an appeal to a fictive ideal past; disdain for human rights; warmongering and celebration of the military; virulent anti-communism; racism; xenophobia; scapegoating perceived domestic and foreign enemies; promotion of heteropatriarchy; suppression of labor unions; support for corporate power; distortions of facts and history; an obsession with crime and security; the use of religion to promote reactionary state policies; control of the media" and "warmongering." While Black Americans have lived under racial fascism, the rise of far-right extremists and the concomitant violence they participate in across the globe has begun to worry white Americans unused to the suppression of their own rights. McDuffie quotes Black poet Haki Madhubuti who stated that Americans "across the socioeconomic and sociodemographic spectrum" are facing challenges resulting from "generational poverty and U.S. empire building."[14] These conditions are the result of bipartisan neoliberal capitalist policies of austerity, and these policies have given rise to a more vocal fascist element committed to delimiting the rights of their fellow citizens and using anti-communism to silence critics.

WAR AND ANTI-WAR IN MEMORY

The paucity of cultural memory about the Korean War is remarkable given that some scholars have described it as an "American Holocaust" and Paul Thomas Chamberlain has described it as one of the "Cold War's Killing fields." The number of Americans killed in Korea, in combat and non-combat roles, stands at 54,249. There were 10,218 Americans missing in action and over 103,000 injured. The Korean and Chinese casualty numbers far outpace US losses: South Korea had 1.3 million casualties and 415,000 deaths. North Korean casualties were nearly 2 million, 1 million of whom were civilians and 520,000 soldiers. These civilians were killed by the US's extensive bombing campaigns along with battle and disease. Nearly 1 million Chinese soldiers were killed. While there was brutality on both sides of the war, South Korean forces participated in a level of carnage that US military officials would prefer to have forgotten given US complicity.[15]

Though Americans have limited historical and cultural memory of the war, its memory is stark and painful in Korea, now two nations at cross purposes. As Choi argues, the official memory of the war in the United States and among officials in South Korea is of a conflict in which the US rescued (some) Koreans from the threat of communism. Because the war is almost wholly absent in US cultural media, there has been virtually no contestation of this official narrative. However, as Haksoon Paik has shown, the war's consequences in Korea have been stark. He argues that the two Koreas, separated by an artificial land barrier since 1945, have become culturally and linguistically distinct. The Korean people had to "concede to the incompleteness of nation-state formation," and the countries' division has had lasting consequences and made it a victim of the Cold War competition. The threat of North Korean attack on the South allowed military and authoritarian rule, with US backing, until the 1990s. This also justified large military expenditures. Not until the end of the Cold War was South Korea able to normalize its relations with other countries and begin to open relations with the North; though this relationship remains tenuous at best. The Korean War also determined the US's relationships with other Pacific nations. It propped up Japan's government as a "rear logistics support base" in the Pacific, and the US forgave WWII reparations. Meanwhile, the US punished China for becoming involved by closing off relations until the late 1970s, but those relations remain strained as current administrations posture for another unwinnable war, and some commentators argue, a new Cold War.[16]

The Korean War led to not only a poor relationship between North and South Korea and the US, but the US's brutality during the war has enabled North Korean leadership to keep civilians in fear of another US attack and thus in a state of constant war preparation. This fear led to the country becoming a nuclear power. The Bill Clinton administration managed to create an agreement with the North Korean government to prevent it from obtaining nuclear weapons, but after George W. Bush described North Korea as part of an axis of evil (along with Iraq and Iran) in 2002, the country began to pursue nuclear tests. In 2006, North Korea successfully tested a nuclear bomb. With each new US administration, that relationship continues to change, but what has not changed is the North Korean memory of US brutality and the government's use of it to keep the nation and its people war ready.[17]

The end of the Cold War loosened the US grip in the Pacific and as Choi argues, the old narrative of anti-communist US heroism has begun to be challenged; but, these "amnesiac, ossified memories of the Korean War have been confronted by newly arising counter-memories." The memories of those still living who witnessed US and South Korean atrocities have led to remembrance of locations like the No Gun Ri massacre site where US troops killed hundreds of Korean civilians. Today a museum has been erected to memorialize the victims and the war's brutality. Another example is the statue of General Douglas MacArthur in Jayu Park in Incheon City, site of the Incheon landing in which MacArthur led troops in an invasion that turned the tide of the war. Choi argues that statues are evidence of how ephemeral historical accounts are; the MacArthur statue became a symbol of US heroism and came to be revered in South Korea. Since the 1990s with the liberalization of South Korean society, activists and "progressive historians" have challenged that mythology and MacArthur's leadership. In 2005, this contest came to a head when activists who wanted the statue taken down clashed violently with veterans and police. In 2022, a North Korean veteran living in South Korea after his release from prison in the 1990s, threatened to set the statue on fire. At a time when younger generations have toppled statues around the globe, the MacArthur statue remains—at least for now.[18]

Though the Korean War does not hold a place in larger US cultural memory, Americans are aware of its existence. This is not true of anti-war activism. This activism, as this book has argued, was part of the larger criticism of anti-communism, imperialism and colonialism, and militarism. To acknowledge it requires acknowledging the precarity of US Cold War commitments, the mythology that committed the US to decades of proxy wars and shifted its economy toward one of constant war resulting in the loss of millions of lives. It requires knowing that behind the US's goal to spread democracy is the reality that the US has most effectively spread terror. It would also require acknowledging that constitutional rights are not durable rights and are subject to the whims of government and legal infrastructures and public opinion. Americans have and continue to consent to the violation of their fellow citizens' rights.

The women in this book were not the only activists opposed to the war; they worked in tandem with other individuals to challenge US anti-communism. They were part of a revolutionary generation that was anti-capitalist, anti-militarist, and anti-imperialist, and they formulated a critique of war and militarism that is useful to contemplate today. As McDuffie argues about Claudia Jones's written work, she provides a "progressive political alternative" to the "cautious incrementalism, neoliberalism, and militarism" and liberal anti-communism that characterizes Democratic administrations—while right-wing Republicanism continues to engage in virulent anti-communism. He believes that in Jones's work there are clues to overcome the US's "moribund fear of socialism and deep-seated white supremacy." She offers a way to undermine historical mythologies that normalized "empire, capitalism, white supremacy, war, and heteropatriarchy." Jones helped to "imagine another world" and to forge a path toward a better future.[19]

Jones was not alone in creating a template for progressives to model. She stands with her comrades Graham Du Bois, Bass, Thompson Patterson, Hansberry, Robeson, and Richardson, among others, in imagining an equitable future grounded in peace. These women argued that the US war state was the antithesis of democratic, that it could not secure democracy elsewhere when it did not exist in its own borders, and that peace meant more than no war, it meant the end of capitalism's stranglehold on the future. They argued that we could not reform our way to emancipation; only with the destruction of capitalist institutions fed by war could we all be liberated. The Korean War is often viewed as an unfinished war, one that has had consequences that continue to the present. A more consequential question to consider is: how has this conflict, and others, perpetuated inequality, empowered lawmakers and capitalists, and alienated oppressed groups from one another? If we ended war and capitalist exploitation, could we all be free? The women in this book argued in the affirmative.

Notes

INTRODUCTION

1. Claudia Jones, "Half the World," *The Worker*, September 2, 1951, 8.
2. Jones, "Half the World," 8; Robert Tomasson, "Truman imposed last wage-price controls in 1951," *New York Times*, August 16, 1971, 15.
3. Jacqueline Castledine, *Cold War Progressives: Women's Interracial Organizing for Peace and Freedom* (Urbana: University of Illinois Press, 2012), 7.
4. Erik S. McDuffie, *Sojourning for Freedom: Black Women, American Communism, and the Making of Black Left Feminism* (Durham, NC: Duke University Press, 2011), 76–77.
5. James A. Miller, Susan D. Pennybackers, and Eve Rosenhaft, "Mother Ada Wright and the International Campaign to free the Scottsboro Boys, 1934–1934," *American Historical Review* 106, no. 2 (April 2001): 387–388.
6. Dennis Childs, "An Insinuating Voice: Angelo Herndon and the Invisible Genesis of the Radical Prison Slave's Neo-Slave Narrative," *Callaloo* 40, no. 4 (2017): 34.
7. Keith Gilyard, *Louise Thompson Patterson: A Life of Struggle for Justice* (Durham, NC: Duke University Press, 2017), 75–76; McDuffie, *Sojourning for Freedom*, 76–77.
8. Charles H. Martin, "Race, Gender, and Southern Justice: The Rosa Lee Ingram Case," *The American Journal of Legal History* 29, no. 3 (July 1985): 252–255.
9. "We'll March: Shout 3000 in Scottsboro Mass Meeting," *Daily Worker*, April 21, 1933, 1.
10. "4500 Jam Hall to hear returned Scottsboro Marchers in New York," *Daily Worker*, May 12, 1932, 2.
11. John S. Portlock, "In the Fabled Land of Make-Believe: Charlotta Bass and Jim Crow Los Angeles," in Brian Purnell, Jeanne Theoharis, Komozi Woodard, *The Strange Careers of the Jim Crow North: Segregation and Struggle Outside of the South* (New York: New York University Press, 2019), 68–69 and Bruce Glasrud, Cary D. Wintz, *African Americans and the White House: The Road to the Presidency* (New York: Routledge, 2010), 48. There is some confusion about Bass' early life, including her birthplace, maiden name, birth date, and the name of her parents. Douglass Flamming settled that debate by arguing that Bass answered all those questions on a 1940 application for Social Security. Douglass Flamming,

Bound for Freedom: Black Los Angeles in Jim Crow America (Berkeley: University of California Press, 2005).

12. Portlock, "In the Fabled Land of Make-Believe," 70–72; "Save the Scottsboro Boys," *The California Eagle*, April 1, 1932, 8; Charlotta Bass, "On the Sidewalk," *The California Eagle*, April 5, 1935, 1; Charlotta Bass, "On the Sidewalk," *The California Eagle*, April 7, 1933, 1.
13. Claudia Jones to William Foster, 6 December 1955, Claudia Jones Vertical File, Tamiment Library, New York University, New York.
14. Douglas O. Linder, "ESSAY ON THE TRIALS OF THE CENTURY: Without Fear or Favor: Judge James Edwin Horton and the Trial of the "Scottsboro Boys" *UMKC Law Review* 68, (Summer, 2000): 549; "Harlem Rallies for Scottsboro Tomorrow," *Daily Worker*, April 7, 1939, 5; "Harlem Rallies for Scottsboro Today," *Daily Worker*, April 8, 1939, 3.
15. Louise Thompson Patterson, "Return to U.S./Scottsboro," 5–6; "4500 Jam Hall to hear returned Scottsboro Marchers in New York," *Daily Worker*, May 12, 1932, 17.
16. Toscano, Alberto. "Incipient Fascism: Black Radical Perspectives." *CLCWeb: Comparative Literature and Culture* 23.1 (2021): https://doi.org/10.7771/1481-4374.4015.
17. Louise Thompson Patterson, "The Paris Conference," 2, Box FF, Louise Thompson Patterson Papers, Archives and Special Collections, Rose Library, Emory University, Atlanta, GA: Richard Wright, "American Negroes in Key Posts of Spain's Loyalist Forces," Daily Worker, September 29, 1937, 2.
18. Mary Washington, *The Other Blacklist: The African American Literary and Cultural Left of the 1950s* (New York: Columbia University Press, 2014), 6–7.
19. Gerald Horne, *Race Woman: The Lives of Shirley Graham Du Bois* (New York: New York University Press, 2000), 38–39. Shirley Graham later marries W. E. B. Du Bois, for the sake of narrative consistency she will be referred to as Graham Du Bois.
20. Horne, *Race Woman*, 92–94, 96.
21. Barbara Ransby, *Eslanda: The Large and Unconventional Life of Eslanda Robeson* (New Haven, CT: Yale University Press, 2013), 179, 184.
22. Ransby, *Eslanda*, 4–5; Imaobong Umoren, "'We Americans are not just American Citizens any longer:' Eslanda Robeson, World Citizenship, and the New World Review in the 1950s," *Journal of Women's History* 30, no. 4 (Winter 2018): 134–35.
23. Soyica Diggs Colbert, *Radical Vision: A Biography of Lorraine Hansberry* (New Haven, CT: Yale University Press, 2021), 4; Michael Anderson, "Lorraine Hansberry, Freedom Family," *American Communist History* 7, no. 2 (2008): 263.
24. Fanon Che Wilkins, "Beyond Bandung: The Critical Nationalism of Lorraine Hansberry, 1950–1965," *Radical History Review* 85 (Spring 2006), 192.
25. McDuffie, *Sojourning for Freedom*, 171–72; Dayo Gore, "A Black Woman Speaks: Beah Richards Life of Protest and Poetry," in Howard Brick, Robbie Lieberman, and Paula Rabinowitz, eds., *Lineages of the Literary Left: Essays in Honor of Alan M. Wald* (Ann Arbor: Michigan Publishing Services, 2015), DOI: http://dx.doi.org/10.3998/maize.13545968.0001.001.

26. Mark Phillip Bradley and Mary L. Dudziak, *Making the Forever War: Marlyn B. Young on the Culture and Politics of American Militarism* (Amherst: University of Massachusetts Press, 2021), 40; Christine Hong, *A Violent Peace: Race, U.S. Militarism, and Cultures of Democratization in Cold War Asia and the Pacific* (Stanford, CA: Stanford University Press, 2020), 24.
27. Suhi Choi, "The New History and the Old Present: Archival Images in PBS documentary Battle for Korea," *Media, Culture & Society* 31, no. 1 (2009): 60–61.
28. Charles Kraus, "American Orientalism in Korea," *Journal of American-East Asian Relations*, Vol. 22 (2015): 149–150; Bradley and Dudziak, *Making the Forever War*, 29; Yi Tae-Jin, "Treaties Leading to Japan's Annexation of Korea: What are the Problems?" *Korea Journal*, 56, no. 4 (Winter 2016): 5.
29. Monica Kim, *The Interrogation Rooms of the Korean War: The Untold History* (Princeton, NJ: Princeton University Press, 2019), 52, 55, 59–60; Bradley and Dudziak, *Making the Forever War*, 29.
30. Bradley and Dudziak, *Making the Forever War*, 29; Mary L. Dudziak, "The Gloss of War" (February 15, 2022), 4. *Michigan Law Review*, http://dx.doi.org/10.2139/ssrn.4049263.
31. Kim, *The Interrogation Rooms of the Korean War*, 35, 46, 49; Vine, *The United States of War*, 6; Mark Clapson, *The Blitz Companion: Aerial Warfare, Civilians, and the City since 1911* (London: University of Westminster Press, 2019), 148. DOI: https://doi.org/10.16997/book26.g.
32. Bradley and Dudziak, *Making the Forever War*, 40–41, 70; Dudziak, "The Gloss of War," 4.
33. Masuda Hajimu, *Cold War Crucible: The Korean Conflict and the Postwar World* (Cambridge, MA: Harvard University Press, 2015), 6; Dudziak, "The Gloss of War," 5–6.
34. Melinda Plastas, *A Band of Noble Women : Racial Politics in the Women's Peace Movement* (Syracuse, NY: Syracuse University Press, 2011), xiii.
35. Joyce Blackwell, *No Peace Without Freedom: Race and the Women's International League for Peace and Freedom, 1915–1975* (Carbondale: Southern Illinois University, 2004), 4–5, 157.
36. Charisse Burden-Stelly and Gerald Horne, *W. E. B. du Bois : A Life in American History* (New York: Bloomsbury Publishing USA, 2019), 76.
37. Shane Smith, "The Crisis in the Great War: W.E.B. Du Bois and his Perception of African-American Participation in World War I," *The Historian* 70, 2 (Summer 2008): 242.
38. Chad Williams, *The Wounded World: W. E. B. Du Bois and the First World War* (New York: Farrar, Straus, and Giroux, 2023), 75, 77–80.
39. Mitchell Lerner, "'It is for this we fought and bled?' The Korean War and the Struggle for Civil Rights," *The Journal of Military History* 82 (2018): 518.
40. Lerner, "'It is for this we fought and bled?'" 518.
41. Hong, *A Violent Peace*, 14–15; Lerner, "'It is for this we fought and bled?'" 518.

42. Lerner, "'It is for this we fought and bled?' 531, 535; Kim, *The Interrogation Rooms of the Korean War*, 315, 345.
43. Lerner, "'It is for this we fought and bled?' 536–538, 545. "Unfairness seen in Courts Martial," *New York Times*, March 2, 1951, 3.
44. Bradley and Dudziak, *Making the Forever War*, 43–44, 47.
45. Leilah Danielson, "Christianity, Dissent, and the Cold War: A. J. Muste's Challenge to Realism and Empire," *Diplomatic History* 30, no. 4 (September 2006): 657.
46. Leilah Danielson, *American Gandhi: A.J. Muste and the History of Radicalism in the Twentieth-Century* (Philadelphia: University of Pennsylvania Press, 2014), 246–248; Leilah Danielson, "'It is a day of judgement:' The Peacemakers, Religion, and Radicalism in Cold War America," *Religion and American Culture: A Journal of Interpretation* 18, no. 2 (Summer 2008): 236; Danielson, "Christianity, Dissent, and the Cold War," 657.
47. Clapson, *The Blitz Campaign*, 151; Yulia Gradskova, *The Women's International Democratic Federation, the Global South, and the Cold War: Defending the Rights of Women of the 'Whole World?'* (London: Routledge, 2021), 88.
48. Bradley and Dudziak, *Making the Forever War*, 69, 79–80.
49. Charisse Burden-Stelly, *Black Scare/Red Scare: Theorizing Capitalist Racism in the United States* (Chicago: University of Chicago Press, 2023), 139.
50. Nick Fischer, *Spider Web: The Birth of American Anticommunism* (Urbana: University of Illinois Press, 2016), 29–30.
51. Fischer, *Spider Web*, 29.
52. Fischer, *Spider Web*, 30, 32, 45.
53. Fischer, *Spider Web*, 67.
54. Burden-Stelly, *Black Scare/Red Scare*, 143.
55. Rhodri Jeffreys-Jones, *The FBI: A History* (New Haven, CT: Yale University Press, 2007), 82–84, it was also in 1935 that FBI agents began carrying weapons; Fischer, *Spider Web*, 250; Donna T. Haverty-Stacke, "Punishment of Mere Political Advocacy: The FBI, Teamsters Local 544, and the Origins of the 1941 Smith Act Case," *The Journal of American History* 100, no. 1 (June 2013): 68–71; Alan Wald, "Review Essay: New Histories of the Old Left," *Journal of Labor and Society* 1, no. 18 (2025): 16.
56. Fischer, *Spider Web*, 30, 32, 45; Athan Theoharis, *Abuse of Power: How Cold War Surveillance and Secret Policy Shaped the Response to 9/11* (Philadelphia: Temple University Press, 2011), 9; Paul Robeson, Section 4, 22, Paul Robeson Sr. file, Federal Bureau of Investigation. As of this writing Paul Robeson's extremely lengthy FBI file is available in the FBI online vault. This document was in part 6 of 31 parts.
57. Bradley and Dudziak, *Making the Forever War*, 69, 79–80.
58. Burden-Stelly, *Black Scare/Red Scare*, 4.
59. Eslanda Robeson deserves a prominent place among these activists as she was a vocal anti-Korean war activist and a central figure in the Progressive Party. Unfortunately, I was denied access to her papers by the Robeson estate located at Howard University. The papers were under contract and not available to researchers. I have

only been able to use the documents available in the Progressive Party Papers and some of her publications. Her role in this book is far smaller than she deserves.

CHAPTER ONE

1. Winston Churchill, "The Sinews of Peace," March 5, 1946, National Archives, Kew, Richmond, United Kingdom.
2. Claudia Jones, "Negro Reaction to Churchill: No!" *Daily Worker*, March 1946, 2.
3. Charlotta Bass, "On the Sidewalk," *The California Eagle*, March 7, 1946, 1.
4. Claudia Jones, "Negro Reaction to Churchill: No!" *Daily Worker*, March 18, 1946, 2; Charlotta Bass, "On the Sidewalk," *The California Eagle*, March 7, 1946, 1.
5. Shirley Graham Du Bois, 37, Part 1, Shirley Graham Du Bois File, Federal Bureau of Investigation file.
6. Paul Diehl, "Exploring Peace: Looking Beyond War and Negative Peace," *International Studies Quarterly* 60, no. 1, (March 2016): 1–2; Jacqueline Castledine, *Cold War Progressives: Women's Interracial Organizing for Peace and Freedom* (Urbana: University of Illinois Press, 2012), 16.
7. Claudia Jones, "'Dirty War': Negro Americans oppose US intervention in Indochina War," *Negro Affairs Quarterly*, June 1954, 2.
8. Robert Frazier, "Kennan, 'Universalism,' and the Truman Doctrine," *Journal of Cold War Studies* 11, no. 2 (Spring 2009): 4
9. Timothy Johnston, "Peace or Pacifism? The Soviet 'Struggle for Peace in all the World,' 1948–1954," *The Slavonic and East European Review* 86, no. 2 (April 2008): 259–60.
10. Draft Paper Prepared in the Department of State, "Soviet 'Peace' Offensive," December 9, 1949, Washington, D.C. Foreign Relations of the United States, 1949; Eastern Europe; The Soviet Union, Volume V, Undersecretary's Meetings, Lot 53, D250.
11. Draft Paper Prepared in the Department of State, "Soviet 'Peace' Offensive," December 9, 1949, Washington, D.C. Foreign Relations of the United States, 1949; Eastern Europe; The Soviet Union, Volume V, Undersecretary's Meetings, Lot 53, D250.
12. Bill V. Mullen, *Un-American: W.E.B. DuBois and the Century of World Revolution* (Philadelphia: Temple University Press, 2015), 155–56.
13. Gerald Horne, *Black Liberation/Red Scare: Ben Davis and the Communist party* (New York: International Publishers, 2021): 78–81.
14. Christina Mislan, "The Imperial 'We': Racial Justice, Nationhood, and Global War in Claudia Jones's *Weekly Review* Editorials, 1938–1943," *Journalism* 18, no. 10 (2017): 1420–21; Erik McDuffie, "For a new Anti-fascist, Anti-imperialist people's coalition: Claudia Jones, Black Left Feminism, and the Politics of Possibility in the era of Trump," in *Post-Cold War Revelations and the American Communist party*, eds. Vernon L. Pedersen, James G. Ryan, and Katherine A. S. Sibley (London: Bloomsbury Academic, 2021), 190–91.

15. Sarah Dunstan and Patricia Owens, "Claudia Jones, International Thinker," *Modern Intellectual History* (April 2021): 8.
16. Jones, "CIO, AFL Unions already endorse Negro Congress," 12; "Call Truman Doctrine threat to Negro People," *Daily Worker*, April 4, 1947, 3.
17. Charisse Burden-Stelly, "Claudia Jones, the Longue Duree of McCarthyism, and the Threat of US Fascism," *Journal of Intersectionality* 3, no. 1 (Summer 2019): 47.
18. Charisse Burden-Stelly, "Theorizing the Structural Location of Blackness," The Caribbean Philosophical Association, April 27, 2023, https://caribbeanphilosophy.org/blog/structural-location-of-blackness; Charisse Burden-Stelly, "In Battle for Peace during Scoundrel Time: W.E.B. Du Bois and United States Repression of Radical Black Peace Activism," *Du Bois Review* 16, no. 2 (2019): 557.
19. Charisse Burden-Stelly, "Constructing Deportable Subjectivity: Antiforeigness, Antiradicalism, and Antiblackness during the McCarthyist Structure of Feeling," *Souls* 19, no. 3: 342–43, 345; Julie Powell, Making 'The Case against the Reds:' Racializing Communism, 1919–1930" in *Historicizing Fear: Ignorance, Vilification, and Othering*, eds., Travis D. Boyce and Winsome M. Chunnu (Louisville: University Press of Colorado, 2019,) 108; McDuffie, "For a new Anti-fascist, Anti-imperialist people's coalition," 190–91.
20. McDuffie, "For a new Anti-fascist, Anti-imperialist people's coalition," 194; Castledine, *Cold War Progressives*, 8–9.
21. Emily R. Cummins and Linda Blum, "Suits to Self-Sufficiency: Dress for Success and Neoliberal Maternalism," *Gender & Society* 29, no. 5 (October 2015): 623–25; Suzy Kim, "The Origins of Cold War Feminism during the Korean War," *Gender & History* 31, no. 2 (July 2019): 473–74.
22. Claudia Jones, "Peace is a Woman's Business," *The Worker*, June 19, 1949, 2, 4; "Kill War Pact, Women Urge," *Daily Worker*, July 14, 1949, 8.
23. Jones, "Peace is a Woman's Business," 2, 4.
24. Barbara Ransby, *Eslanda: The Large and Unconventional Life of Eslanda Robeson* (New Haven, CT: Yale University Press, 2013), 180–181.
25. Pearl S. Buck, *American Argument with Eslanda Robeson* (New York: The John Day Company, 1949), 66–67.
26. McDuffie, "For a new Anti-fascist, Anti-imperialist people's coalition," 191–92.
27. Claudia Jones, *An End to the Neglect of the Problems of the Negro Woman!* (New York: Political Affairs, 1949), 17.
28. Jones, *An End to the Neglect of the Problems of the Negro Woman*, 18; Jones, "Women's Organizations in the Struggle for Peace," 1.
29. Claudia Jones, "A Hot Radio Debate on Military Training," *Daily Worker*, August 4, 1947, 11.
30. Claudia Jones, "International Women's Day and the Struggle for Peace," *Political Affairs*, March 1950, 32–33.
31. Jones, "International Women's Day and the Struggle for Peace," 34–35.
32. Jones, "International Women's Day and the Struggle for Peace," 35–36.

33. Jones, "International Women's Day and the Struggle for Peace," 39; Denise Lynn, "Framing Women: American Communism, the Women's Charter, and the Equal Rights Amendment, 1936–1938," *Women's History Review* 8, no. 2 (April 2014): 1–16.
34. Jones, "International Women's Day and the Struggle for Peace," 41–42, 45.
35. Robert A. Lanier, "When Henry Wallace Came to Memphis: A Research Note on Race and Politics in the Post World War II Era," *The Tennessee Historical Quarterly*, 74, no. 4 (Winter 2015): 300; Mary Hamilton, "A Pennsylvania Newspaper Publisher in 'Gideon's Army': J.W. Gitt, Henry Wallace, and the Progressive party of 1948," Vol. 61, No. 1. *Pennsylvania History: A Journal of Mid-Atlantic States*, (January 1994), 18, 19, 21–22; Ada Belle. Letter from Ada Belle Jackson to Shirley Graham, December 19, 1947. W. E. B. Du Bois Papers (MS 312). Special Collections and University Archives, University of Massachusetts Amherst Libraries; Du Bois, W. E. B. (William Edward Burghardt), 1868–1963. Letter from W. E. B. Du Bois to Progressive Citizens of America, January 10, 1947. W. E. B. Du Bois.
36. Cover Page to Speech from Secretary of Commerce (H. Wallace) to Truman. July 23, 1946, Box 19, Clark M. Clifford Papers, Truman Library, Independence, Missouri; Hamilton, "A Pennsylvania Newspaper Publisher in 'Gideon's Army,'" 19.
37. Hamilton, "A Pennsylvania Newspaper Publisher in 'Gideon's Army,'" 26; Keith Gilyard, *Louise Thompson Patterson: A Life of Struggle for Justice* (Durham, NC: Duke University Press, 2017), 159.
38. Hamilton, "A Pennsylvania Newspaper Publisher in 'Gideon's Army,'" 25, 28; Ada Belle. Letter from Ada Belle Jackson to Shirley Graham, December 19, 1947. W. E. B. Du Bois Papers (MS 312). Special Collections and University Archives, University of Massachusetts Amherst Libraries; Du Bois, W. E. B. (William Edward Burghardt), 1868–1963. Letter from W. E. B. Du Bois to Progressive Citizens of America, January 10, 1947. W. E. B. Du Bois.
39. Hamilton, "A Pennsylvania Newspaper Publisher in 'Gideon's Army,'" 25, 28; Jackson, Papers (MS 312). Special Collections and University Archives, University of Massachusetts Amherst Libraries.
40. Henry Wallace, "Militarization in the US," 1948, Series X, Box 73, Henry Wallace Papers, University of Iowa, Iowa City, Iowa.
41. "Speech by Henry Wallace before Evansville Wallace Committee," April 6, 1948, Series X, Box 68, Henry Wallace Papers, University of Iowa, Iowa City, Iowa.
42. Castledine, *Cold War Progressives*, 98; Shirley Graham Du Bois, "Speech, Progressive party Founding Convention," July 23, 1948, Shirley Graham Du Bois Papers, Box 25, Folder 21, Schlesinger Library, Radcliffe Institute, Harvard University, Boston, Massachusetts.
43. Shirley Graham Du Bois, "Speech, Progressive party Founding Convention," July 23, 1948, Shirley Graham Du Bois Papers, Box 25, Folder 21, Schlesinger Library, Radcliffe Institute, Harvard University, Boston, Massachusetts; "Civil and Political

Rights," Series X, Box 73, Henry Wallace Papers, University of Iowa, Iowa City, Iowa; Castledine, *Cold War Progressives*, 76.
44. Charlotta Bass, "Acceptance Speech," July 6, 1952, Charlotta A. Bass Papers, Southern California Library for Social Studies and Research (Los Angeles).
45. Douglas Flamming, *Bound for Freedom: Black Los Angeles in Jim Crow America* (Berkeley: University of California Press, 2006), 366–67; "Kinloch's Corner," *The California Eagle*, November 28, 1946, 1.
46. "A Clarion Call," *The California Eagle*, January 8, 1948, 1; Charlotta Bass, "On the Sidewalk," *The California Eagle*, 29 January 1948, 1; Charlotta Bass, "Autobiography," 313–14, Charlotta A. Bass Papers, Southern California Library for Social Studies and Research (Los Angeles).
47. Charlotta Bass, "Autobiography," 313, Charlotta A. Bass Papers, Southern California Library for Social Studies and Research (Los Angeles); Flamming, *Bound for Freedom*, 366–67.
48. Charlotta Bass, "Autobiography," 313, Charlotta A. Bass Papers, Southern California Library for Social Studies and Research (Los Angeles); Flamming, *Bound for Freedom*, 366–67.
49. Christina Pérez Jiménez, "Los Amigos de Wallace: Henry Wallace's 1948 Presidential Campaign and the bid to capture the Latino vote," *Latino Studies* 19 (2021): 286, 288. DOI: https://doi.org/10.1057/s41276-021-00335-2.
50. Charlotta Bass, "Autobiography," 313–17, Charlotta A. Bass Papers, Southern California Library for Social Studies and Research (Los Angeles); Charlotta Bass, "The Dawn of a New Century," *The California Eagle*, 5 August 1948, 6; "Get on the Wallace Train," *The California Eagle*, October 7, 1948, 6.
51. Charlotta Bass, "Autobiography," 313–317, Charlotta A. Bass Papers, Southern California Library for Social Studies and Research (Los Angeles).
52. Robbie Lieberman, "Measure them Right: Lorraine Hansberry and the Struggle for Peace," *Science & Society* 75, no. 2 (April 2011): 218, 221; Michael Anderson, "Lorraine Hansberry, Freedom Family," *American Communist History* 7, no. 2 (2008): 264; Lorraine Hansberry to Edyth, July 31, 1948, Box 2, Folder 11, Lorraine Hansberry Papers, Schomburg Center for Research in Black Culture, Harlem, New York.
53. Ransby, *Eslanda*, 179, 184.
54. "Paul Robeson Show Stopped," *The Terra Haute Tribune*, January 11, 1948, 14; "Wallace," *Rushville Republican*, April 6, 1948, 4; Ransby, *Eslanda*, 185–86; Castledine, *Cold War Progressives*, 86.
55. Robert E. Hartley, *Battleground 1948: Truman, Stevenson, Douglas, and the Most Surprising Election in Illinois History* (Carbondale: Southern Illinois University Press, 2013), 194; Randy Mills, "'The Real Violence at Evansville': The Firing of Professor George F. Parker," *Indiana Magazine of History* XCIV (June 2003): 129–54; Thomas W. Devine, *Henry Wallace's 1948 Presidential Campaign and the future of Postwar Liberalism* (Chapel Hill: University of North Carolina Press, 2013), 273, 289.

56. Hartley, *Battleground 1948*, 194.
57. Charlotta Bass, "Autobiography," 317–18, Charlotta A. Bass Papers, Southern California Library for Social Studies and Research (Los Angeles).
58. "Throngs Cheer Wallace at Garment Area Rally," *Daily Worker*, October 29, 1948, 11; Claudia Jones, "CIO, AFL Unions already endorse Negro Congress," *Daily Worker*, May 26, 1946, 12.
59. Henry Wallace, "Personal Statement on the Korean Situation," and Progressive party, "National Committee Text on Korea and China," *National Guardian*, July 19, 1950, 4.
60. Robbie Lieberman, "Does that make Peace a Bad Word?' American Responses to the Communist Peace Offensive, 1949–1950," *Peace & Change* 17, no. 2: 199–200.
61. Michael Cox and Carolyn Kennedy-Pipe, "The Tragedy of American Diplomacy?" *Journal of Cold War Studies* 7, no. 1 (Spring 2005): 109–110.
62. Shirley Graham Du Bois, *His Day is Marching On: A Memoir of W.E.B. Du Bois* (Philadelphia: J.B. Lippincott and Company, 1971), 105, 116; "Program, The Cultural and Scientific Conference for World Peace," 25–27 March 1949, Shirley Graham Du Bois Papers, Schlesinger Library, Radcliffe Institute, Harvard University, Boston, Massachusetts.
63. Shirley Graham Du Bois, *His Day is Marching On: A Memoir of W.E.B. Du Bois* (Philadelphia: J.B. Lippincott and Company, 1971), 105, 116; "Program, The Cultural and Scientific Conference for World Peace," 25–27; Committee on Un-American Activities, U.S. House of Representatives, "Review of the Scientific and Cultural Conference for World Peace," April 19, 1949, Washington, DC, 9, 11, 19, 33, 41–42, 46, 55, 58.
64. Gao Yunxiang, *Arise Africa, Roar China: Black and Chinese Citizens of the World in the Twentieth Century* (Chapel Hill: University of North Carolina Press, 2021), 34; Graham Du Bois, *His Day is Marching On*, 104, 107; Charles Grutzner, "Cultural Visas Denied to British," *New York Times*, March 22, 1949, 1; Lieberman, "Does that make Peace a Bad Word?' 204; Phillip Deery, "Shostakovich, the Waldorf Conference, and the Cold War," *American Communist History* 11, no. 2 (2012): 168.
65. Graham Du Bois, *His Day is Marching On*, 105, 116.
66. National Council of Arts, Sciences, and Professions, "Cultural and Scientific Conference for World Peace Program, March 27, 1949, 82, W. E. B. Du Bois Papers, University of Massachusetts, Amherst, Massachusetts; Gerald Horne, *Race Woman: The Lives of Shirley Graham Du Bois* (New York: New York University Press, 2000), 110–11.
67. Deery, "Shostakovich, the Waldorf Conference, and the Cold War," 162–63, 165, 170–71.
68. Deery, "Shostakovich, the Waldorf Conference, and the Cold War," 162–63, 165, 170–71; Lieberman, "Does that Make Peace a Bad Word?" 205.
69. Lieberman, "Does that Make Peace a Bad Word?" 205; House Committee on Un-American Activities, "The Communist 'Peace' Offensive: A Campaign to Disarm

and Defeat the United States," U.S. House of Representatives, Washington, DC, April 1, 1951, 11.

70. W. E. B. Du Bois, *In Battle for Peace: The Story of my 83rd Birthday*, 29. Shirley Graham Du Bois Papers, Schlesinger Library, Radcliffe Institute, Harvard University, Boston, Massachusetts.

71. Gerald Horne, *Paul Robeson: The Artist as Revolutionary* (New York: Pluto Press, 2015), 115; Graham Du Bois, *His Day is Marching On*, 108–109.

72. Graham Du Bois, *His Day is Marching On*, 117; Charisse Burden-Stelly, ""In Battle for Peace during 'Scoundrel Time': W.E.B. Du Bois and United States Repression of Radical Black Peace Activism," *Du Bois Review* 16, no. 2 (2019): 559.

73. Graham Du Bois, *His Day is Marching On*, 118–119; "Strengthen the Peace Front Everywhere," *In Defence of Peace*, August 1949, 1–2, World Peace Council Collected Records, 1949–1996, Swarthmore College Peace Collection, Swarthmore, Pennsylvania.

74. Graham Du Bois, *His Day is Marching On*, 118–119; "Strengthen the Peace Front Everywhere," *In Defence of Peace*, August 1949, 1–2, World Peace Council Collected Records, 1949–1996, Swarthmore College Peace Collection, Swarthmore, Pennsylvania; W. E. B. Du Bois, *In Battle for Peace: The Story of my 83rd Birthday*, 31. Shirley Graham Du Bois Papers, Schlesinger Library, Radcliffe Institute, Harvard University, Boston, Massachusetts

75. "Organization and Action of the World Committee of Partisans of Peace," *In Defence of Peace*, August 1949, 31, World Peace Council Collected Records, 1949–1996, Swarthmore College Peace Collection, Swarthmore, Pennsylvania; Graham Du Bois, *His Day is Marching On*, 120.

76. Graham Du Bois, *In Battle for Peace*, 30–31; Graham Du Bois, *His Day is Marching On*, 122, 124.

77. Graham Du Bois, *His Day is Marching On*, 121.

78. "Open Letter from Lubya Kosmodemyanskaya to Elizabeth Moos," July 1949, W. E. B. Du Bois Papers, Special Collections and University Archives, University of Massachusetts, Amherst, Amherst, Massachusetts; "Dear Lyubov Kosmodemyanskaya, Mother of Zoya and Alexander, Noble Woman of the Soviet Union," Shirley Graham Du Bois Papers, Schlesinger Library, Radcliffe Institute, Harvard University, Boston, Massachusetts.

79. Horne, *Paul Robeson*, 121–24; Joseph Fronczak, "The Fascists Game: Transnational Political Transmission and the Genesis of the U.S. Modern Right," *Journal of American History* (December 2018): 563–65, 586; Samuel White, "Popular Anticommunism and the UE in Evansville, IN" in *American Labor and the Cold War: Grassroots Politics and Postwar Political Culture*, eds., Robert Cherny, William Issel, Kiernan Walsh Taylor (New Brunswick: Rutgers University Press, 2004), 142–43; "Dear Lyubov Kosmodemyanskaya, Mother of Zoya and Alexander, Noble Woman of the Soviet Union," Shirley Graham Du Bois Papers, Schlesinger Library, Radcliffe Institute, Harvard University, Boston, Massachusetts; Shirley

Graham Du Bois, 22, Part 1, Shirley Graham Du Bois File, Federal Bureau of Investigation file.
80. Committee on Un-American Activities, "Report on the Communist 'Peace' Offensive: A Campaign to Disarm and Defeat the United States," April 1, 1951, U.S. House of Representatives: Washington, DC. 16–18.
81. Graham Du Bois, *His Day is Marching On*, 123; Shirley Graham Du Bois, 22, Part 1, Shirley Graham Du Bois File, Federal Bureau of Investigation file; "The Battle for Peace," *In Defence of Peace*, August 1949, 29, World Peace Council Collected Records, 1949–1996, Swarthmore College Peace Collection, Swarthmore, Pennsylvania; Graham Du Bois, *In Battle for Peace*, 33.

CHAPTER TWO

1. Claudia Jones, "Warmakers fear America's women," *Daily Worker*, August 7, 1951, 5.
2. Jones, "Warmakers fear America's women," 5.
3. Jones, "Warmakers fear America's women," 5.
4. Mary L. Dudziak, "The Gloss of War" (February 15, 2022), 4. *Michigan Law Review*, http://dx.doi.org/10.2139/ssrn.4049263.
5. Bruce Cumings, *The Korean War: A History* (New York: The Modern Library, 2010), 51–55.
6. Cumings, *The Korean War*, 58; Bruce Cumings, "A Murderous History of Korea," *London Review of Books* 39, no. 10–18 (May 2017): 3.
7. Oliver Elliott, *The American Press and the Cold War: The Rise of Authoritarianism in South Korea, 1945–1954* (Cham, Switzerland: Palgrave MacMillan, 2018), 10; Cumings, *The Korean War*, 58, 106; Cumings, "A Murderous History of Korea," 3.
8. Elliott, *The American Press and the Cold War*, 13; Cumings, "A Murderous History of Korea," 3.
9. Cumings, *The Korean War*, 139, 141, 144–45; Cumings, "A Murderous History of Korea," 3.
10. Vincent Intondi, *African Americans Against the Bomb: Nuclear Weapons, Colonialism, and the Black Freedom Movement* (Stanford, CA: Stanford University Press, 2015), 10–11.
11. Leilah Danielson, *American Gandhi: A.J. Muste and the History of Radicalism in the Twentieth Century* (Philadelphia: University of Pennsylvania Press, 2014), 242–243; Intondi, *African Americans Against the Bomb*, 12.
12. Albert Einstein, "Arms Can Bring No Security," *Bulletin of Atomic Scientists* 76, no. 6 (2020): 350. Reprint of articles from March 1950 edition.
13. Intondi, *African Americans Against the Bomb*, 13–15.
14. Robbie Lieberman, "'Measure them Right:' Lorraine Hansberry and the Struggle for Peace," Vol 75, 2 *Science & Society* (April 2011): 218; Shirley Graham Du Bois, *His Day is Marching On: A Memoir of W.E.B. Du Bois* (Philadelphia: Lippincott,

1971), 90; "What Other Papers Say," *California Eagle*, September 20, 1945, 6; Charlotta Bass, "The Sidewalk," *The California Eagle*, August 25, 1950, 3.
15. Graham Du Bois, *His Day is Marching On*, 90.
16. Graham Du Bois, *His Day is Marching On*, 124.
17. Peace Information Center. Peace-gram vol. 1, no.1, ca. May 12, 1950. W. E. B. Du Bois Papers (MS 312). Special Collections and University Archives, University of Massachusetts Amherst Libraries; Intondi, *African Americans Against the Bomb*, 32.
18. Claudia Jones, "Women Crusade for Peace," *The Worker*, March 12, 1950, 1.
19. Jones, "Women Crusade for Peace," 10.
20. Jones, "Women Crusade for Peace," 1.
21. Christina Mislan, "Claudia Jones Speaks to '"Half the World":' Gendering Cold War Politics in the *Daily Worker*, 1950–1953," *Feminist Media Studies* 17, no. 2 (2017): 283, 285.
22. Claudia Jones, "Half of the World," *Daily Worker*, April 2, 1950, 11.
23. "Peace Drive Discussed by Women's Meet," *Daily Worker*, April 9, 1950, 9; Claudia Jones, "Half of the World," *Daily Worker*, May 21, 1950, 11.
24. Danielson, *American Gandhi*, 258; "Fast for Peace Begun," *New York Times*, April 2, 1950, 32; Intondi, *African Americans Against the Bomb*, 36–37.
25. Shirley Graham Du Bois, 23, Part 1, Shirley Graham Du Bois File, Federal Bureau of Investigation file; "Nationwide Peace Drive Opens," *The Worker*, June 11, 1950, 3; Mark Phillip Bradley and Mary L. Dudziak, eds., *Making the Forever War: Marilyn B. Young on the Culture and Politics of American Militarism* (Amherst: University of Massachusetts Press, 2021).
26. 100 Negro Leaders Hit Intervention in Korea as War for Slavery," *Daily Worker*, July 24, 1950, 8.
27. David Vine, *The United States of War: A Global History of America's Endless Conflicts, From Columbus to the Islamic State* (Oakland: University of California Press, 2020), 6, 168, 195.
28. Matthew Farish, "The Ordinary Cold War: The Ground Observer Corp and Midcentury Militarization in the United States," *Journal of American History* (December 2016): 642; Masuda Hajimu, *Cold War Crucible: The Korean Conflict and the Postwar World* (Cambridge, MA: Harvard University Press, 2015), 6.
29. Vine, *The United States of War*, 132.
30. Du Bois, *In Battle for Peace*, 40.
31. Charlotta Bass, "The Sidewalk," *California Eagle*, August 25, 1950, 3; Charlotta Bass, section 2, page 67, section 3, page 59–61, Charlotta Bass Federal Bureau of Investigation File.
32. Du Bois, *In Battle for Peace*, 40; Peace Information Center. Partial list of prominent Americans endorsing the World Peace Appeal, August 14, 1950. W. E. B. Du Bois Papers (MS 312). Special Collections and University Archives, University of Massachusetts Amherst Libraries; Charlotta Bass, "The Sidewalk," *California Eagle*, 1 September 1950, 3.

33. Mary Dudziak, *Wartime: An Idea, its History, and its Consequences* (Oxford, UK: Oxford University Press, 2012), 4.
34. Du Bois, W. E. B. (William Edward Burghardt), 1868-1963. Letter from W. E. B. Du Bois to United States Department of State, July 14, 1950. W. E. B. Du Bois Papers (MS 312). Special Collections and University Archives, University of Massachusetts Amherst Libraries; "US Press Cites Fraud in Communist Peace Petition," Information Bulletin, September 1950, 43.
35. Peace Information Center. The meaning of the case against the Peace Information Center, ca. 1951. W. E. B. Du Bois Papers (MS 312). Special Collections and University Archives, University of Massachusetts Amherst Libraries.
36. Shirley Graham Du Bois, "In Defense of the Peace Information Defendants," 1952, W. E. B. Du Bois Papers, University of Massachusetts, Amherst, Massachusetts; SAC, Los Angeles to Director of the FBI, July 23, 1951, "Dr. W.E.B. Du Bois; Shirley Graham aka Mrs. W.E.B. Du Bois," Security Matter-C, 1-2, Shirley Graham Du Bois FBI file; Du Bois, W. E. B. (William Edward Burghardt), 1868-1963. We can now speak for peace in the United States, May 9, 1952. W. E. B. Du Bois Papers (MS 312). Special Collections and University Archives, University of Massachusetts Amherst Libraries.
37. For more on the Du Bois' book see: W. E. B. Du Bois. *In Battle for Peace: The Story of My 83rd Birthday*. New York: Masses and Mainstream, 1952 and Denise Lynn and Phillip Luke Sinitiere, "W.E.B. Du Bois's *In Battle for Peace*: Historical and Political Perspectives," *American Communist History* 21, no. 3-4 (2022): 145-149. The issue of the journal is devoted to Du Bois's book.
38. Committee on Un-American Activities, "Report on the Communist 'Peace' Offensive: A Campaign to Disarm and Defeat the United States," April 1, 1951, U.S. House of Representatives: Washington, DC. 29, 31-32.
39. Shirley Graham Du Bois, 25, Part 1, Shirley Graham Du Bois File, Federal Bureau of Investigation file; Shirley Graham Du Bois to Veb Bibliographisches Institut, January 30, 1956, Shirley Graham Du Bois Papers, Radcliffe Institute for Advanced Study, Harvard University, Boston, Massachusetts.
40. National Council of Arts, Sciences, and Professions, "Cultural and Scientific Conference for World Peace Program, March 27, 1949, 82, W. E. B. Du Bois Papers, University of Massachusetts, Amherst, Massachusetts.
41. John Pittman, "The Negro and America's Wars: The Long Struggle for Peace," *The Masses & Mainstream*, 1952, 38.
42. Pittman, "The Negro and America's Wars," 39.
43. Erik McDuffie, "For a New Anti-fascist, Anti-imperialist People's Coalition: Claudia Jones, Black Left Feminism, and the Politics of Possibility in the Era of Trump," in *Post-Cold War Revelations and the American Communist Party*, eds. Vernon L. Pedersen, James G. Ryan, and Katherine A. S. Sibley (London: Bloomsbury Academic, 2021), 194-195.
44. Claudia Jones, "Half the World," *The Worker*, May 13, 1951, 8.
45. John Galtung, "An Editorial," *Journal of Peace Research*, Vol. 1, 1 (1964): 1-4.

46. Claudia Jones, "Half the World," *The Worker*, April 22, 1951, 8; Harry Truman, "Recall of General MacArthur," Recall of General MacArthur, August 2017, 1, https://search.ebscohost.com/login.aspx?direct=true&AuthType=sso&db=pwh&AN=21212903&site=eds-live&scope=site&authtype=sso&custid=s8876348.
47. Claudia Jones, "Half the World," *The Worker*, June 17, 1951, 8.
48. Claudia Jones, "Half the World," *Daily Worker*, July 16, 1950, 11; Claudia Jones, "Half the World," *The Worker*, August 19, 1951, 11.
49. Taewoo Kim, "Frustrated Peace: Investigatory Activities by the Commission of the Women's International Democratic Federation in North Korea during the Korean War," *Sungkyun Journal of East Asian Studies*, Vol. 20, 1 (April 2020): 87; Yulia Gradskova, *Democratic Federation, the Global South, and the Cold War: Defending the Rights of Women of the "Whole World?"* (London: Routledge, 2021), 90.
50. Suzy Kim, "The Origins of Cold War Feminism during the Korean War," *Gender & History*, Vol. 31, 2 (July 2019): 460, 462, 473–474.
51. Kim, "Frustrated Peace, 87; Gradskova, *Democratic Federation, the Global South, and the Cold War*, 90.
52. "Hear Testimony today against Arm-Americas Bill," *Daily Worker*, July 22, 1946, 1; "Dennis urges Senate to kill War Pact; Urges Arms Cuts," *Daily Worker*, May 12, 1949, 3; "Joint Conference formed against Intervention," *Daily Worker*, March 19, 1947, 2; "Kill war Pact, Women Urge," *Daily Worker*, July 14, 1949, 8; Kate Weigand, *Red Feminism: American Communist and the Making of Women's Liberation* (Baltimore: Johns Hopkins University Press, 2001), 48.
53. Congress of American Women, "International Women's Day," March 8, 1949, Series III, CAW, Betty Millard Papers, Sophia Smith Collection, Smith College, Northampton, Massachusetts.
54. Weigand, *Red Feminism*, 48–49, 55; House Committee on Un-American Activities, "Report on the Congress of American Women," (Washington D.C.: United States Government Printing Office, 1949), 69–71, 73, 83, 91–92, 98, 107, 115.
55. Jones, "Women Crusade for Peace," 1.
56. Claudia Jones, "Women's Organizations in the Struggle for Peace," *Daily Worker*, 13 February 1951, 1; "A New Stage in the Struggle for Peace," WIDF *Information Bulletin*, March–April 1950, 1, and "To the Women of Korea," WIDF *Information Bulletin*, June 1950, 1, Box 4, Folder 5, Women's International Democratic Federation Papers, Sophia Smith Collection, Smith College, Northampton, Massachusetts.
57. Claudia Jones, "Women's Organizations in the Struggle for Peace," *Daily Worker*, 13 February 1951, 1.
58. Charlotta Bass, "The Sidewalk" 28 September 1950, *The California Eagle*, p. 3; Francisca de Haan, "Eugenie Cotton, Pak Chong-ae, and Claudia Jones: Rethinking Transnational Feminism and International Politics," Vol. 25, No. 4, *The Journal of Women's History*, (Winter 2013), 179.
59. Clapson, *The Blitz Campaign*, 151; Gradskova, *The Women's International Democratic Federation, the Global South, and the Cold War*, 88; Eric Talmadge,

"64 Years after Korean War, North Still Digging up Bombs," Associated Press, July 24, 1917, https://apnews.com/article/international-news-asia-pacific-ap-top-news-north-korea-dd6256bad51e458cb2e8a1bf64b5c2b6.
60. Gradskova, *Democratic Federation, the Global South, and the Cold War*, 66; Women's International Democratic Federation, *We Accuse!* Berlin, Germany: Women's International Democratic Federation, 1951, 6–7.
61. Claudia Jones, "Half the World," *The Worker*, August 5, 1951, 8.
62. Claudia Jones, "Half the World," *The Worker*, August 5, 1951, 8; Elizabeth Gurley Flynn, "'Half the World', Guest Column," *The Worker*, June 10, 1951, 8.
63. Claudia Jones, "Half the World," *The Worker*, December 9, 1951, 8.
64. Kim, "Frustrated Peace," 92, 106; Claudia Jones, "Half the World," *The Worker*, December 9, 1951, 8.
65. Gradskova, *Democratic Federation, the Global South, and the Cold War*, 66; Elizabeth B. Armstrong, *Bury the Corpse of Colonialism: The Revolutionary Feminist Conference of 1949* (Berkeley: University of California Press, 2023), 137; Claudia Jones, "Half the World," *The Worker*, December 9, 1951, 8.
66. "Korean Women accuse Aerial Pirates," *Freedom*, February 1951, 6.
67. Kim, "Frustrated Peace," 83, 88; Carl R. Weinberg, "Massacre at No Gun Ri?: American Military Policy toward Civilian Refugees during the Korean War," *OAH Magazine of History* (October 2008): 58–60; McDuffie, "For a new Anti-fascist, Anti-imperialist people's coalition," 194.
68. Claudia Jones, "Half the World," *The Worker*, December 9, 1951, 8; Kim, "Frustrated Peace," 89, 92; Monica Kim, *The Interrogation Rooms of the Korean War: The Untold History* (Princeton, NJ: Princeton University Press, 2019), 59–60.
69. Kim, "Frustrated Peace," 83, 88.
70. Armstrong, *Bury the Corpse of Colonialism*, 140.
71. Bradley and Dudziak, *Making the Forever War*, 39.
72. Hajimu, *Cold War Crucible*, 6; Dudziak, *Wartime*, 92.
73. Claudia Jones, "Half the World," *The Worker*, August 19, 1951, 11.
74. Claudia Jones, "The Struggle for Peace in the United States," *Political Affairs*, February 1952, 2.
75. Jones, "The Struggle for Peace in the United States," 2.
76. Jones, "The Struggle for Peace in the United States," 2–3.
77. Graham Du Bois, *His Day is Marching On*, 123; Jones, "The Struggle for Peace in the United States," 2–3, 20; Charisse Burden-Stelly and Gerald Horne, "Third World Internationalism and the Global Color Line," in *The Cambridge History of America and the World, Volume IV, 1945 to the Present*, editors, David C. Engerman, Max Paul Friedman, and Melanie McAlister, 370–396 (Cambridge, UK: Cambridge University Press, 2021).
78. Beulah Richardson, *A Black Woman Speaks . . . of White Womanhood of White Supremacy of Peace* (New York: American Women for Peace, 1951), 3–6.
79. Richardson, *A Black Woman Speaks*, 9; Claudia Jones, *An End to the Neglect of the Problems of the Negro Woman* (New York: Political Affairs, 1949), 17.

80. Richardson, *A Black Woman Speaks*, 10; Beulah Richardson, "Genocide," pp. 1–2, Box 27 Folder 9, Civil Rights Congress Papers, Gale Cengage.
81. Erik McDuffie, "A "New Freedom Movement of Negro Women:' Sojourning for Truth, Justice, and Human Rights during the Cold War," *Radical History Review*, 101 (Spring 2008): 82; McDuffie, *Sojourning for Freedom*, 173; Dayo Gore, "The Danger of Being an Active Anti-Communist:' Expansive Black Left Politics and the Long Civil Rights Movement," *American Communist History*, Vol. 11, 1 (2012): 47; James Smethhurst, "Claudia Jones, The West Indian Gazette and Afro-Asian Caribbean News and the Rise of a New Black Radicalism in the UK and US," *Science & Society*, Vol. 87, 2 (April 2023): 266.
82. McDuffie, *Sojourning for Freedom*, 174.
83. McDuffie, *Sojourning for Freedom*, 174.
84. Sojourners for Truth and Justice, "A Call to Negro Womanhood," Box 12, Folder 17, Louise Thompson Patterson Papers, Special Collections, Robert W. Woodruff Library, Emory University, Atlanta, GA; Charlotta Bass, "Why We're Going to Washington," *Daily Worker*, September 27, 1951, 2.
85. Sojourners for Truth and Justice, "A Call to Negro Womanhood," Box 12, Folder 17, Louise Thompson Patterson Papers, Special Collections, Robert W. Woodruff Library, Emory University, Atlanta, GA.
86. Sojourners for Truth and Justice, "A Call to Negro Womanhood," Box 12, Folder 17, Louise Thompson Patterson Papers, Special Collections, Robert W. Woodruff Library, Emory University, Atlanta, GA.
87. Lorraine Hansberry, "Women Voice Demands in Capital Sojourner," *Freedom*, October 1951, 6.
88. "Where was the FBI? Women Demand Justice be done," *Freedom*, October 1951, 6.
89. Beulah Richardson, Initiating Committee, STJ to Alexander Pace, Secretary of War, War Department, September 25, 1951; Beulah Richardson, Initiating Committee to the White House, September 25, 1951, Box 12, Folder 17, Louise Thompson Patterson Papers, Special Collections, Robert W. Woodruff Library, Emory University, Atlanta, GA. Richardson's language in the letter is pointed and a bit dated, which might have been intentional. She called it the War department and the Secretary of War which had changed in 1947 to the Department of Defense and the Secretary of Defense, clearly more intentional labels.
90. "Sojourners for Truth and Justice," September 27, 1951; Mr. F.J. Baumgadner to Mr. A.H. Belmont, October 18, 1951, Sojourners for Truth and Justice file, Federal Bureau of Investigation.
91. Carole Boyce Davies, *Left of Karl Marx: The Political Life of Black Communist Claudia Jones* (Durham, NC: Duke University Press, 2007): 82–83; Claudia Jones, "Half the World," *The Worker*, November 25, 1951, 8.
92. Claudia Jones, "Half the World," *The Worker*, November 25, 1951, 8.
93. Claudia Jones, "Sojourners for Truth and Justice," *The Worker*, February 10, 1952, 8.

94. Claudia Jones, "Half the World," *The Worker*, November 25, 1951, 8; "We Negro Women Demand the Following," Box 12, Folder 17, Louise Thompson Patterson Papers, Special Collections, Robert W. Woodruff Library, Emory University, Atlanta, GA.
95. Richard O. Boyer, "Why 6 Negro Leaders Defend Claudia Jones," *Daily Worker*, February 25, 1952, 5.
96. "Mrs. Bass Urges support to move to free Claudia Jones," *Daily Worker*, 3 April 1955, 13; "Claudia Jones denied diet prescribed for heart illness," *Daily Worker*, 7 March 1955, 6; "Hear Health Plea Monday by Claudia Jones, Jacob Mandel," Daily Worker, 23 January 1955, 2.
97. Soyica Diggs Colbert, *Radical Vision: A Biography of Lorraine Hansberry* (New Haven, CT: Yale University Press, 2021), 48; Lorraine Hansberry, "'Illegal' Conference Shows Peace is Key to Freedom," *Freedom*, April 1952, 3; Lorraine Hansberry, "Speech at American Peace Congress," May 28, 1952, Box 3, Folder 66, Lorraine Hansberry Papers, Schomburg Center for Research in Black Culture, Harlem, New York.
98. Lorraine Hansberry, "'Illegal' Conference Shows Peace is Key to Freedom," *Freedom*, April 1952, 3.
99. Lorraine Hansberry, "Untitled," 1952, Box 3, Folder 66, Lorraine Hansberry Papers, Schomburg Center for Research in Black Culture, Harlem, New York.
100. State Department, "Refusal," Passport Application, March 13, 1952, Box 5, Folder 72, Lorraine Hansberry Papers, Schomburg Center for Research in Black Culture, Harlem, New York; Lorraine Hansberry, "A Negro Woman Speaks for Peace," *The Worker*, June 22, 1952, 8.

CHAPTER THREE

1. Monica Kim, *The Interrogation Rooms of the Korean War: The Untold History* (Princeton, NJ: Princeton University Press, 2019), 7–8; Eslanda Robeson, "Southern Officers treat Korean POWs like Negroes in the South," *Freedom*, July 1952, 5.
2. Kim, *The Interrogation Rooms of the Korean War*, 171–174; Robeson, "Southern Officers Treat Korean POWs like Negroes in the South," 5.
3. Kim, *The Interrogation Rooms of the Korean War*, 12; Robeson, "Southern Officers Treat Korean POWs like Negroes in the South," 5.
4. C.B. Baldwin, Secretary and Campaign Manager, Progressive Party to Members of Congress, May 29, 1952, Folder 11, Box 126, and "Text of the Red Cross Report on Koje PW Incident", reprint from *The Daily Compass*, May 27, 1952), 27 May 1952, Mixed Materials, Box 147, Jessie Lloyd O'Connor papers, Sophia Smith Collection, SSC-MS-00254, Smith College Special Collections, Northampton, Massachusetts.
5. Kim, *The Interrogation Rooms of the Korean War*, 263, 287, 304–5.
6. Christine Hong, *A Violent Peace: Race, U.S. Militarism, And Cultures of Democratization in Cold War Asia and the Pacific* (Stanford, CA: Stanford University Press, 2020), 48, 49, 51.

7. Charisse Burden-Stelly, *Black Scare/Red Scare: Theorizing Capitalist Racism in the United States* (Chicago: University of Chicago Press, 2023), 96–97.
8. Hong, *A Violent Peace*, 24.
9. "Demand Army investigate discrimination in Asia," *The California Eagle*, August 11, 1950, 2.
10. Brief for the Civil Rights Congress as Amicus Curae, p. 1, *Gilbert v. United States*, Box 7, A. 116, Civil Rights Congress Papers, Schomburg Center for Research in Black Culture, Harlem, New York; Mitchell Lerner, "'It is for this we fought and bled?' The Korean War and the Struggle for Civil Rights," *The Journal of Military History*, Vol. 82 (2018): 531, 535.
11. Brief for the Civil Rights Congress as Amicus Curae, p. 1–2, *Gilbert v. United States*; Lerner, "'It is for this we fought and bled?'" 531, 535.
12. "Free Lieutenant Gilbert," *California Eagle*, December 14, 1950, 5.
13. Lerner, "'It is for this we fought and bled?'" 536–38, 545; "Lt. Gilbert says: Jimcrow killed my baby," *Daily Worker*, January 29, 1951, 4; Keith Gilyard, *Louise Thompson Patterson: A Life of Struggle for Justice* (Durham, NC: Duke University Press, 2017), 159; Brief for the Civil Rights Congress as Amicus Curae, p. 1–2, *Gilbert v. United States*.
14. Brief for the Civil Rights Congress as Amicus Curae, p. 1–2, 5–6, *Gilbert v. United States*.
15. Thurgood Marshall, "Summary Justice—The Negro GI in Korea," *The Crisis*, Vol. 58 (May 1951): 298.
16. Lerner, "'It is for this we fought and bled?'" 536–38, 545; "Unfairness seen in Courts Martial," *New York Times*, March 2, 1951, 3.
17. Lerner, "'It is for this we fought and bled?'" 536–38, 545; Marshall, "Summary Justice—The Negro GI in Korea," 300.
18. Lerner, "'It is for this we fought and bled?'" 536–538, 545; "Unfairness seen in Courts Martial," *New York Times*, March 2, 1951, 3; Marshall, "Summary Justice—The Negro GI in Korea," 300–305.
19. Claudia Jones, "Half the World," *The Worker*, April 22, 1951, 8; "Urge Truman Free Victim of Jim Crow," *California Eagle*, November 10, 1950, 1.
20. "Lt. Gilbert says: Jimcrow killed my baby," *Daily Worker*, January 29, 1951, 4; Gilyard, *Louise Thompson Patterson*, 159; Beulah Richardson, Initiating Committee, STJ to Alexander Pace, Secretary of War, War Department, September 25, 1951, Box 12, Folder 17, Louise Thompson Patterson Papers, Special Collections, Robert W. Woodruff Library, Emory University, Atlanta, GA.
21. William Patterson, "A Letter to Mrs. Gilbert," *Daily Worker*, March 7, 1951, 2; Burden-Stelly, *Black Scare/Red Scare*, 223.
22. William T. Bowers, William M. Hammond, and George L. MacGarrigle. *Black Soldiers, White Army: The 24th Infantry Regiment in Korea* (Washington, DC.: Center of Military History, United States Army, 1996), 186, 267.
23. Charisse Burden-Stelly, "In Battle for Peace During Scoundrel Time: W.E.B. Du Bois and United States Repression of Radical Black Peace Activism," *Du Bois*

Review 16, no. 2: 559; Civil Rights Congress, "Jim Crow in New York and Korea," 1950, Folder 116, Box 7, Civil Rights Congress Papers, Schomburg Center for Research in Black Culture, Harlem, New York.

24. Jones, "For the Unity of Women in the Cause of Peace," 159; "Midwest College Students Hear Jones on McGee Case," *Daily Worker*, 25 May 1951, 2; "Willie McGee," *Daily Worker*, 20 May 1952, 8; Leandra Zarnow, "Braving Jim Crow to Save Willie McGee: Bella Abzug, the Legal Left, and Civil Rights Innovation, 1948–1951," *Law & Social Inquiry* 33, no. 4: (Fall 2008) 1006–7.
25. "Mrs. McGee Tells Story of Pursuit by White Woman," *California Eagle*, April 26, 1951, 1, 6.
26. Civil Rights Congress, "Fact Sheet on the Willie McGee Case," April 15, 1949, Box 44, Folder 4, Mary Kaufmann Papers, Sophia Smith Collection, Smith College, Northampton, Massachusetts.
27. Zarnow, "Braving Jim Crow to Save Willie McGee," 1006–7, 1010, 1031; "Midwest College Students Hear Jones on McGee Case," *Daily Worker*, May 25, 1951, 2.
28. *Willie McGee v. J.P. Coleman, et. al*, United States District Court for the Southern District of Mississippi, Box 44, Folder 8, Mary Kaufmann Papers, Sophia Smith Collection, Smith College, Northampton, Massachusetts.
29. Jackson Daily News, "An Animal We Don't Know," July 20, 1950, Box 44, Folder 4, Mary Kaufmann Papers, Sophia Smith Collection, Smith College, Northampton, Massachusetts.
30. Zarnow, "Braving Jim Crow to Save Willie McGee," 1006–7; Erik McDuffie, *Sojourning for Freedom: Black Women, American Communism, and the Making of Black Left Feminism* (Durham, NC: Duke University Press, 2011) 11; Dayo Gore, "A Black Woman Speaks: Beah Richards Life of Protest and Poetry," in Howard Brick, Robbie Lieberman, and Paula Rabinowitz, eds., *Lineages of the Literary Left: Essays in Honor of Alan M. Wald* (Ann Arbor: Michigan Publishing Services, 2015); Beulah Richardson, "A Black Woman Speaks ... of White Womanhood, of White Supremacy, of Peace," (New York: American Women for Peace, 1951), p. 2; Jones, "For the Unity of Women in the Cause of Peace," 159; "Midwest College Students Hear Jones on McGee Case," *Daily Worker*, May 25, 1951, 2; "Willie McGee," *Daily Worker*, May 20, 1952, 8.
31. Charlotta Bass, "The Sidewalk" July 28 1950, *The California Eagle*, 3–4.
32. Claudia Jones, "Half the World," *The Worker*, May 27, 1951, 8; McDuffie, *Sojourning for Freedom*, 183.
33. Richardson, "A Black Woman Speaks ... of White Womanhood, of White Supremacy, of Peace," 9–10.
34. Claudia Jones, "Half the World," *The Worker*, April 22, 1951, 8; Richardson, "A Black Woman Speaks ... of White Womanhood, of White Supremacy, of Peace," 2; Claudia Jones, "Half the World," *The Worker*, May 27, 1951, 8.
35. Claudia Jones, "Half the World," *The Worker*, May 27, 1951, 8.
36. Civil Rights Congress, "A Wife Pleads to Nation for Innocent Husband: 'Please don't let Willie McGee die,'" October 31, 1949, and "Statement of Rosalee McGee,"

July 25, 1950, Box 44, Folder 4, Mary Kaufmann Papers, Sophia Smith Collection, Smith College, Northampton, Massachusetts.
37. Claudia Jones, "Half the World," *The Worker*, May 27, 1951, 8.
38. Zarnow, "Braving Jim Crow to Save Willie McGee," 1003; Lorraine Hansberry, "Freedom," Box 57, Folder 9, Lorraine Hansberry Papers, Schomburg Center for Research in Black Culture, Harlem, New York; Soyica Diggs Colbert, *Radical Vision: A Biography of Lorraine Hansberry* (New Haven, CT: Yale University Press, 2021), 42–43.
39. Shirley Graham, "Oh No Brother, No One is Going to Forget About Willie McGee," *Freedom*, June 1951, 1.
40. Graham, "Oh No Brother, No One is Going to Forget About Willie McGee," 1, 2.
41. "Negro Leaders Wife also Dies in Bombing," *New York Times*, January 4, 1952, 14; Jake C. Miller, "Harry T. Moore's Campaign for Racial Equality," *Journal of Black Studies* 31, no. 2: (November 2000) 214; James C. Clark, "Civil Rights Leader Harry T. Moore and the Ku Klux Klan in Florida," *The Florida Historical Quarterly* 73, no. 2: 166.
42. Gloster B. Current, "Martyr for a Cause," NAACP Pamphlet, May 1952.
43. "Bias Report cites Bombing in Florida," *New York Times*, December 30, 1951, 16; Clarence Mitchell, "The People vs. Winstead of Mississippi," *The Crisis*, May 1952, 308.
44. Claudia Jones, "Sojourners for Truth and Justice," *The Worker*, February 10, 1952, 8.
45. "Shown at Newark on New Years Eve," *Daily Worker*, January 4, 1952, 3; Betty Feldman, "North or South, It's the same vile foe," *The Worker*, March 2, 1952, 8.
46. Feldman, "North or South, It's the same vile foe," 8.
47. Feldman, "North or South, It's the same vile foe," 8.
48. "12 States send Mourners to Mrs. Moore's Funeral," *Daily Worker*, January 7, 1952, 1.
49. Charlotta Bass Speech, January 1952, Progressive Party 1952 Speeches, Charlotta A. Bass Papers, Southern California Library for Social Studies and Research, Los Angeles, California.
50. Charlotta Bass Speech, January 1952, Progressive Party 1952 Speeches, Charlotta A. Bass Papers, Southern California Library for Social Studies and Research, Los Angeles, California.
51. "Officials Jittery as fight mounts against Florida terror," *Daily Worker*, January 20, 1952, 4; Charlotta Bass Speech, January 1952, Progressive party 1952 Speeches, Charlotta A. Bass Papers, Southern California Library for Social Studies and Research, Los Angeles, California.
52. Charlotta Bass Speech, January 1952, Progressive Party 1952 Speeches, Charlotta A. Bass Papers, Southern California Library for Social Studies and Research, Los Angeles, California.
53. Charlotta Bass Speech, January 1952, Progressive Party 1952 Speeches, Charlotta A. Bass Papers, Southern California Library for Social Studies and Research, Los Angeles, California; Erik S. McDuffie, *Sojourning for Freedom: Black Women,*

American Communism, and the Making of Black Left Feminism (Durham, NC: Duke University Press, 2011), 176.
54. McDuffie, *Sojourning for Freedom*, 176.
55. Denise Lynn, "Gender Violence as Genocide: the Rosa Lee Ingram Case and We Charge Genocide Petition," *Radical Americas* 7, 1 (2022): 1. DOI: https://doi.org/10.14324/111.444.ra.2022.v7.1.001.
56. "Delegation to Georgia will Aid Negro Mother," *The Worker*, March 14, 1948, 2-A; Abner Berry, "White House Refuses to Aid Doomed Negro Mother, Sons," *Daily Worker*, March 18, 1948, 3; Lynn, Gender Violence as Genocide: the Rosa Lee Ingram Case and We Charge Genocide Petition"; Dayo Gore, *Radicalism at the Crossroads: African American Women Activists in the Cold War* (New York: New York University Press, 2011), 75.
57. Gore, *Radicalism at the Crossroads*, 75–76.
58. Jacqueline Castledine, "'In a Solid Bond of Unity:' Anticolonial Feminism in the Cold War Era," *Journal of Women's History* 20, no. 4 (Winter 2008): 66.
59. Erik McDuffie, "A 'New Freedom Movement of Negro Women:' Sojourning for Truth, Justice, and Human Rights during the Cold War," *Radical History Review*, 101 (Spring, 2008): 83–84; Cheryl Higashida, *Black Internationalist Feminism: Women Writers of the Black Left, 1945–1995* (Urbana: University of Illinois Press, 2011), 44.
60. Claudia Jones to Betty Millard, November 11, 1947, Betty Millard Papers, Sophia Smith Collection, Smith College, Northampton, Massachusetts; Claudia Jones, "An End to the Neglect of the Problems of the Negro Woman," *Political Affairs*, June 1949, 16.
61. Danielle McGuire, *At the Dark End of the Street: Black Women, Rape, and Resistance—a New History of the Civil Rights Movement from Rosa Parks to the Rise of Black Power* (New York: Random Books, 2010), 33–35; Allison Berg, "Trauma and Testimony in Black Women's Civil Rights Memoirs: The Montgomery Bus Boycott and the Women who started it, Warriors Don't Cry, and From the Mississippi Delta," *Journal of Women's History* 21, 3 (2009): 84–86; Jones, "An End to the Neglect of the Problems of the Negro Woman,"16.
62. Jones, "An End to the Neglect of the Problems of the Negro Woman,"16; McDuffie, "A 'New Freedom Movement of Negro Women," 84.
63. National Committee to Free the Ingram Family. Letter from National Committee to Free the Ingram Family to W. E. B. Du Bois, April 13, 1949, and National Committee to Free the Ingram Family. Petition from National Committee to Free the Ingram Family to President Harry S. Truman, ca. 1949, W. E. B. Du Bois Papers (MS 312). Special Collections and University Archives, University of Massachusetts Amherst Libraries.
64. Claudia Jones, "Peace is a Woman's Business," *Worker*, June 19, 1949, 4; Dr. Andrea Andreen, "The Struggle for the Winning of Women's Rights as Mothers Workers and Citizens," in WIDF, World Congress of Women, June 1953, 21, Box 2, Folder 3, and WIDF, *For their Rights as Mothers, Workers, Citizens*, 4, 33, Box 2,

Folder 19, WIDF Papers, Sophia Smith Collection, Smith College, Northampton, Massachusetts.

65. Constitution and By-Laws, Sojourners for Truth and Justice, and Charlotta Bass and Louise Thompson Patterson to New Member, January 14, 1952, Folder 17, Box 12, Louise Thompson Patterson Papers, Stuart A. Rose Manuscript, Archives, and Rare Book Library, Emory University, Atlanta, GA.

66. Claudia Jones, "Half the World," November 25, 1951, *The Worker*, 11; Claudia Jones, "Sojourners for Truth and Justice," February 10, 1952, *The Worker*, 8.

67. Sojourners for Truth and Justice, 26, Part 5, Sojourners for Truth and Justice, Federal Bureau of Investigation file.

68. Sojourners for Truth and Justice, 26–27, Part 5, Sojourners for Truth and Justice, Federal Bureau of Investigation file.

69. Sojourners for Truth and Justice, 29–34, 51–58, 79–93, Part 5, Sojourners for Truth and Justice, Federal Bureau of Investigation file.

70. McDuffie, "A 'New Freedom Movement of Negro Women,' 97–98; Sojourning for Truth, Justice 13, 50, Part 1, 5–13, 40, 29–34, 51–58, 79–93, Part 5, Sojourners for Truth and Justice, Federal Bureau of Investigation file; "Georgia Official Hints at Release of Ingrams," *Daily Worker*, June 13, 1957, 1; "Georgia Ignoring Ingrams," *Pittsburgh Courier*, October 5, 1957, 2; "11 Year Battle Wins Freedom of Mrs. Ingram," *Daily Worker*, September 6, 1959, 2.

71. William Patterson, *The Man who Cried Genocide: An Autobiography of William L. Patterson* (New York: International Publishers, 1971), XXVI, 175.

72. Hong, *A Violent Peace*, 170, 174–75, William Patterson, ed., *We Charge Genocide: The Crime of Government Against the Negro People* (New York: International Publishers, 1951), XIX.

73. Beulah Richardson, "Genocide," 5–10, Box 27 Folder 9, Civil Rights Congress Papers, Gale Cengage.

74. "Make the Rules of this Nation Heed!" *Freedom*, February 1952, 1; Charles H. Martin, "Internationalizing 'The American Dilemma': The Civil Rights Congress and the 1951 Genocide Petition to the United Nations," *Journal of American Ethnic History* 16, no. 4 (Summer 1997): 54.

75. Jones, "An End to the Neglect of the Problems of the Negro Woman," 16.

CHAPTER FOUR

1. Charlotta Bass, "Acceptance Speech," 1–2, July 1952, Charlotta A. Bass Papers, Southern California Library for Social Studies and Research, Los Angeles, California.

2. John S. Portlock, "In the Fabled Land of Make-Believe: Charlotta Bass and Jim Crow Los Angeles," in *The Strange Careers of the Jim Crow North: Segregation and Struggle Outside of the South*, editors Brian Purnell, Jeanne Theoharis and Komozi Woodard, 79–80 (New York: New York University Press, 2019); Roger Streitmatter, *African-American Women Journalists Who Changed History* (Lexington: University Press of Kentucky, 1994), 102–4.

3. Mitchell Lerner, "Is It for This We Fought and Bled? The Korean War and the Struggle for Civil Rights," *The Journal of Military History* 82 (April 2018): 515–16.
4. Charlotta Bass, "Uncle Tom is Not Dead," *The California Eagle*, July 14, 1950, 1.
5. Charlotta Bass, "Uncle Tom is Not Dead," 1, 4.
6. Charlotta Bass, "The Sidewalk" *The California Eagle*, July 28, 1950, 3–4.
7. The Korean People's Army, The Chinese People's Volunteers, "Negro Soldiers! There's a Letter for you inside, Read it!" circa 1950–1952, Box 1 Folder 13, Edward A Podesta Collection, University of California, Santa Cruz. University Library. Special Collections and Archives Santa Cruz, California 95064; Monica Kim, *The Interrogation Rooms of the Korean War: The Untold History* (Princeton, NJ: Princeton University Press, 2019), 307.
8. House Committee on Un-American Activities, "Testimony of Raphael Konigsberg," June 27 and 18, 1955, Investigation of Communist Activities in the California Area, (Washington: United States Government Printing Office, 1955), 1657; Raphael Konigsberg, "Who Do They Think They Are?" *The California Eagle*, September 8, 1950, 6: Raphael Konigsberg, "National Containment," *The California Eagle*, December 28, 1950, 5.
9. Konigsberg, "National Containment," 5; Raphael Konigsberg, "Truth will Rise," *The California Eagle*, December 7, 1950, 6.
10. Raphael Konigsberg, "Negroes Know Fascism," *The California Eagle*, September 14, 1950, 6; Charlotta Bass, "On the Sidewalk," *The California Eagle*, July 28, 1950, 3.
11. House Committee on Un-American Activities, "Testimony of Raphael Konigsberg," June 27 and 18, 1955, Investigation of Communist Activities in the California Area, (Washington: United States Government Printing Office, 1955), 1656–1666; Burt A. Folkart, "Raphael Konigsberg: Politics delayed admission to Bar," Los Angeles Times, June 12, 1991; Raphael Konigsberg v. State Bar of California, April 24, 1961, Legal Information Institute, Cornell Law School, https://www.law.cornell.edu/supremecourt/text/366/36.
12. Elizabeth Armstrong, "Before Bandung: The Anti-Imperialist Women's Movement in Asia and the Women's International Democratic Federation," *Signs* 41, no. 2 (Winter 2016): 307.
13. "Iota presentation," *The California Eagle*, December 8, 1949, 8; Charlotta Bass, "Autobiography," 349–350, Charlotta A. Bass Papers, Southern California Library for Social Studies and Research, Los Angeles, California; Elizabeth Armstrong, *Bury the Corpse of Colonialism: The Revolutionary Feminist Conference of 1949* (Oakland: University of California Press, 2023), 81.
14. "Miss Bass in Europe to Report on Continental Conditions," *The California Eagle*, August 18, 1950, 3; Charlotta Bass, "The Sidewalk," August 25, 1950, *The California Eagle*, 3.
15. Charlotta Bass, "The Sidewalk" 1 September 1950, *The California Eagle*, 3.
16. "Resolution of Solidarity with Korea, Speech by Lieutenant Colonel Kan Puk," Charlotta A. Bass Papers, Southern California Library for Social Studies and Research, Los Angeles, California.

17. Charlotta Bass, "Europe as I Saw It," *The California Eagle*, December 14, 1950, 3.
18. Charlotta Bass, "Autobiography," 362, 265, Charlotta A. Bass Papers, Southern California Library for Social Studies and Research, Los Angeles, California; Keeanga Yamatta-Taylor, *Race for Profit: How Banks and the Real Estate Industry Undermined Black Homeownership* (Chapel Hill: University of North Carolina Press, 2020), 57.
19. Charlotta Bass, "Autobiography," 367–369, Charlotta A. Bass Papers, Southern California Library for Social Studies and Research, Los Angeles, California; Streitmatter, *African-American Women Journalists Who Changed History*, 104.
20. Charlotta Bass, "Europe as I Saw It," *The California Eagle*, December 14, 1950, 3; Charlotta Bass, "Autobiography," 375, Charlotta A. Bass Papers, Southern California Library for Social Studies and Research, Los Angeles, California;.
21. Charlotta Bass, "Autobiography," 357, Charlotta A. Bass Papers, Southern California Library for Social Studies and Research, Los Angeles, California; House Committee on Un-American Activities, "Report on the Congress of American Women," (Washington D.C.: United States Government Printing Office, 1949), 36.
22. Charlotta Bass, "Autobiography," 375, Charlotta A. Bass Papers, Southern California Library for Social Studies and Research (Los Angeles).
23. Charlotta Bass, "Autobiography," 375, Charlotta A. Bass Papers, Southern California Library for Social Studies and Research (Los Angeles); "Mrs. Bass for Congress in 14th," The California Eagle, September 21, 1950, 1; "Enthusiastic Campaign for Election of Mrs. Bass Under Way," *The California Eagle*, September 28, 1950, 2.
24. Progressive party National Committee, "A time of danger to our country . . . such as America has never known," 1, September 16–17, 1950, Box 126, Folder 11, Jessie Lloyd O'Connor papers, Sophia Smith Collection, Smith College Special Collections, Northampton, Massachusetts.
25. Progressive party National Committee, "A time of danger to our country . . . such as America has never known," 2–3.
26. Shirley Graham Du Bois, *His Day is Marching On: A Memoir of W.E.B. Du Bois* (Philadelphia: Lippincott, 1971), 131.
27. Eslanda Robeson, "Loyalty: Lost and Found," Box 46, Folder 200, Progressive Party Papers, University of Iowa; "Mrs. Robeson will Speak at Rally at West Middle School," *Hartford Courant*, October 11, 1950, 25.
28. Eslanda Robeson, "Loyalty: Lost and Found," Box 46, Folder 200, Progressive Party Papers, University of Iowa.
29. "Vote for the People's party candidates," *Hartford Courant*, November 5, 1950, 7; Charlotta Bass, "On the Sidewalk," The California Eagle, October 26, 1950, 1.
30. Charlotta Bass, "On the Sidewalk," The California Eagle, October 26, 1950, 1: "Benton, Bush trade Verbal Punches; Crowd Hoots and Jeers Debaters," *Meriden Record*, October 24, 1950, 10; "Vote for the People's party candidates," *Hartford Courant*, November 5, 1950, 7.
31. Charlotta Bass, "Autobiography," 380–382, Charlotta A. Bass Papers, Southern California Library for Social Studies and Research, Los Angeles, California.

32. Du Bois, W. E. B. (William Edward Burghardt), 1868-1963. The Progressive Party convention, October 22, 1950. W. E. B. Du Bois Papers (MS 312). Special Collections and University Archives, University of Massachusetts Amherst Libraries.
33. "Supporters cheer Mrs. Bass in opening campaign rally," *The California Eagle*, October 19, 1950, 11.
34. Graham Du Bois, *His Day is Marching On*, 130; Greg Mitchell, *Tricky Dick and the Pink Lady: Richard Nixon vs. Helen Gahagan Douglas—Sexual Politics and the Red Scare, 1950* (New York: Random House, 1998); Barbara Ransby, *Eslanda: The Large and Unconventional Life of Mrs. Paul Robeson* (New Haven, CT: Yale University Press, 2013), 186.
35. Charlotta Bass, "One the Sidewalk," *The California Eagle*, February 2, 1951, 1, 5.
36. "Congratulations—40 Years of Service," *The California Eagle*, April 26, 1951, 4.
37. Flamming, *Bound for Freedom*, 368; Charlotta Bass, "On the Sidewalk," *The California Eagle*, April 26, 1951, 5.
38. John Hudson Jones, "Negro Woman Leader hits attack on Peace Fighters," *Daily Worker*, June 27, 1951, 8.
39. Flamming, *Bound for Freedom*, 369-70; Peter Afrasiabi, "Immigration's Collusion with Labor in the Legal Arena: How the Legal System failed Labor Leader Harry Bridges and why it matters today," *Labor Law Journal* 68, no. 2 (Summer 2017): 135-38.
40. Bass, "Acceptance Speech," 2-3.
41. Bass, "Acceptance Speech,", 3.
42. Bass, "Acceptance Speech,", 4-5.
43. Bass, "Acceptance Speech,", 6-7.
44. Bass, "Acceptance Speech,", 9-10.
45. Louise Patterson to Sojourners, June 12, 1952, Box 12, Folder 17, Louise Thompson Patterson Papers, Emory University, Atlanta, Georgia.
46. Arnold Perl, "For Immediate Release," April 21, 1952, Box 126, Folder 11, and Progressive party, "Which is your Candidate?" Box 126, Folder 13, Jessie Lloyd O'Connor papers, Sophia Smith Collection, Smith College Special Collections, Northampton, Massachusetts.
47. Progressive Party, "For Immediate Release," July 11, 1952, Box 126, Folder 13, and "Statement on Negro Representation as Adopted at the Third National Convention of the National Progressive party," July 4-6, 1952, Box 127, Folder 1, Jessie Lloyd O'Connor papers, Sophia Smith Collection, Smith College Special Collections, Northampton, Massachusetts.
48. Progressive Party, "Peace will be on the Ballot in '52," Box 126, Folder 11, Jessie Lloyd O'Connor papers, Sophia Smith Collection, Smith College Special Collections, Northampton, Massachusetts.
49. Charlotta Bass, "Autobiography,", 333.
50. Delegates National Assembly for Peace, Washington, DC, April 1, 1952, Box 126, Folder 11, Jessie Lloyd O'Connor papers, Sophia Smith Collection, Smith College Special Collections, Northampton, Massachusetts.

51. Progressive Party, Progressive Party Peace Platform, 1952, Box 126, Folder 11, and Progressive Party, "For Immediate Release," June 25, 1952, Box 126, Folder 13, Jessie Lloyd O'Connor papers, Sophia Smith Collection, Smith College Special Collections, Northampton, Massachusetts.
52. Progressive Party, "For Immediate Release," May 27, 1952, Box 126, Folder 13, Progressive party, "Progressive party Platform," July 4–6, 1952, Box 127, Folder 1, Jessie Lloyd O'Connor papers, Sophia Smith Collection, Smith College Special Collections, Northampton, Massachusetts.
53. "The Women Are in There Campaigning," *The Worker*, (1952), 8; Charlotte William, "New Star on the Horizon," *The Worker*, (1952), 8.
54. Beulah Richardson, "Progressives Name Mrs. Bass: First Woman V.P. Candidate," *Freedom*, April 1952, 1, 4.
55. Eslanda Robeson, "Radio Broadcast," 1–5, October 29, 1952, Box 126, Folder 15, Jessie Lloyd O'Connor papers, Sophia Smith Collection, Smith College Special Collections, Northampton, Massachusetts.
56. Robeson, "Radio Broadcast," 5–8.
57. Doris Matthews, "Candidette," *New York Times*, April 20, 1952, SM40; Betty Feldman, "Women ARE the Presidential Race," *The Worker* (1952), 8.
58. Feldman, "Women ARE the Presidential Race," 8.
59. Feldman, "Women ARE the Presidential Race," 8.
60. Charlotta Bass, "Address to Committee of Women, American Labor party," April 28, 1952, Box 126, Folder 15, Jessie Lloyd O'Connor papers, Sophia Smith Collection, Smith College Special Collections, Northampton, Massachusetts.
61. Charlotta Bass, "Autobiography," 335–336
62. "Address by Mrs. Charlotta Bass, American Labor party Rally, Madison Square Garden," October 27, 1952, 2–4. Charlotta A. Bass Papers, Southern California Library for Social Studies and Research (Los Angeles).
63. Charlotta Bass, "For Release after October 16, 1952," Progressive party of the District of Columbia, 2–3, Charlotta A. Bass Papers, Southern California Library for Social Studies and Research (Los Angeles); and "Address by Mrs. Charlotta Bass, American Labor party Rally, Madison Square Garden," 5–6.
64. Bass, "For Release after October 16, 1952," 2–3; "Address by Mrs. Charlotta Bass, American Labor party Rally, Madison Square Garden," 7–9.
65. "Address by Mrs. Charlotta Bass, American Labor party Rally, Madison Square Garden," 2.
66. "Address by Mrs. Charlotta Bass, American Labor party Rally, Madison Square Garden," 9–11.
67. "Address by Mrs. Charlotta Bass, American Labor party Rally, Madison Square Garden," 13–17.
68. "Address by Mrs. Charlotta Bass, American Labor party Rally, Madison Square Garden," 13–17.
69. Progressive party, "Minutes of Meeting of National Committee," November 29–30, 1950, Box 126, Folder 9, Jessie Lloyd O'Connor papers, Sophia Smith Collection, Smith College Special Collections, Northampton, Massachusetts.

70. Bass, "Autobiography," 335; "Progressives Protest," *New York Times*, June 14, 1952, 10; "Progressives Lists Plans," *New York Times*, August 28, 1952, 13; "Illinois Bars Dry party," *New York Times*, August 29, 1952, 11.
71. Progressive party, "For Immediate Release," November 30, 1952, Box 126, Folder 13, Jessie Lloyd O'Connor papers, Sophia Smith Collection, Smith College Special Collections, Northampton, Massachusetts.
72. "National Committee of the Progressive party, Secretary's Report," November 29, 1952, Box 126, Folder 14, Jessie Lloyd O'Connor papers, Sophia Smith Collection, Smith College Special Collections, Northampton, Massachusetts.

CHAPTER FIVE

1. Peter Andreas, "The Mexicanization of the US-Canada Border: Asymmetric Interdependence in a changing security context," *International Journal* 60, no. 2 (Spring 2005): 449–62.
2. Bruce Mickelburgh to Shirley Graham Du Bois, June 10, 1952, W. E. B. Du Bois Papers, University of Massachusetts, Amherst, Amherst, Massachusetts; Federal Bureau of Investigation, Memo on Shirley Graham Du Bois, 99, Shirley Graham Du Bois FBI File, Federal Bureau of Investigation.
3. Nick Fischer, *Spider Web: The Birth of American Anticommunism* (Urbana: University of Illinois Press, 2016); Ellen Schrecker, *Many are the Crimes: McCarthyism in America* (New York: Little, Brown, 1998); Charisse Burden-Stelly, *Black Scare/Red Scare: Theorizing Capitalist Racism in the United States* (Chicago: University of Chicago Press, 2023), 139.
4. Phillip Jenkins, *Cold War at Home: The Red Scare in Pennsylvania, 1945–1960* (Chapel Hill: University of North Carolina Press, 1999), 9; Masuda Hajimu, *Cold War Crucible: The Korean Conflict and the Postwar World* (Cambridge, MA: Harvard University Press, 2015), 203.
5. Mary Dudziak, *Wartime: An Idea, its History, its Consequences* (Oxford, UK: Oxford University Press, 2012), 8; Suhi Choi, "The New History and the Old Present: Archival Images in PBS documentary Battle for Korea," *Media, Culture & Society* 31, no. 1 (2009): 60–61.
6. Christine Hong, *A Violent Peace: Race, U.S. Militarism, and Cultures of Democratization in Cold War Asia and the Pacific* (Stanford, CA: Stanford University Press, 2020), 3, 6, 7, 9.
7. Gerald Horne, *Black Liberation/Red Scare: Ben Davis and the Communist Party* (Newark: University of Delaware Press, 1994), 13.
8. Erick McDuffie, "Black and Red: Black Liberation, the Cold War, and the Horne Thesis," *Journal of African American History* 96, no. 2 (March 2011): 236–237.
9. Dayo Gore, "The Danger of Being an Active Anticommunist: Expansive Black Left Politics and the Long Civil Rights Movement," *American Communist History* 11, no. 1 (2012): 45–48; Gerald Horne, *Race Woman: The Lives of Shirley Graham Du Bois* (New York: New York University Press, 2000), 112.

10. Robbie Lieberman, "The Long Black and Red Scare: Anti-communism and the African American Freedom Struggle," in *Little 'Red Scares:' Anti-Communism and Political Repression in the United States, 1921–1946,"* eds., Robert Justin Goldstein (London: Taylor & Francis, 2016), 262–263; Nick Fischer, *Spider Web: The Birth of American Anticommunism* (Urbana: University of Illinois Press, 2016).
11. Kirsten Marie Delegard, *Battling Miss Bolsheviki: The Origins of Female Conservatism in the United States.* (Philadelphia: University of Pennsylvania Press, 2012); K. A. Cuordileone, "'Politics in the Age of Anxiety': Cold War Political Culture and the Crisis in American Masculinity, 1949–1960," *The Journal of American History* 87, no. 2 (September 2000): 528.
12. Charisse Burden-Stelly, "In Battle for Peace During Scoundrel Time: W.E.B. Du Bois and United States Repression of Radical Black Peace Activism," *Du Bois Review*, Vol. 16, 2 (2019): 555–57.
13. Charisse Burden-Stelly, "Modern U.S. Racial Capitalism: Some Theoretical Insights," *Monthly Review*, 1 July 2020, https://monthlyreview.org/2020/07/01/modern-u-s-racial-capitalism/; Burden-Stelly, *Black Scare/Red Scare*, 209.
14. Charisse Burden-Stelly, "Constructing Deportable Subjectivity: Antiforeigness, Antiradicalism, and Antiblackness during the McCarthyist Structure of Feeling," *Souls*, 19, no. 3 (July-September 2017): 342–43, 345; Charisse Burden-Stelly, "Claudia Jones, the Longue Duree of McCarthyism, and the Threat of US Fascism," *Journal of Intersectionality* 3, no. 1 (Summer 2019): 62–63.
15. Charisse Burden-Stelly, "Modern U.S. Racial Capitalism: Some Theoretical Insights," *Monthly Review*, July 1, 2020, https://monthlyreview.org/2020/07/01/modern-u-s-racial-capitalism/; Burden-Stelly, "Claudia Jones, the Longue Duree of McCarthyism, and the Threat of US Fascism," 62.
16. Joyce Blackwell, *No Peace Without Freedom: Race and the International League for Peace and Freedom, 1915–1975* (Carbondale: Southern Illinois University Press, 2004), 156–57.
17. John Munro, "Imperial Anticommunism and the African American Freedom Movement in the Cold War," *History Workshop Journal* 79 (February 2015): 54–55.
18. Haverty-Stacke, "Punishment of Mere Political Advocacy," 68–71; Schrecker, *Many are the Crimes*, 130; Michael J. Ybarra, Washington Gone Crazy: Senator Pat McCarren and the great American Communist Hunt (Hanover, NH: Steerforth Press, 2004), 743; Burden-Stelly, "Constructing Deportable Subjectivity," 346.
19. Michael Hanchard, *The Spectre of Race: How discrimination haunts Western Democracy* (Princeton, NJ: Princeton University Press, 2018), 161–63.
20. Fischer, *Spider Web*, 251; Burden-Stelly, "Constructing Deportable Subjectivity," 345.
21. Athan Theoharis, "The FBI and the Politics of Anti-Communism, 1920–1945: Prelude to Power," in *'Little Red Scares:' Anti-Communism and Political Repression in the United States, 1921–1946*, ed. Robert Justin Goldstein (London: Routledge, 2014), 32–33.

22. SAC New York, "Claudia Jones," Part 3, Volume 2, 36, 43–46, Claudia Jones File, Federal Bureau of Investigation. As of this writing in 2021, Jones's file is available on the FBI Reading Room website (https://vault.fbi.gov/reading-room-index). "Part" refers to how it is labeled on the website, "Volume" refers to the internal document, and page numbers are the page number in the actual file. Authors of documents are redacted so "SAC New York" refers to the Special Agent in Charge in New York which is where most of the monitoring of Jones took place. Bureau files are not consistent.
23. SAC New York, "Claudia Jones," Part 1, Volume 1, 5–26, Claudia Jones File, Federal Bureau of Investigation.
24. SAC New York, "Claudia Jones," Part 2, Volume 1, 16, 22, 26, 48–49, 62, Claudia Jones File, Federal Bureau of Investigation.
25. SAC New York, "Claudia Jones," Part 3, Volume 2, 46, Claudia Jones File, Federal Bureau of Investigation.
26. Miss Jones Statement," *Daily Worker*, 14 September 1948, 11; Elizabeth Gurley Flynn, "Life of the party," *Daily Worker*, 17 September 1948, 10; Robert Lichtman, "Louis Budenz, the FBI, and the "List of 400 Concealed Communists": an Extended Tale of McCarthy Era Informing," *American Communist History* 3, no. 1 (2004): 25–54; Denise Lynn, "Deporting Black Radicalism: Claudia Jones's Deportation and Policing Blackness in the Cold War," *Twentieth Century Communism*, Issue 18 (2020): 48–49.
27. John Gate, "Claudia Jones Writes from Ellis Island," *Daily Worker*, November 8, 1950, 2, 9; "A Letter from Ellis Island," *Daily Worker*, November 12, 1950, 7; "McCarran Victims Urge Intensified Repeal Drive," *Daily Worker*, December 4, 1950, 4.
28. SAC New York, "Claudia Jones," Part 6, Volume 3, 10–26, Claudia Jones File, Federal Bureau of Investigation; Lydia Lindsey, "Red Monday: The Silencing of Claudia Jones in 20th Century Feminist Revolutionary Thought," *Journal of Intersectionality* 3, no. 1 (Summer 2019): 14.
29. SAC New York, "Claudia Jones Report," Part 6, Volume 3, 14–43, Claudia Jones File, Federal Bureau of Investigation; "Ouster Ordered of Claudia Jones," *New York Times*, December 22, 1950; Lynn, "Deporting Black Radicalism," 48.
30. Ted Morgan, *Reds: McCarthyism in America* (New York: Random House, 2004), 314; Schrecker, *Many are the Crimes*, 190–96; Russell Porter, "11 Communists Convicted of Plot," *New York Times*, October 15, 1949, 1.
31. "Claudia Jones ill, Trial of 16 postponed," *Daily Worker*, 17 June 1952, 1; Marika Sherwood, *Claudia Jones: A Life in Exile* (London: Lawrence & Wishart, 1999), 21; Claudia Jones to "Comrade Foster," 6 December 1955, Schomburg Library, Claudia Jones Memorial Collection; Elizabeth Gurley Flynn, *My Life as a Political Prisoner: The Rebel Girl Becomes "No 11710"* (New York: International Publishers, 2019), 25–41
32. William Foster, "Matusow confesses perjury," *Daily Worker*, February 1, 1955, 3; Claudia Jones, *13 Communists Speak to the Court* (New York: New Century

Publishers, 1953), 19–26; Virginia Gardner, "Will send 3 women leaders to West Virginia Jail," *Daily Worker,* January 21, 1955, 2; "3 Women Prisoners due in Alderson Today," *Daily Worker,* January 25, 1955, 2; Gregory S. Taylor, *The Life and Lies of Paul Crouch: Communist, Opportunist, Cold War Snitch* (Gainesville: University Press of Florida, 2014), 235–37, 245; Burden-Stelly, *Black Scare/Red Scare,* 217.

33. SAC New York, "Claudia Jones," Part 8, Volume 7, 21; Part 9, Volume 8, 78, 99–105, Claudia Jones File, Federal Bureau of Investigation.

34. Augusta Strong, "Hundreds Say Last Goodbye to Claudia Jones, Who Sails Today," *Daily Worker,* December 9, 1955, 3; "200 at Pier Bid farewell to Claudia Jones," *Daily Worker,* December 12, 1955, 3; Carole Boyce Davies, *Left of Karl Marx: The Political Life of Black Communist Claudia Jones* (Durham, NC: Duke University Press, 2007), 3.

35. Bass's file, though not all of it, is available (as of 2021) at the FBI Reading Room. Only 51 pages were made available to me and are available on the FBI vault website. I contacted others who wrote about a lengthy file in manuscripts that included Bass, each of them told me they were quoting Roger Streitmatter. Streitmatter told me that he lost the file in an office flood. Thankfully I was contacted by Charles Holm, who was given a copy of her file by a distant relative of Bass. This is the second time I was given only a partial (and very insubstantial) part of an FBI file, and I have also been encouraged by the Bureau FOIA officers to accept limited file releases. I have written about this challenge for Nursing Clio: https://nursingclio.org/2019/11/20/fbi-files-and-historical-practice/. Roger Streitmatter, *African-American Women Journalists Who Changed History* (Lexington: University Press of Kentucky, 1994).

36. A.H. Belmont to D.H. Ladd, May 25, 1951, and A.H. Belmont to D.H. Ladd, June 6, 1951, 57–62, Part 3, Charlotta Bass file, Federal Bureau of Investigation.

37. Report on Charlotta Bass, 6, Part 3, Charlotta Bass file, Federal Bureau of Investigation.

38. Sojourners for Truth and Justice, 1–2, Part 5, Sojourners for Truth and Justice, Federal Bureau of Investigation file. There is no consistency in filing among FBI files, the SJT file is not available online and was released in five parts in backwards chronological order. Though the file is not labeled "Part 5" that is how I am labeling it for consistency; the Bureau did not give this file any volume numbers.

39. Sojourners for Truth and Justice, 5–13, 40, Part 5, Sojourners for Truth and Justice, Federal Bureau of Investigation file.

40. Veronica Wilson, "'To Tell All My People:' Race, Representation, and John Birch Society Activist Julia Brown," in *Women of the Right: Comparisons and Interplay Across Borders* eds., Kathleen Blee and Sandra McGee Deutsch (University Park: Penn State University Press, 2012), 244–45.

41. Julia Brown, *I Testify: My Years as an Undercover Agent for the FBI* (Boston: Western Islands Publishers, 1966), 43, 49.

42. Brown, *I Testify,* 50, 58.

43. Brown, *I Testify,* 62–63.

44. Wilson, "'To Tell all my People,'" 245.
45. Sojourners for Truth and Justice, 61, 65, Part 5, 14, 59, 84, Part 4, Sojourners for Truth and Justice, Federal Bureau of Investigation file.
46. Sojourners for Truth and Justice, 13, 50, Part 1, Sojourners for Truth and Justice, Federal Bureau of Investigation file.
47. Report of SA William White, "Charlotta Bass," July 3, 1967; Report of SA William Brady, "Charlotta Bass," June 17, 1968; SAC Los Angles to J. Edgar Hoover, June 17, 1968; Part 8, Charlotta Bass file, Federal Bureau of Investigation; Sojourners for Truth and Justice, 13, 50, Part 1, Sojourners for Truth and Justice, Federal Bureau of Investigation file. The final section of Bass's file, section 8, includes the Bureau's notations on her last will and testament and the work of her attorney, Ben Margolis, in settling the estate.
48. Shirley Graham Du Bois, 4–7, Part 1, Shirley Graham Du Bois File, Federal Bureau of Investigation file. As of this writing in 2021, Graham Du Bois's file has been made available here: http://omeka.wustl.edu/omeka/exhibits/show/fbeyes/duboisshirley. Citations follow the filing on the website with "Part 1" indicating the first part of the file.
49. Robert Lichtman, "Louis Budenz, the FBI, and the "List of 400 Concealed Communists': an Extended Tale of McCarthy Era Informing," *American Communist History* 3, no. 1 (2004): 25, 29; Denise Lynn, *Where is Juliet Stuart Poyntz? Gender, Spycraft, and Anti-Stalinism in the Early Cold War* (Amherst: University of Massachusetts Press, 2021), 113–15.
50. Shirley Graham Du Bois, *His Day is Marching On: A Memoir of W.E.B. Du Bois* (Philadelphia: Lippincott, 1971), 104–09; s Grutzner, "Cultural Visas Denied to British," *New York Times*, March 22, 1949, 1.
51. Committee on Un-American Activities, U.S. House of Representatives, "Review of the Scientific and Cultural Conference for World Peace," April 19, 1949, Washington, DC, 3–6.
52. Graham Du Bois, *His Day is Marching On*, 188; Horne, *Race Woman*, 136, 142–46; Andreas, "The Mexicanization of the US-Canada Border," 449–62; Michael J. Ybarra, Washington Gone Crazy: Senator Pat McCarren and the great American Communist Hunt (Hanover, NH: Steerforth Press, 2004), 743; "Kent and Briehl v. Dulles," *The American Journal of International Law* 53, 1 (January 1959): 171–77.
53. Gerald Horne, *Race Woman: The Lives of Shirley Graham Du Bois* (New York: New York University Press, 2000), 136, 142–46, 152, 168.
54. Barbara Ransby, *Eslanda: The Large and Unconventional Life of Mrs. Paul Robeson* (New Haven, CT: Yale University Press, 2013), 5.
55. Paul Robeson, Referrals Section, 45, Paul Robeson Sr. File, Federal Bureau of Investigation. Eslanda Robeson's file is included with Paul's; Ransby, *Eslanda*, 224.
56. TESTIMONY OF ESLANDA GOODE ROBESON (ACCOMPANIED BY HER COUNSEL, MILTON H. FRIEDMAN), July 7, 1953, Senate Permanent Subcommittee on Investigations of the Committee on Government Operations, Washington, DC; Ransby, *Eslanda*, 5.

57. TESTIMONY OF ESLANDA GOODE ROBESON (ACCOMPANIED BY HER COUNSEL, MILTON H. FRIEDMAN), July 7, 1953, Senate Permanent Subcommittee on Investigations of the Committee on Government Operations, Washington, DC; Ransby, *Eslanda*, 224.
58. Louise Thompson Patterson, 46, 48, Section 2, Louise Thompson Patterson File, Federal Bureau of Investigation.
59. Athan Theoharis, *Abuse of Power: How Cold War Surveillance and Secret Policy Shaped the Response to 9/11* (Philadelphia: Temple University Press, 2011), 10–11.
60. Louise Thompson Patterson, 51, 62, Section 2, Louise Thompson Patterson File, Federal Bureau of Investigation.
61. Louise Thompson Patterson, 79–81, Section 2, Louise Thompson Patterson File, Federal Bureau of Investigation.
62. Gerald Horne, *Black Revolutionary: William Patterson and the Globalization of the African American Freedom Struggle* (Champaign: University of Illinois Press, 2013), 121–122.
63. New York Field Office Memo, "Juliet Stuart Poyntz," 11, 24–25 June 1954, 1–7, Federal Bureau of Investigation. Sam Tanenhaus Papers, Box 53 Folder 1, Hoover Institution Archives, Stanford University, Stanford, CA; Keith Gilyard, *Louise Thompson Patterson: A Life of Struggle* (Durham, NC: Duke University Press, 2017), 169.
64. Louise Thompson Patterson, 91–92, Section 2, Louise Thompson Patterson File, Federal Bureau of Investigation.
65. Gilyard, *Louise Thompson Patterson*, 177–79.
66. Beah Richards, 3, Beah Richards File, Federal Bureau of Investigation file. Richardson's file is substantially shorter than her peers coming in at 317 pages; this is at least what the FBI has recently released. There are no separate parts or any other divisions indicated in the file.
67. Horne, *Race Woman*, 38; Beah Richards, 10, Beah Richards File, Federal Bureau of Investigation file.
68. Dayo Gore, "A Black Woman Speaks: Beah Richards Life of Protest and Poetry," in Howard Brick, Robbie Lieberman, and Paula Rabinowitz, eds., *Lineages of the Literary Left: Essays in Honor of Alan M. Wald*. (Ann Arbor: Michigan Publishing Services, 2015); Beah Richards, 13–15, 26, 29, 37, 60, 63, Beah Richards File, Federal Bureau of Investigation file.
69. Beah Richards, 13–15, 26, 29, 37, 60, 63, Beah Richards File, Federal Bureau of Investigation file.
70. Beah Richards, 117, 120, Beah Richards File, Federal Bureau of Investigation file.
71. Beah Richards, 125, 139, 149, Beah Richards File, Federal Bureau of Investigation file.
72. Beah Richards, 149, 153, 162 Beah Richards File, Federal Bureau of Investigation file; "Beah Richards; Obituary," *The Guardian*, 25 October 2000.
73. Lorraine Hansberry, Part 1 of 3, 180, Lorraine Hansberry file, Federal Bureau of Investigation; Beverly Gage, *G-Man: J. Edgar Hoover and the Making of the American Century* (New York: Penguin Random House, 2022), 384.

74. Robbie Lieberman, "Measure them Right: Lorraine Hansberry and the Struggle for Peace," *Science and Society* 75, no. 2 (April 2011): 218, 220; Soyica Diggs Colbert, *Radical Vision: A Biography of Lorraine Hansberry* (New Haven, CT: Yale University Press, 2021), 51.
75. Lorraine Hansberry, Part 1 of 3, 82, 93–95, Lorraine Hansberry file, Federal Bureau of Investigation.
76. Lorraine Hansberry, Part 1 of 3, 131–50, Lorraine Hansberry file, Federal Bureau of Investigation.

CONCLUSION

1. Shirley Graham Du Bois, "We Too, Want Peace," *Soviet Woman* (1959): 17, Shirley Graham Du Bois Papers, Radcliffe Institute for Advanced Study, Harvard University, Boston, Massachusetts.
2. Elizabeth Armstrong, *Bury the Corpose of Colonialism: The Revolutionary Feminist Conference of 1949* (Berkeley: University of California Press, 2023), 3; Elizabeth Armstrong, "Before Bandung: The Anti-Imperialist Women's Movement in Asia and the Women's International Democratic Federation," *Signs: Journal of Women in Culture and Society 2016* 41, no. 2 (2016): 307.
3. Armstrong, "Before Bandung," 305, 308.
4. Gao Yunxiang, "W.E.B. Du Bois and Shirley Graham Du Bois in Maoist China," *Du Bois Review* 10, no. 1 (2013): 66.
5. Fanon Che Wilkins, "Beyond Bandung: The Critical Nationalism of Lorraine Hansberry, 1950–1965," *Radical History Review*, Issue 95 (Spring 2006): 193–95.
6. Imaobong Umoren, "'We Americans Are Not Just American Citizens Any Longer:' Eslanda Robeson, World Citizenship, and the *New World Review* in the 1950s," *Journal of Women's History* 30, no. 4 (Winter 2018): 140–41.
7. Zifeng Liu, "Claudia Jones and Black Internationalism during the Sino-Soviet Split," *Black Feminist Internationalism and Eurasian Knowledge Production*, Issue 1 (2023): 34; Gao Yunxiang, "W.E.B. Du Bois and Shirley Graham Du Bois in Maoist China," 61; Gao Yunxiang, *Arise, Africa! Roar, China!: Black and Chinese Citizens of the World in the Twentieth Century* (Chapel Hill: University of North Carolina Press, 2021), 5.
8. Liu, "Claudia Jones and Black Internationalism during the Sino-Soviet Split," 35.
9. Suhi Choi, "The New History and the Old Present: Archival Images in PBS documentary Battle for Korea," *Media, Culture & Society* 31, no. 1 (2009): 60–61; Charisse Burden-Stelly, "Claudia Jones, the Longue Duree of McCarthyism, and the Threat of US Fascism," *Journal of Intersectionality* 3, no. 1 (Summer 2019): 53; Charisse Burden-Stelly, *Black Scare/Red Scare: Theorizing Capitalist Racism in the United States* (Chicago: University of Chicago Press, 2023), 149, 165.
10. Beverly Gage, *G-Man: J. Edgar Hoover and the Making of the American Century* (New York: Penguin Random House, 2022), 384.
11. Ruth Wilson Gilmore, Brenna Bhandar, and Alberto Toscano, eds, *Abolition Geography: Essays Toward Liberation* (London: Verso, 2022): 185; Michael Brenes,

For Might and Right: Cold War Defense Spending and the Remaking of American Democracy (Amherst: University of Massachusetts Press, 2020), 4; Burden-Stelly, *Black Scare/Red Scare*, 244.

12. Eleana J. Kim, *Making Peace with Nature: Ecological Encounters Along the Korean DMZ* (Durham, NC: Duke University Press, 2022), 155; Olive Belcher, Patrick Bigger, Ben Neimark, and Cara Kennelly, "Hidden Carbon Costs of the 'everywhere war': Logistics, geopolitical ecology, and the carbon boot-print of the US military," *Transactions of the Institute of British Geographers* 45, no. 1 (June 2019): 65–80; Ho Chih Lin, Nick Buxton, Mark Akkerman, Deborah Burton, Wendela de Vries, Climate Crossfire, 17 October 2023, https://www.tni.org/en/publication/climate-crossfire.

13. Mark Phillip Bradley and Mary L. Dudziak, *Making the Forever War: Marlyn B. Young on the Culture and Politics of American Militarism* (Amherst: University of Massachusetts Press, 2021), 39; Mary Dudziak, *Wartime: An Idea, its History, and its Consequences* (Oxford: Oxford University Press, 2012), 93; Mary L. Dudziak, "The Gloss of War" (February 15, 2022), 47–48. *Michigan Law Review*, http://dx.doi.org/10.2139/ssrn.4049263.

14. Erik McDuffie, "For a New Anti-fascist, Anti-imperialist People's Coalition: Claudia Jones, Black Left Feminism, and the Politics of Possibility in the era of Trump," in *Post-Cold War Revelations and the American Communist party*, eds. Vernon L. Pedersen, James G. Ryan, and Katherine A. S. Sibley (London: Bloomsbury Academic, 2021), 196–97.

15. Mark Clapson, *The Blitz Companion: Aerial Warfare, Civilians, and the City since 1911* (London: University of Westminster Press, 2019), 152. DOI: https://doi.org/10.16997/book26.g; Paul Thomas Chamberlain, *The Cold War's Killing Fields: Rethinking the Long Peace* (New York: Harper Collins, 2018); Dudziak, "The Gloss of War," 37–38; For a breakdown of US deaths in Korea see: Defense Casualty Analysis System, "U.S. Military Casualties—Korean War Casualty Summary," May 2, 2024, https://dcas.dmdc.osd.mil/dcas/app/conflictCasualties/korea/koreaSum.

16. Suhi Choi, *Embattled Memories: Contested Meanings in Korean War Memorials* (Omaha: University of Nevada Press, 2014), 4; Haksoon Paik, "Superpower Rivalry and the Victimization of Korea: The Korean War and the North Korean Crisis" 38–41, in *Superpower Rivalry and Conflict: The Long Shadow of the Cold War on the 21st Century*, ed, Chandra Chari (London: Taylor & Francis 2010), 38–41; Constantin Simon and Aruna Popuri, "China Seas: A New Cold War Brewing?" *France 24*, March 8, 2024, https://www.france24.com/en/tv-shows/reporters/20240308-asia-pacific-region-the-brewing-of-a-new-cold-war; Alexander Panetta, "Will a wildly popular app become a casualty of the new Cold War between China and the US?" *Canadian Broadcasting Corporation*, April 24, 2024, https://www.cbc.ca/news/world/tik-tok-crackdown-becomes-law-1.7183042.

17. Paik, "Superpower Rivalry and the Victimization of Korea," 37, 96–96. In 2021, North and South Korea agreed "in principle" to the end of the war. "South Korea:

End to Korean War agreed to in principle," CNN, December 13, 2021, https://www.bbc.com/news/world-asia-59632727.
18. Choi, *Embattled Memories*, 4; Andrew Jeong, "A 91-year-old North Korean loyalist's lonely battle against a long-dead US general," *Washington Post*, February 20, 2022.
19. McDuffie, "For a new Anti-fascist, Anti-imperialist people's coalition," 198.

Index

Abzug, Bella, 104
Acheson, Dean, 41, 51, 68, 72, 81, 91
ACLU (American Civil Liberties Union), 5, 194
AFL-CIO, 194
Africa, 9
African diaspora, 9
African liberation, 10
Alabama, 4
Albert, Nathan, 40
Alien Anarchist Exclusion Act, 21
Alien Enemies Act, revival of, 21
Alien Registration Act. *See* Smith Act (Alien Registration Act)
Alpha Kappa Lambda sorority, 140
American and British Federation of Atomic Scientists, 69
American Committee for Cultural Freedom, 53
American Committee for the Protection of the Foreign Born (ACPFB), 170–71
American Communist Party, 69, 165, 184
American Federation of Labor (AFL), 69. *See also* AFL-CIO
American Labor Party, 157, 159
American Legion, 23, 57
American Peace Congress, 94
American Peace Crusade, 162
American People's Peace Congress, 86
American Women for Peace, 117
Amigos de Wallace, 47
Andreen, Andrea, 117
anti-Blackness, 166
anti-Black violence, 97

anti-Cold War activism, 25, 173
anti-communism, 1, 2, 9, 11, 14–15, 18–19, 24, 26, 39; anti-communist laws, 21, 22; anti-communist policy, 121; anti-communist propaganda, 23; anti-communist purges, 20; anti-communist trials, 22; Cold War and, 97, 163; McCarthyism and, 180; repression and, 20–23, 92–93, 163, 165; war effort and, 84–86
anti-fascism, 3, 7–8, 10–11
Anti-feminists, 165
anti-imperialism, 7, 16
anti-Korean War movement, 14–20, 23, 79
anti-lynching bill, 6
anti-nuclear movement, 25
anti-racism, 3
antiradicalism, 15, 23, 166
anti-subversive laws, 21
anti-Vietnam War movement, 15, 18, 23
anti-war activism, 18, 24–25, 52, 65, 103, 191–93; anti-Vietnam War movement, 15, 18, 23; Black leaders and, 69
Aptheker, Herbert, 74
Armstrong, Elizabeth, 83, 139–40, 191
Asian Women's Conference in Beijing, 191
Atlee, Clement, 142
Austin, Warren, 82

Baldwin, C. B., 154
Bandung Conference, 140, 191–92
Ban the Bomb campaign, 25, 60–61, 64–74, 72, 77, 148

Bass, Charlotta, 2, 8–9, 24, 26, 30–32, 124, 177, 182–83, 189, 190–91, 199, 201–2n11; 1950 congressional campaign and, 143–48; American Labor candidate, 146; *The California Eagle*, 5–6, 30, 46, 48, 50, 65, 79, 103, 105, 135–39, 143, 148, 175; campaign platform, 145; Congressional Campaign of 1950, 143–48; death of, 177; denied right to travel to China, 71; "Europe as I saw it," 140; FBI and, 174, 230n35; Hallinan and, 155, 160; Jones and, 30; Leon Gilbert and, 102; moved to Harlem, 148; organizing for Henry Wallace, 46; PP and, 42, 46–48, 50, 143–49, 154–56, 157, 158–59; on Security Index, 182; "On the Sidewalk" column, 30, 47, 137; Soviet Union and, 142–43; speech at Madison Square Gardon, 159; speech at Progressive party convention, 149; speech in New Jersey, 152; STJ and, 87, 92, 100, 112–13, 116, 174–77; surveillance of, 169, 174; travel visa denied, 140; for vice president, 134–35, 148–61; Wendell Wilke campaign and, 46; at World Congress in Prague, 77

Bass, Joseph, 6
Bates, Ruby, 4–5, 7
Beah Richards. *See* Richardson, Beulah
Beloved, 187
Benton, William, 146
Berg, Allison, 116
Berkman, Alexander, 21
Bill of Rights, 153
birth control, restrictions on, 7
Black Americans, 3–4, 39–40, 60, 52, 74, 94, 96–98, 143, 150, 154, 157, 164; failure of federal government to protect, 113–14; in Florida, 111–12; genocide of, 113; Ingram case and, 115; injustices faced by in Korea, 110; "legal lynching" of, 106; lynch law and, 108; military and, 25, 137; in New York, 112; poverty and, 151; at Progressive Party convention in LA, 48; racial fascism and, 7; racism and, 35; surveillance of, 169; unprosecuted deaths of, 120; yet to enjoy fruits of democracy, 27

Black Belt Thesis, 98
Black Freedom Struggle, 49, 53, 91, 93, 134–35, 151, 153, 163, 169
Black internationalism, 9–10
Black Left Feminism, 87, 88
Black liberation, 2, 27
Black nationalism, 88
Black peace activism, 14–19
Black Popular Front, 8
Black press, 6, 17
Black Prisoners of War (POWs), 18
Black radical activists, 10, 18, 25, 52, 61, 92, 166; radicals, becoming, 3–11; scholarship on, 3; stigmatization of, 20–21. *See also specific groups, movements, and individuals*
Black Scare, 23–24, 35, 98, 166
Black soldiers, 16; military and, 136; POWs, 18; racism and, 26; segregation and, 16; treatment of in WWII, 8–9; trials in Japan, 101
Blackwell, Joyce, 15–16, 167
Bolshevik revolution, 165
Boyce Davies, Carole, 91
Brando, Marlon, 52
Brenes, Michael, 194
Bridges, Harry, 149
Brooks, Robert, lynching of, 150
Brown, Julia Clarice, 176, 177, 184; *I Testify: My Years as an Undercover FBI Agent*, 176
Brownell, Herbert, 172
Bryson, Hugh, 46
Buck, Pearl S., *American Argument*, 38
Budenz, Louis, 177
Bulletin of Atomic Scientists, 64, 69
Burden-Stelly, Charisse, 20, 22–24, 35, 54, 98, 103, 163, 166–67, 194
Bureau of Investigation (BI), 22
Bush, George W., 197
Bush, Prescott, 146

California Bar Association, 139
The California Eagle, 5–6, 30, 46, 48, 50, 65, 79, 103, 105, 135–39, 143, 175; "Koreans vs. Willie McGee," 105; sale of, 148; "On the Sidewalk" column, 30, 47, 137
California Progressive Party, 48
"A Call to Negro Women" march, 88, 175
Canadian Peace Congress, 162
capitalism, 2–3, 7–8, 11, 19–20, 27
Castledine, Jacqueline, 36, 45, 115
Catholic Church, 67
Catholic Workers Organization, 69
Central Intelligence Agency (CIA), 23, 44, 53, 71, 134
Chamberlain, Paul Thomas, 196
Chattanooga, Tennessee, 4
Chicago, Illinois, 10
Chicago Defender, 136–37
childcare, 41
Childress, Alice, 88, 187
China, 11, 18, 71, 139, 192, 193, 197
Chinese Americans, 48
Chinese Communist Party, 62
Choi, Suhi, 11–12, 194, 197–98
Churchill, Winston, 29–30, 35, 150
civil liberties, 19, 92
civil rights: attacks on, 11, 18; hopes for extension of, 18
Civil Rights Congress (CRC), 4, 56, 88, 100, 102–5, 107, 110–12, 119–20, 176–77, 183–85, 188
civil rights movement, 17
Civil War, 154
Clapson, Mark, 20
class oppression, 7
Cleveland Call and Post, 135
Clinton, Bill, 197
Cohn, Roy, 180
Colbert, Soyica Diggs, 9–11, 109
Cold War, 1, 9–11, 51–52, 57, 72, 95–97, 106, 163, 173, 193–94, 198; anti-communism and, 89, 98, 105, 167, 169; Black opposition to, 54; as fascist, 134; militarism and, 89, 164; opposition to, 14–15; peace movement and, 31, 36, 51, 162; policy during, 3, 10, 14–19, 32, 35, 39, 67–71, 77, 85, 88–89, 92, 96–97, 99, 119, 121, 134, 135, 150, 153, 162–64, 166–67; repressive legislation during, 27; surveillance and, 179; US and, 143; women's rights advocates, 36
colonialism, 8–9, 13, 15
Commerce Department, 1
Committee for Non-Violent Action, 18
Communism, 2, 12, 26, 34, 52, 70
Communist International (COMINTERN), 8, 62
Communist Party, 1, 8, 14, 53, 59, 87–88, 154; Black Belt Thesis, 98
Communist Party of Great Britain (CPGB), 20
Communists, 7, 20
Confederate Constitution, 158
Conference of the Women of Asia, 139
Congress, 96; Black representation in, 144
Congress of American Women (CAW), 37, 77–78, 117, 140, 183
Constitution, 145
containment policy, 19, 52
Continental Congress for World Peace, 57
Cooke, Marvin, 88
"cooperation alongside struggle," 17
The Cosby Show, 187
Cotton, Eugenie, 77, 79
Council on African Affairs (CAA), 4, 88, 183
Cousins, Norman, 52–53
CPUSA (Communist Party of the United States), 3, 22, 24, 40, 84, 154, 170, 174, 176, 181, 187; anti-fascism and, 10–11; Ban the Bomb petition and, 60, 69; Black women in, 3–4; criticism of US military behemoth, 20; *Daily Worker*, 94, 118, 149, 177; Du Bois's turn toward, 73; Jones and, 6; leaders of arrested, 172; members tracked by FBI, 183–85; Mother's

CPUSA (*continued*)
    Day and, 75; National Women's Work Commission, 78; policy shift of, 34–35; responsibility to organize and empower women to lead, 37; Scottsboro case and, 4, 10–11. *See also* Jones, Claudia
The Crisis magazine, 16
Crouch, Paul, 172
Crouch Index, 172
Cuba Peace Conference, 179
Cultural Revolution, 193
Cumberbatch, Claudia. *See* Jones, Claudia
Cumberbatch, Yvonne, 170
Cumings, Bruce, 62
Curie, Joliet, 140, 142
Custodial Detention program, 182

Daily Worker, 1, 102, 154, 171
Danielson, Leilah, 19, 64
Davis, Almena, 148
Davis, Angela, 185
Davis, Ben, 35, 103
Dawson, William, 146
Day, Dorothy, 64
Declaration of Independence, 145
Deery, Phillip, 53
defense spending, 20
Delegates National Assembly for Peace, 153
Democratic Party, 43–44, 143, 145, 151–52, 156–60, 164
Dennis v. US, 172
Department of Defense, 44, 95
Department of Justice, 114
Department of Labor, 149
deportations, 21, 26, 162, 170–71, 173, 193
desegregation, 6
DETCOMM, 182
Devine, Thomas, 49
Dewey, Thomas, 48, 183
Dickerson, Angie, 90
Dies, Martin, 22
Dies Committee, 22
Dillingham-Hardwick Act, 21

Dodd, Francis, 95
Doomsday clock, 64
"Double V" campaign, 17
Douglas, Helen Gahagan, 147
Douglass, Frederick, 90, 148
Du Bois, Shirley Graham, anti-war stance of, 16
Du Bois, W. E. B., 16–17, 44, 122, 129, 130, 138, 153, 177, 179, 188, 193; arrest of, 175; Ban the Bomb petition and, 60, 66, 71–72; blacklisting of, 73; *Black Reconstruction*, 34; campaign as American Labor candidate, 146–48; deported from Canada, 162; Foreign Agents Registration Act, 134; *In Battle for Peace*, 73; indictment and exoneration of, 72, 91–92; Ingram appeal, 117; marriage to Shirley, 72; at NCASP peace conference, 52; run for Senator on Labor Party ticket, 144; travel documents and, 168, 192; turns toward CPUSA, 73; *We Charge Genocide* petition, 119
Dudziak, Mary, 13–14, 163, 195
Dunstan, Sarah, 34

Einstein, Albert, 52, 65
Eisenhower, Dwight, 151, 155, 157–58, 160, 195
Elliott, Oliver, 62–63
Ellis Island, 171
Emma Lazarus Foundation, 112
Equal Rights Amendment (ERA), 41
Espionage Act, 21
Ethiopia, 8
Europe, Communist influence in, 51
exclusion, 7
Executive Order 9835 (Loyalty pledge), 35
Executive Order 9981, integration of US military, 164

Fair Employment Practices Committee (FEPC), 18, 46, 50, 89, 137, 145–46, 151, 154
family separation, 26
fascism, 3, 7–8, 10–11, 26, 35, 41, 147

INDEX 241

fascist triple K (*Kinde-Küche-Kirche*), 41
Fast, Howard, 52
Federal Bureau of Investigation (FBI), 10, 22–23, 52, 134, 149, 169, 188; Bass and, 174–75, 182, 230n35; Brown and, 176, 177; Graham Du Bois and, 57, 69; Hansberry and, 94; Jones and, 59, 76, 171, 173; KKK and, 113; McCarthyism and, 180–81; Richardson and, 169, 175–76, 185–88; STJ and, 90–91, 118–19, 231n38; study on Black soldiers, 98; Thompson Patterson and, 169, 181–85; tracking of CPUSA membership, 183–85, 186–87
Federation of American Scientists, 64
Federation of British Scientists, 64
Feldman, Betty, 155–57
Fellowship of Reconciliation (FOR), 18, 69
Felship, Max, 112
femininity, traditional, 3
feminism, Marxism and, 42
Field, Jean, 59
Fifteenth Amendment, 89, 180
Fifth Amendment, 180, 184
Fischer, Nick, 21, 165, 168
Flamming, Douglass, 201–2n11
Flynn, Elizabeth Gurley, 78, 173
Forbes, Kenneth Ripley, 112
Foreign Agents Registration Act, 22, 72
forever war, 14
Fort Huachuca, Arizona, 8–9
foundational narratives, rejection of, 12
Fourteenth Amendment, 89, 104
Fourteenth Congressional District of California, 143, 147
"frame-up" trials, 6
Franco, Francisco, US support for government of, 144
freedom, peace and, 15–16
Freedom (newspaper), 90, 92–93, 154, 188, 192
Freedom of Information Act (FOIA), 174

Gage, Beverly, 194
Gallup Poll, 64, 84
Galtung, Johan, 3
Gannett, Betty, 173
Gao Yunxiang, 193
Garvin, Vicki, 88
gender, 3, 7
General Electric, 44
Geneva Convention, 80
Georgia, 4
Germany, 7, 81
Gilbert, Kay, 99, 102
Gilbert, Leon, 26, 98–103, 109–10; arrest and prosecution of, 96–97, 99; death sentence commuted, 103; defense of, 100; stillborn child of, 102
Gilbert case, 119
Gilmore, Ruth Wilson, 195
Gilyard, Keith, 183–85
global peace movement, 25
Global South, 77
Goldman, Emma, 21
Gore, Dayo, 10, 88, 115, 165
Graham, Shirley, 8. *See also* Graham Du Bois, Shirley
Graham Du Bois, Shirley, 2, 8–9, 24, 30–32, 60, 122, 130, 189, 193, 199; accusations of communism and, 57, 178–79; Ban the Bomb campaign and, 64–66, 71; blacklisting of, 73; bus trip in Europe, 55–56; campaign to defend Du Bois, 134; as "concealed Communist:, 177; death of, 179; deported from Canada, 162; as "director of negro work" with YWCA-USO, 8–9; FBI and, 57, 69, 73; left US for Ghana, 179; marriage to Du Bois, 72; at Moore's funeral, 111; "Oh No Brother, No One is Going to Forget about Willie McGee," 109; at peace conferences, 51–57; PP and, 42, 44, 45; reflections of, 190; on Security Index, 182; on silencing of peace movement, 85; speech at Progressive Party convention, 45; speech in Philadelphia, 48; STJ and, 87, 116, 175, 176; travel documents and, 168, 179, 192; warns of "Atlantic Curtain," 30

Gray, Rosa Lee, 92
Great Acceleration, 195
Great Depression, 22, 169
Greenlee, Charles, 110

Hajimu, Masuda, 14, 70, 163
Haksoon Paik, 197
Hallinan, Vincent, 26, 149, 156
Hallinan, Vivian, 149, 154, 155, 160
Hamilton, Mary, 44
Hansberry, Lorraine, 2, 9–10, 24, 32, 65, 126, 169, 182, 185–89, 190, 192, 199; Communist Party and, 49; *Freedom* (newspaper), 105; Henry Wallace campaign and, 48; "Lynchsong," 108; PP and, 43; *A Raisin in the Sun*, 10, 188; on Security Index, 182; STJ and, 87, 89–90, 92–94; travel documents and, 94, 134, 192; University of Wisconsin, 48; Young Progressive of American, 48–49
Hansberry v. Lee, 10
Harlem, 6
Harlem Renaissance, 4
Harrison, Hubert, 17
Harvard University, 51
Haven, Dorothy, 145
Haverty-Stacke, Donna, 22
Hawkins, Wileta, 103–4, 106–7, 109
Healey, Dorothy, 59
Higashida, Cheryl, 115
Hiroshima, attack on, 65
Hiss, Alger, 159
historiography, 11–14
Hitler, Adolf, 29–30, 39, 41, 56, 81, 120
Hitlerism, 150
Holiday, Billie, "Strange Fruit" (anti-lynching song), 139
Holm, Charles, 230n35
Hong, Christine, 11, 17, 98, 120, 164
Hoover, J. Edgar, 22, 98, 182, 194
Horne, Gerald, 8–9, 52, 164–65, 167
House Un-American Activities Committee (HUAC), 22, 46, 53–54, 57, 73, 78, 139, 167, 169, 175, 177; "Communist 'Peace' Offensive" (report), 53

Howard, Charles, 48
Hunt, Amy, 114
hydrogen bomb, 25, 69, 70

Immigration and Naturalization Services (INS), 149, 170–71
Immigration or Anarchist Exclusion Act, 21
imperialism, 2–3, 10, 11, 93, 120
Independent Progressive Party, California State Executive Committee, 143
Indochina, 77, 144, 150
Indonesia, 70, 150
Information Bulletin, 72
Ingram, Charles, 114
Ingram, James, 114
Ingram, Rosa Lee, 26, 97, 114–19, 120, 151, 160
Ingram, Sammy Lee, 114
Ingram, Wallace, 114
Ingram case, 115, 119–20
integration of US military, 17–18
Inter-Continental Peace Congress Conference, Montevideo, Uruguay, 92, 188
Internal Security Act (McCarran Act), 168, 171
internationalism, 9–10
International Labor Defense (ILD), 4–5, 100
International Women's Day, 40, 67, 75, 78
International Workers Order (IWO), 4, 116, 182, 183–84
Intondi, Vincent, 65
Irvin, Walter Lee, 110, 118
Italy, 8

Jackson, Ada Belle, 44
Jackson Daily News, 104
Japan, 2, 12, 18; Korea and, 12–13; military "Special Kim Detachment," 62; US bombing of, 25, 64
Japanese, prejudice against, 65
Japanese Americans, at Progressive Party convention in LA, 48
Jefferson School of Social Science, 186

Jeffries, Louise, 92
Jenkins, Phillip, 163
Jim Crow laws, 7, 15, 52, 111, 134, 158, 165
job loss, 26
Johnson, Lyndon, 174
Johnson, Manning, 54
Johnston, Timothy, 32
Joint Congressional Committee Report, 1
Jones, Claudia, 1–2, 6–8, 24, 29, 31–32, 121, *123*, 148, 180, 188–89, 190, 198–99; activism of, 76–77; anti-war position, 40; arrest and trial of, 172; Ban the Bomb campaign and, 67–69; CAW and, 78; charged under Smith Act, 76; "The Children of Korea Call to the Women of the world," 81; CPUSA and, 3, 6, 50, 78; death of, 173; deportation from US and, 170–71, 173, 193; "An End to the Neglect of the Problems of the Negro Woman," 87, 39, 115; family of, 170; on Gilbert case, 102; "Half the World" column, 67–68, 75, 80, 91, 102; imperialism and, 167; imprisonment of, 173, 192; indictment under Smith Act, 92; Ingram and, 114, 116, 118; on Ingram case, 116; International Women's Day speech and article, 40, 75, 171, 172; Korean War, 39, 84; on McGee, 116; McGee and, 103, 105–8; Moore and, 110–11; on Mother's day, 75; "Peace Is a Woman's Business," 37; protests against, 76; Roosevelt College speech in Chicago, 76; on Security Index, 182; Soviet Union and, 40; STJ and, 74, 78, 82, 84, 86–87, 90–91; "The Struggle for Peace in the United States," 84–85; surveillance and persecution of, 169–73; theorization of peace and, 33–42; trial of, 134; "For the Unity of Women in the Cause of Peace," 172; Wallace campaign and, 50; "Warmakers fear women" article, 59–60; *The Woman Today*, 91; women and banning the H Bomb, 68; "Women Crusade for Peace," 75, 78

Jones, John Hudson, 149
journalism, anti-war activism and, 24–25
Justice department, 90

Kahn, Albert, 111, 144
Kan Puk, 141
Katz, Maude White, 116–17
Kaufmann, Mary, 172
Kennan, George, 51
Kent, Rockwell, 69
Kent v. Dulles, 179
Kim, Eleana, 195
Kim, Monica, 13, 83, 95
Kim, Suzy, 36–37, 77
Kim, Taewoo, 77, 83
Kim Il Sung, 62, 63
Kim Sok-Won, 63
Kinloch, John, 46
Koje Island POW camp, South Korea, 95–96, 154
Konigsberg, Raphael, 138–39, 147
Korea, 12–13, 56, 63, 66, 70, 113; demarcation line between North and South, 61; Democratic People's Republic, 61; independence of, 12; Japan and, 12–13, 62
Korean Civil War, 64
Korean Democratic Women's League (DWL), 82
Korean Democratic Women's Union (DUKW), 79
Korean People's Army, 137
Koreans, repatriation of, 154
Korean War Red Scare, 163
Kraus, Charles, 12
Ku Klux Klan, 6, 18, 87, 111–13, 155

Landon, Al, 46
Latin America, 93
Latinx coalition, 47
legal lynching, 25–26
legal system, racism in, 8
Lerner, Mitchell, 17–18, 100, 102, 135
liberation movements, 2–3
Lichtman, Robert, 177
Lieberman, Robbie, 48, 51, 65, 165

Lincoln, Abraham, 155
Lindsey, Lydia, 171
Liu, Zifeng, 193
Loeb, Charles, 136
Los Angeles Tribune, 148
Luce, Henry, 63
Lusk Committee (NY), 22
lynching, 104, 115, 119, 150. *See also* lynch law
lynch law, 4, 11, 25–26, 88, 94, 96–97, 103, 106–8, 117, 118, 121

MacArthur, Douglas, 75, 76, 101–2, 149, 198
Madhubuti, Haki, 196
Mailer, Norman, 52
Malaya, 70
Mao Tse-Tung, 130
Mao Zedong, 139, 192–93; "Statement Supporting the Afro-American in Their Just Struggle Against Racial Discrimination by U.S. Imperialism," 193
Marcantonio, Vito, 144, 183
Margolis, Ben, 177
Marshall, George, 51
Marshall, Thurgood, 101–2
Marshall Plan, 51, 53, 67, 78, 143
Marxism, 42, 87, 186
Marxist Leninism, 87
Mateo Hubbard, 90
maternity, 37–38
Matthews, Doris, 155
Matusow, Harvey, 172
McCall, Sheriff, 113
McCarran Act, 145–46, 152
McCarran-Walter Act, 168
"McCarran Wing," 171
McCarthy, Joseph, 152, 159, 180, 188
McCarthyism, 12, 22, 163, 180, 194
McDuffie, Erik, 3, 34, 36, 39, 74, 87–88, 113, 115, 119, 165, 196, 198
McGee, Rosalie, 103, 105, 107, 118
McGee, Willie, 25–26, 97, 103–9, 120
McGee case, 119–20
McGuire, Danielle, 116
McKinley, William, assassination of, 21

memory, 196–99
Mexican Americans, 48
militarism, 2, 17, 20–21, 53, 89, 164, 193–96
"militarized multiculturalism," 17
military, integration of, 167
Millard, Betty, "Save Our Sons" campaign, 83
Miller, Arthur, 52
Mislán, Christina, 34, 67
misogyny, 2
Montgomery, Olen, 4
Montgomery Bus Boycott, 186
Moore, Audley, 35, 114
Moore, Harriette, 26, 97, 109–14, 138, 151, 176
Moore, Harry, 26, 97, 109–14, 138, 151, 176
Moore case, 114, 119
Moore murders, 113, 121
Moos, Elizabeth, 66, 72
Munro, John, 167
Muste, A. J., 18–19, 64, 69

NAACP (National Association for the Advancement of Colored People), 5, 10, 16, 47, 65, 99, 101, 109–10, 112, 114, 119, 149, 151–52, 169, 194
Nagasaki, attack on, 65
Nash, Phileo, 114
National Committee for the Defense of the Ingram Family (NCDIF), 116–17
National Committee to Defend Negro Leadership, 170
National Council of the Arts, Sciences, and Professions (NCASP), 51, 53–54
National Defense Committee for Claudia Jones, 92
National Equal Rights League, 16
National Lawyers Guild, 177
National Negro Congress (NNC), 88, 119
national press, 18
National Security Act of 1947, 44
National Security Agency (NSA), 44
National Student Peace Conference, 141
Naval Intelligence, 91

Nazi fascism, 34, 139
Negro History Week, 91
"Negro Soldiers! There's a letter for you inside, Read it!" pamphlet, 137
Neimore, Joseph, 5–6
neo-colonialism, 2, 17, 27
New Challenges, 188
New Deal state, 2, 153, 191
New World Review, 192
New York, 4, 6
New York State, anti-communist laws in, 22
New York State Insurance Department, 184
New York Wallace for President committee, 45
Nexo, Martin Andersen, 55
Nixon, Richard, 147, 152
No Gun Ri massacre, 82, 198
non-alignment, 191–93
"nonpeace organizations," 15–16
non-violent resistance, 16
Norris, Clarence, 4, 6
North Atlantic Treaty Organization (NATO), 29, 37–38, 51, 68, 195
North Korea, 12, 60–63, 73–74, 83, 95, 137, 141, 197–98
North Korean military, 63, 137
nuclear weapons, 18, 25, 64
Nuremberg laws, 7

O'Casey, Sean, *Juno and the Paycock*, 48
Office of Naval Intelligence, 23, 175
Office of Strategic Services, 63
Office of the US High Commissioner of Germany, 72
Owens, Patricia, 34

Pace, Alexander, 90
Pace, Frank, 99
pacifists, 14, 18–19
Padget, Willie, 110
Paint Rock, Alabama, 4
Parent Teacher's Association, 112
Paris Peace Conference, 55–56, 66, 179
patriotism, 23
Patten, Frank, 174

Patterson, Heywood, 4, 6
Patterson, William, 4–5, 10, 100, 121, 184; arrest of, 175; detention in federal penitentiary, 185; indictment of, 183; *We Charge Genocide* petition, 87
peace: as "absence of war" and "presence of justice," 3, 24–27; anti-racist, anti-sexist, anti-capitalist conception of, 3; criminalization of, 19–24; freedom and, 15–16; high price of, 162–89; theorizing, 33–42, 74–86; through defense spending, 19; USSR and, 32–33
peace conferences, 25, 51–58, 139–43
Peace Information Center (PIC), 66, 72–73, 162, 168, 175, 179
The Peacemakers, 18, 69
peace movements, 163
Pearl Harbor, 64
People's Front of Struggle Against War and Fascism, 8. *See also* Popular Front
People's Republic of China, 71, 139. *See also* China
People's Republic of Korea, 13
Pérez Jiménez, Christina, 47
Permanent Committee of the Partisans of Peace, 66
Perry, Imani, 105
Philippines: Libel Law in, 21; US colonial wars in, 21
Picasso, Pablo, 52
Pittman, John, 75; "The Negro and America's Wars: The Long Struggle for Peace," 74
Pittsburgh Courier, 17
Plastas, Melinda, 15
Popular Front, 7, 8
Powell, Clive, 6
Powell, Julie, 36
Powell, Ozie, 4
presidential campaign of 1948, 23–24, 26, 42–51
presidential campaign of 1952, 26, 134–35, 148–61
Price, Victoria, 4

Prisoners of War (POWs), 95–96, 154; Black, 18
prison time, 26
Progressive Citizens of American (PCA), 43–44
Progressive Party (PP), 24, 26, 45–47, 49–51, 96, 100, 112, 175, 179, 180; 1948 campaign, 43; atomic bomb and, 50; Bass and, 42, 46–48, 50, 146–49, 154–56, 158–59; Bass as candidate for, 134–61; civil rights platform, 45, 48; Graham Du Bois and, 42, 44, 45; Hansberry and, 43; Korean War and, 50, 143–44, 153–54; National Committee, 160–61; Peace Candidates, 152, 154; platform of, 156; Robeson and, 49
propaganda, 23
Protestants, 19
Puerto Rico, 49

race, 7
racial fascism, 7
racial justice, 25
racism, 2–3, 7, 9, 26, 33, 36, 88, 117; in criminal legal system, 8; military, 17; racist violence, 18, 25
Randolph, A. Phillip, 69
Ransby, Barbara, 9, 38, 49, 180
Reconcentration Act, 21
Reconstruction amendments, 89
Red Army, 141
red-baiting, 162–69
Red Cross investigation, 96
Red Scare, 23–24, 35, 98
Republican Party, 43–44, 46–47, 145–46, 151–52, 156–60
Republic of Korea (ROK), 61
"Resolution of Solidarity with Korea," 141
restrictive covenants, 10
Revolutionary Radicalism, 22
Rhee, Syngman, 13, 62–63, 138, 141
Richards, Beah, *125*. *See also* Richardson, Beulah
Richardson, Beulah, 2, 9–10, 24–25, *125*, 199; Bass and, 148, 154–55; "A Black Woman Speaks . . . of White Womanhood of White Supremacy of Peace," 86, 105, 185; FBI and, 169, 175–76, 185–88; "Genocide" (performance poem), 120; McGee and, 106; on Security Index, 182, 186; STJ and, 61, 86–87, 100, 102, 175–76; *We Charge Genocide* petition, 186
Roberson, Willie, 4
Robeson, Eslanda Goode, 2, 9, 24, 32, 39, 116, *127*, *132*, *133*, 179–81, 188, 190, 192, 199, 204–5n59; *American Argument*, 38; Dodd abduction and, 95–96; Henry Wallace campaign and, 49; marriage to Paul, 145; "Peace and the Right to Work for Peace" (speech), 144–45; PP and, 42, 49, 146–48, 155; run for congress representing Hartford, CT, 144; STJ and, 87–88, 175, 177; surveillance of, 169; travel documents and, 134, 168, 179, 192; "Walk on Georgia," 118
Robeson, Paul, 9–10, 23, 52, 69, 93, 124, *127*, 138, 177, 193; accusations of communism and, 54, 56; attacks on, 56–57, 187; at Delegates National Assembly for Peace meeting, 153; *Freedom* (newspaper), 82, 92; PP and, 42, 48, 145; revocation of passport and, 92, 134, 168, 179–80, 192; surveillance of, 169; *We Charge Genocide* petition and, 120–21
Robeson, Paul Jr., *127*, 145
Robinson, Jackie, 57
Robinson, Theresa, 92
Roosevelt, Franklin, 9, 43, 46, 50, 169
Roosevelt College, Chicago, 76
Russo-Japanese War, 12
Rustin, Bayard, 69

Sanford and Son, 187
San Francisco National Union of Marine Cooks and Stewards, 46
Scholnick, Abraham, 169
Scholnick, Claudia. *See* Jones, Claudia
Schrecker, Ellen, 172
Schuyler, George, 65, 69
Scientific and Culture Conference for Peace in New York City, 177

Scottsboro case, 3–5, 25, 155; Bass and, 5–6; CPUSA and, 10–11; Jones and, 6, 8; Thompson Patterson and, 4–5
Secretary of Defense, 44
Secret Service, 23, 90, 175, 177
Security Index, 182–83, 186
Sedition Act, 21
segregation, in US military, 8, 16, 18
self-determination, 2, 9, 13
Senate Permanent Subcommittee on Investigations, 180
sexism, 7, 26
sexual assault, 89
Shapley, Harlow, 52
Sheen, Fulton, 177
Shepherd, Samuel, 110, 118
Shostakovich, Dimitri, 53
Sino-Korean army, 62
Smethurst, James, 87
Smith, Shane, 16
Smith Act (Alien Registration Act), 22, 59, 76, 89, 92, 172, 176
socialism, 3, 8, 20, 24, 26–27
Socialist Workers Party, 22
social justice, 2–3, 24–25
Social Workers, 1
Sojourners for Truth and Justice (STJ), 59, 61, 102, 105, 110–16, 118–21, 148–49, 151, 184–85, 188; Bass and, 87, 92, 100, 112–13, 116, 174–77; FBI and, 90–91, 118–19, 231n38; Graham Du Bois and, 87, 116, 175, 176; Hansberry and, 87, 89–90, 92–94; Jones and, 74, 78, 82, 84, 86–87, 90–91; military segregation and, 89; New York "Report Back" meeting, 91; protection of Black women against sexual assault, 117; Richardson and, 61, 86–87, 100, 102, 175–76; Robeson and, 87–88, 175, 177; Sojourners March, 176; surveillance of, 91; Thompson Patterson and, 25, 175, 177
South Africa, 49, 70, 115, 150
Southern Democrats, 164
South Korea, 62–63, 73, 83, 141, 197–98
Soviet Union, 2, 9, 14, 19, 23–24, 42, 145, 153, 192, 194; atomic bomb and, 64; Ban the Bomb campaign and, 71–72; Cold War and, 51, 53, 68, 78, 134–35; escalation of conflict with, 20; labor unions, 168; Nazi invasion of, 34; nuclear program, 32; nuclear weapons and, 60; peace and, 32–33; Struggle for Peace campaign, 32; US tensions with, 40; *We Charge Genocide* petition and, 121
Soviet Women, 190
Spain, 7–8
Spanish Civil War, 8
Sparkman, John, 152
Spear, Charlotta, 5. *See also* Bass, Charlotta
Springarn, Joel, 16
Stack, Loretta Starvus, 59
Stalin, Josef, 53, 62–63
Stanton, Elizabeth Cady, 156
State Department, 11, 32–33, 52, 62, 72, 92, 94, 117, 139, 162, 168, 174–75, 188
State's Rights Party (Dixiecrats), 50
Stevenson, Adlai, 151–52, 155, 157–59
Stockholm Peace Appeal, 60, 66, 79, 141
Stockholm peace petition, 25
Stratford, John, 114–16
Streitmatter, Roger, 230n35
Subversive Activities Control Board (SACB), 168
Supreme Court, 139, 172
surveillance state, 22
Survey of Racial Conditions in the United States (RACON), 98, 169

Taft-Hartley Act, 145
Taylor, Glen, 44
Taylor, Pauline, 90, 92
Tennessee, 4
Terrell, Mary Church, 15, 116
Thirteenth Amendment, 89
Thomas, Ernest, 110
Thompson Patterson, Louise, 2, 4, 7–10, 24, 61, 87, *128*, *131*, 148, 187, 189, 190, 199; CPUSA and, 3; CRC and, 100, 102; FBI and, 169, 181–85; ILD and, 4–5; Ingram and, 114, 115, 116; McGee and, 105; Scottsboro campaign and, 6–7; in Spain, 8; STJ and, 25, 175, 177

Thurmond, Strom, 50
Toscano, Alberto, 7
travel papers, seizure of, 26
treason, accusations of, 19
triple oppression paradigm, 7
Trotter, William Monroe, 16–17
Trudeau, Clyde, 145
Truman, Harry, 1, 13–14, 20, 24–25, 47, 50, 69, 83, 102–3, 117, 195; administration of, 61, 85, 164; Ban the Bomb campaign and, 66; commits to the war, 63; hydrogen bomb and, 40, 64; integration of US military and, 17, 99; labor vote and, 49; lobbied to pardon Ingram and sons, 116; loyalty oaths, 46; MacArthur and, 75–76; thermonuclear weapons and, 60; "Truman-Acheson doctrine," 41; Truman Doctrine, 32, 35, 43, 51, 78, 114, 144
"Truman-Acheson doctrine," 41
Truman Doctrine, 32, 35, 43, 51, 78, 114, 144
Truth, Sojourner, 148, 156
Tubman, Harriet, 89, 148, 156
Twenty-Fifth Division, 99
Twenty-Fourth Infantry Regiment, 99, 101

Umoren, Imaobong, 9
United Nations, 8, 13, 43, 70, 82–83, 95, 117, 119, 192
United States, 53, 67, 71, 74; anticommunism, 62; claims of decolonization from Japanese, 13; Cold War policy of, 3; fascism and, 39, 67; freedom struggle in, 70; incomes in, 1; military budget of, 11; racial fascism and, 97; racist policy of, 8. *See also specific branches, agencies, departments of government*
United States Army Counterintelligence Corps, 175
Universal Military Training Bill, 110, 153
Urban League, 10
US Army Counterintelligence Corps, 23, 91

US Congress, 13–14; 1950 congressional campaign, 143–48; Senate Permanent Subcommittee on Investigations, 180; war powers and, 13–14, 195
US Constitution, 45
US intelligence agencies, 18–20
US military, 70; budget of, 52; desegregation and, 98; integration of, 17–18, 110; as Jim Crow army, 91; as neocolonial force, 94; proliferation and, 44; segregation in, 2, 8, 16, 18, 110; suppression of criticism of, 23–24
USSR. *See* Soviet Union
US Supreme Court, 10

Vasquez, Leonor Aguilar, 93
Veterans of Foreign Wars, 53
Vietnam War, 12, 15, 18
Vine, David, 70
The Voice, 17

Wachter, Lilly, 83
Waldorf Conference, 51, 53
Wallace, Henry, 26, 31, 42–51, 132, 134–35, 150–51; 1948 Peace Tour, 49; campaign of, 44, 48–49; candidacy of, 46; Korean War and, 50; political loss and, 49; presidential campaign of, 23–24; "progressive capitalism," 44; racism and, 49; resignation of, 43; "The Way to Peace" (speech at Madison Square Garden), 43
war: capitalism and, 19; committing to, 61–63; "war of intervention," 13. *See also specific conflicts*
war powers, 13–14
War Powers Act, 195
Warren, Fuller, 111, 112
War Resister's League, 69
Washington, D.C., march of May 8, 1932, 5
Washington, Mary Helen, 8
We Charge Genocide petition and, 119–21, 148
Weems, Charlie, 4, 6
Weigand, Kate, 77
Western Women, 77

West Indian Gazette and Afro-Asian-Caribbean News, 173
White, Samuel, 56
White, Walter, 47, 57, 110, 149
whites: poor, 7; white activists, 15; white women, 39, 106
white supremacists, 4
white supremacy, 11, 16, 35, 75, 115, 139
Wilkie, Wendell, 46
Wilkins, Fanon Che, 10, 192
Wilkins, Roy, 99
William, Charlotte, 154
Williams, Chad, 16
Williams, Eugene, 4
Wilson, Charles, 44
Winstead amendment, 110
Winston Churchill Iron Curtain speech, 174
women's emancipation, Marxism and, 42
Women's International Democratic Federation (WIDF), 36–37, 61, 77–79, 82–84, 91, 93, 102, 117, 139–40, 191; anti-Korean war campaign, 80; delegation to North Korea, 80; executive Council meeting report, 81; Korean branch of, 81; letter to American women, 79; *We Accuse!* report, 80, 83
Women's International Democratic Federation (WIDF) (Swedish), 117; *For their Rights as Mothers, Workers, Citizens* (report), 117

Women's International League for Peace and Freedom (WILPF), 15–16, 18, 41, 67, 167
women's liberation, 2, 27
Women's Peace Party (WPP), 16, 18
Woodson, Carter G., 74
Worker magazine, 67
working classes, 7
World Committee of the Defenders of Peace, 140
World Congresses, 77
World Congress of the Partisans of Peace, 54, 57
World Partisans of Peace, 71
World Peace Congress, 66
World Peace Council, 57, 73, 140
World War I, 17; African territory and, 16
World War II, 12, 17, 25, 34, 41, 46, 62, 64, 70, 77, 98, 107, 163–64, 169; Black Americans and, 74; "Black militancy" and, 8; US treatment of Black soldiers, 8–9, 98
Wright, Andy, 4, 6
Wright, Roy, 4

Yergan, Max, 54
Yorty, Samuel, 147
Young, Marilyn, 12–14, 18, 20, 23, 84, 195–96
Young Communist League, 6
Young Progressive of American, 48
YWCA-USO, 8–9

DENISE LYNN is professor and chair of the History Department, director of Gender and Sexuality Studies, and director of Africana Studies at the University of Southern Indiana in Evansville, Indiana. Her research focuses on women in the American Communist Party. Dr. Lynn is vice president of the Historians of American Communism and the editor of its journal, *American Communist History*. She is the author of *Where is Juliet Stuart Poyntz? Gender, Spycraft, and Anti-Stalinism in the Early Cold War* and *Claudia Jones: Visions of a Socialist America*.

www.ingramcontent.com/pod-product-compliance
Lightning Source LLC
Chambersburg PA
CBHW030535230426
43665CB00010B/902